Risk in International Finance

Risk has become *the* lens through which financial market activity is understood in the post-Bretton Woods monetary order, largely because risk management financial instruments permit financial and commodity exchange in a global economy characterized by rapid capital mobility and volatility in foreign exchange rates. This book analyzes the evolution and impact of the concept of risk on processes of transnational banking and financial market regulation, as well as the externalities generated by speculative financial activity in developing and emerging market economies.

The author provides an alternative theory for the study of international financial market regulation by applying elements of a post-structural methodology to the topic. Inspired by Michel Foucault's framework of critical discourse analysis in *The History of Sexuality*, the argument dissects the rules of formation that govern the evolving discourse on risk. The author argues that the apparently abstract and mathematically formal technology of risk emerges from within specific institutions, events, perspectives, and economic formations; thereby limiting its utility in the regulation of global financial markets. Exploring how the applied technology of risk has been implicated for fueling a major financial crisis, his work also demonstrates how the regulation of global financial markets and abstruse financial instruments in advanced industrialized countries impacts the lives of the poorest people in developing countries and emerging markets.

This informative study is relevant to subject areas such as international political economy, international finance and globalization studies and is useful, specifically, for modules relating to global governance and international financial market regulation.

Vikash Yadav is Assistant Professor of Political Science at Hobart and William Smith Colleges in Geneva, New York.

Routledge Frontiers of Political Economy

1 **Equilibrium versus Understanding**
Towards the rehumanization of economics within social theory
Mark Addleson

2 **Evolution, Order and Complexity**
Edited by Elias L. Khalil and Kenneth E. Boulding

3 **Interactions in Political Economy**
Malvern after ten years
Edited by Steven Pressman

4 **The End of Economics**
Michael Perelman

5 **Probability in Economics**
Omar F. Hamouda and Robin Rowley

6 **Capital Controversy, Post Keynesian Economics and the History of Economics**
Essays in honour of Geoff Harcourt, volume one
Edited by Philip Arestis, Gabriel Palma and Malcolm Sawyer

7 **Markets, Unemployment and Economic Policy**
Essays in honour of Geoff Harcourt, volume two
Edited by Philip Arestis, Gabriel Palma and Malcolm Sawyer

8 **Social Economy**
The logic of capitalist development
Clark Everling

9 **New Keynesian Economics/ Post Keynesian Alternatives**
Edited by Roy J. Rotheim

10 **The Representative Agent in Macroeconomics**
James E. Hartley

11 **Borderlands of Economics**
Essays in honour of Daniel R. Fusfeld
Edited by Nahid Aslanbeigui and Young Back Choi

12 **Value, Distribution and Capital**
Essays in honour of Pierangelo Garegnani
Edited by Gary Mongiovi and Fabio Petri

13 **The Economics of Science**
Methodology and epistemology as if economics really mattered
James R. Wible

14 **Competitiveness, Localised Learning and Regional Development**
Specialisation and prosperity in small open economies
Peter Maskell, Heikki Eskelinen, Ingjaldur Hannibalsson, Anders Malmberg and Eirik Vatne

15 **Labour Market Theory**
A constructive reassessment
Ben J. Fine

16 **Women and European Employment**
Jill Rubery, Mark Smith, Colette Fagan, Damian Grimshaw

17 **Explorations in Economic Methodology**
From Lakatos to empirical philosophy of science
Roger Backhouse

18 **Subjectivity in Political Economy**
Essays on wanting and choosing
David P. Levine

19 **The Political Economy of Middle East Peace**
The impact of competing trade agendas
Edited by J.W. Wright, Jnr

20 **The Active Consumer**
Novelty and surprise in consumer choice
Edited by Marina Bianchi

21 **Subjectivism and Economic Analysis**
Essays in memory of Ludwig Lachmann
Edited by Roger Koppl and Gary Mongiovi

22 **Themes in Post-Keynesian Economics**
Essays in honour of Geoff Harcourt, volume three
Edited by Claudio Sardoni and Peter Kriesler

23 **The Dynamics of Technological Knowledge**
Cristiano Antonelli

24 **The Political Economy of Diet, Health and Food Policy**
Ben J. Fine

25 **The End of Finance**
Capital market inflation, financial derivatives and pension fund capitalism
Jan Toporowski

26 **Political Economy and the New Capitalism**
Edited by Jan Toporowski

27 **Growth Theory**
A philosophical perspective
Patricia Northover

28 **The Political Economy of the Small Firm**
Edited by Charlie Dannreuther

29 **Hahn and Economic Methodology**
Edited by Thomas Boylan and Paschal F. O'Gorman

30 **Gender, Growth and Trade**
The miracle economies of the postwar years
David Kucera

31 **Normative Political Economy**
Subjective freedom, the market and the state
David Levine

32 **Economist with a Public Purpose**
Essays in honour of John Kenneth Galbraith
Edited by Michael Keaney

33 **Involuntary Unemployment**
The elusive quest for a theory
Michel De Vroey

34 **The Fundamental Institutions of Capitalism**
Ernesto Screpanti

35 **Transcending Transaction**
The search for self-generating markets
Alan Shipman

36 **Power in Business and the State**
An historical analysis of its concentration
Frank Bealey

37 **Editing Economics**
Essays in honour of Mark Perlman
Hank Lim, Ungsuh K. Park and Geoff Harcourt

38 **Money, Macroeconomics and Keynes**
Essays in honour of Victoria Chick, volume one
Philip Arestis, Meghnad Desai and Sheila Dow

39 **Methodology, Microeconomics and Keynes**
Essays in honour of Victoria Chick, volume two
Philip Arestis, Meghnad Desai and Sheila Dow

40 **Market Drive and Governance**
Reexamining the rules for economic and commercial contest
Ralf Boscheck

41 **The Value of Marx**
Political economy for contemporary capitalism
Alfredo Saad-Filho

42 **Issues in Positive Political Economy**
S. Mansoob Murshed

43 **The Enigma of Globalisation**
A journey to a new stage of capitalism
Robert Went

44 **The Market**
Equilibrium, stability, mythology
S. N. Afriat

45 **The Political Economy of Rule Evasion and Policy Reform**
Jim Leitzel

46 **Unpaid Work and the Economy**
Edited by Antonella Picchio

47 **Distributional Justice**
Theory and measurement
Hilde Bojer

48 **Cognitive Developments in Economics**
Edited by Salvatore Rizzello

49 **Social Foundations of Markets, Money and Credit**
Costas Lapavitsas

50 **Rethinking Capitalist Development**
Essays on the economics of Josef Steindl
Edited by Tracy Mott and Nina Shapiro

51 **An Evolutionary Approach to Social Welfare**
Christian Sartorius

52 **Kalecki's Economics Today**
Edited by Zdzislaw L. Sadowski and Adam Szeworski

53 **Fiscal Policy from Reagan to Blair**
The left veers right
Ravi K. Roy and Arthur T. Denzau

54 **The Cognitive Mechanics of Economic Development and Institutional Change**
Bertin Martens

55 **Individualism and the Social Order**
The social element in liberal thought
Charles R. McCann Jnr.

56 **Affirmative Action in the United States and India**
A comparative perspective
Thomas E. Weisskopf

57 **Global Political Economy and the Wealth of Nations**
Performance, institutions, problems and policies
Edited by Phillip Anthony O'Hara

58 **Structural Economics**
Thijs ten Raa

59 **Macroeconomic Theory and Economic Policy**
Essays in honour of Jean-Paul Fitoussi
Edited by K. Vela Velupillai

60 **The Struggle Over Work**
The "end of work" and employment alternatives in post-industrial societies
Shaun Wilson

61 **The Political Economy of Global Sporting Organisations**
John Forster and Nigel Pope

62 **The Flawed Foundations of General Equilibrium Theory**
Critical essays on economic theory
Frank Ackerman & Alejandro Nadal

63 **Uncertainty in Economic Theory**
Essays in honor of David Schmeidler's 65th Birthday
Edited by Itzhak Gilboa

64 **The New Institutional Economics of Corruption**
Edited by Johann Graf Lambsdorff, Markus Taube & Matthias Schramm

65 **The Price Index and its Extension**
A chapter in economic measurement
S. N. Afriat

66 **Reduction, Rationality and Game Theory in Marxian Economics**
Bruce Philp

67 **Culture and Politics in Economic Development**
Volker Bornschier

68 **Modern Applications of Austrian Thought**
Edited by Jürgen G. Backhaus

69 **Ordinary Choices**
Individuals, incommensurability, and democracy
Robert Urquhart

70 **Labour Theory of Value**
Peter C. Dooley

71 **Capitalism**
Victor D. Lippit

72 **Macroeconomic Foundations of Macroeconomics**
Alvaro Cencini

73 **Marx for the 21st Century**
Edited by Hiroshi Uchida

74 **Growth and Development in the Global Political Economy**
Social structures of accumulation and modes of regulation
Phillip Anthony O'Hara

75 **The New Economy and Macroeconomic Stability**
A neo-modern perspective drawing on the complexity approach and Keynesian economics
Teodoro Dario Togati

76 **The Future of Social Security Policy**
Women, work and a citizens basic income
Ailsa McKay

77 **Clinton and Blair**
The political economy of the third way
Flavio Romano

78 Marxian Reproduction Schema
Money and aggregate demand in a capitalist economy
A. B. Trigg

79 The Core Theory in Economics
Problems and solutions
Lester G. Telser

80 Economics, Ethics and the Market
Introduction and applications
Johan J. Graafland

81 Social Costs and Public Action in Modern Capitalism
Essays inspired by Karl William Kapp's theory of social costs
Edited by Wolfram Elsner, Pietro Frigato and Paolo Ramazzotti

82 Globalization and the Myths of Free Trade
History, theory and empirical evidence
Edited by Anwar Shaikh

83 Equilibrium in Economics: Scope and Limits
Edited by Valeria Mosini

84 Globalization
State of the art and perspectives
Edited by Stefan A. Schirm

85 Neoliberalism
National and regional experiments with global ideas
Edited by Ravi K. Roy, Arthur T. Denzau, Thomas D. Willett

86 Post-Keynesian Macroeconomics Economics
Essays in honour of Ingrid Rima
Edited by Mathew Forstater, Gary Mongiovi and Steven Pressman

87 Consumer Capitalism
Anastasios S. Korkotsides

88 Remapping Gender in the New Global Order
Edited Marjorie Griffin Cohen and Janine Brodie

89 Hayek and Natural Law
Eric Angner

90 Race and Economic Opportunity in the Twenty-First Century
Edited by Marlene Kim

91 Renaissance in Behavioural Economics
Harvey Leibenstein's impact on contemporary economic analysis
Edited by Roger Frantz

92 Human Ecology Economics
A new framework for global sustainability
Edited by Roy E. Allen

93 Imagining Economics Otherwise
Encounters with identity/difference
Nitasha Kaul

94 Reigniting the Labor Movement
Restoring means to ends in a democratic labor movement
Gerald Friedman

95 The Spatial Model of Politics
Norman Schofield

96 The Economics of American Judaism
Carmel Ullman Chiswick

97 Critical Political Economy
Christian Arnsperger

98 Culture and Economic Explanation
Economics in the US and Japan
Donald W. Katzner

99 Feminism, Economics and Utopia
Time travelling through paradigms
Karin Schönpflug

100 Risk in International Finance
Vikash Yadav

Risk in International Finance

Vikash Yadav

Routledge
Taylor & Francis Group
LONDON AND NEW YORK

First published 2008
by Routledge
2 Park Square, Milton Park, Abingdon, Oxon OX14 4RN

Simultaneously published in the USA and Canada
by Routledge
270 Madison Ave, New York, NY 10016

Routledge is an imprint of the Taylor & Francis Group, an informa business

Typeset in Times New Roman by
Taylor & Francis Books
Printed and bound in Great Britain by
Antony Rowe Ltd, Chippenham, Wiltshire

British Library Cataloguing in Publication Data
A catalogue record for this book is available from the British Library

Library of Congress Cataloging in Publication Data
Yadav, Vikash.
Risk in international finance / Vikash Yadav.
p. cm.
Includes bibliographical references and index.
1. International finance. 2. Financial risk. 3. Financial services industry–Risk management. I. Title.
HG3881.Y32 2008
332′.042–dc22 2007038430

ISBN 978-0-415-77519-9 (hbk)
ISBN 978-0-203-92923-0 (ebk)

Contents

Tables

Preface

This book analyzes the evolution and impact of the concept of risk on processes of transnational banking and financial market regulation, as well as the externalities generated by speculative financial activity in emerging market economies. I argue that the concept of risk is *the* lens through which financial market activity is understood in the post-Bretton Woods monetary order. The proliferation and regulation of the complex financial instruments related to risk management are central to the monetary order because they permit financial and commodity exchange in an international economy characterized by rapid capital mobility and volatility in foreign exchange rates. In large part, my work is an attempt to theorize the relationship between the evolving concept of risk and public/private regulation.

My research seeks to apply elements of a post-structural methodology to the study of international financial market regulation. Inspired by Michel Foucault's framework of critical discourse analysis in *The History of Sexuality*, my argument dissects the rules of formation that govern the evolving discourse on risk. My application of Foucault's theoretical framework is actually an extension of the work of some of his most prominent colleagues and students. In particular, the works of Francois Ewald on "Insurance and Risk," Daniel Defert on "Insurance Technology," and Robert Castel on "Dangerousness and Risk" were all sources of insight that led me to study the concept of risk in international finance.

My aim throughout has been to apply post-structural theory to advance understanding and provide a critique of the dynamic politics of the regulation of risk. For the reader who is unfamiliar with post-structural theory and methodology, I have attempted to remove jargon and minimize the dense prose associated with this advanced theory. The advantages of a post-structural outlook are that it allows the scholar to unearth the political and cultural artifacts buried inside the positivist temple architecture and to analyze de-centralized and fluid power relations.

A common critique of the Foucaudian framework(s) is its pessimism regarding individual freedom and political liberation. As a result, the approach does not usually generate practical policy injunctions. Rather, its strength is to deliver an unflinching examination of the intimate and extensive relationship of power and knowledge. Following in this tradition, this book traces the cunning of power in one section of the international monetary order; I do not offer simple solutions to "fix" the international financial architecture. Proponents of global public policy reform initiatives (e.g. the Tobin Tax on transnational capital flows) often fail to grasp the constantly evolving relationship between power and knowledge in the international political economy that generate loopholes and spaces of defection. The international political economy is not a static object which can be "fixed" by tinkering.

Similarly, the peddlers of prosperity, like Frederic S. Mishkin, who argue that financial liberalization "done right" will help disadvantaged nations "get rich," deal in truisms. Neo-liberal policy prescriptions contingent on the suppression of existing political and economic interests are mere abstractions. A socially disembedded financial system will not long survive untarnished in the agonistic realm of public life even if it can be implemented. Moreover, to the extent that advocates of financial globalization do not confront candidly the political and economic interests of foreign financial institutions, their arguments rehearse an all too familiar colonial rubric. Finally, it must be acknowledged that the structure of the international monetary order makes the challenge of financial integration incredibly complex and generally stacked against the emerging markets. The existence of a hierarchy of currencies and the recurrent flights to quality during financial crises severely constrain the ability of countries to get financial liberalization "right," even when property rights are secure and prudential regulations are in place. Access to foreign capital and the import of foreign financial institutions in an emerging economy does not obviate the need for an emerging economy to establish a credible currency domestically and internationally. In an economy without a credible currency, financial liberalization/globalization is unlikely to create the virtuous circle where the end of financial repression leads to increased liquidity, higher interest rates, increased savings, efficient investment, and higher rates of absolute and relative growth. The reason is that the absence of a credible currency combined with unfettered access to foreign capital often invites speculative assaults which are associated with real costs to the economy and society. A robust financial sector populated by a diverse array of financial institutions is not the precondition for a credible currency; a vibrant financial sector is the product of a credible monetary economy. Financial depth develops gradually through increasing confidence in the credit status of borrowers, a growing network of relationships among state and market institutions, and predictable public policies. For several emerging market economies a policy of financial restraint (without financial repression), which entails setting the deposit rate below the national competitive average to encourage the development of the franchise value of private banks and limiting competition from international banks, may be more appropriate to promoting financial depth and economic development than a blanket policy of financial liberalization/globalization. Channeling existing interests and institutions to promote financial deepening through domestic competition is more practical than attempting to suppress and overwhelm domestic interests with foreign competition. The main point is that existing political interests and institutions cannot be evacuated in order to implement an idealized slate of financial policy reforms.

Of course, an awareness of the ubiquity of power relations as well as the resilience of governance structures and interests within countries and the broader financial order does not constitute an endorsement of their social and economic effects. This book rejects the panglossian outlook of political economists who marvel at the rapid evolution of regulatory structures that have permitted global financial markets to withstand a series of major financial crises. Unlike Ethan Kapstein, the infamous author of the 1996 *Foreign Affairs* article "Shockproof: The End of Financial Crisis," I do not seek to announce the "elimination of financial contagion" by diligent state regulators or to trivialize the social consequences of recurrent financial crises as "tragic" but ultimately inconsequential to the systemic order. Financial crises have long-term and asymmetric impacts on some of the most vulnerable segments of society in the emerging economies. From the standpoint of social justice, the effects of these crises herald the need for thorough reform of the international monetary order.

A transformation of the international monetary order will require much more than public policy tinkering or the adoption of rose colored glasses. It will require a critical reexamination of the "moral sentiments" which address the gap between the behavior and belief of subjects. Of course, a new ethical system modeled on a moral/juridical code is no longer tenable in an age where philosophy has failed to produce firm foundations, and economics has adopted a reductive vision of the subject. An ethical system based on self-referential practices within a network of social relations might suggest possibilities for the future, but a new ethical subject cannot emerge without first exposing the perpetual spiral of limit and transgression in which the current discourse on risk is trapped. It is my hope that this book will contribute to the critique of the present monetary order and help to advance substantive reform.

Acknowledgments

> The foundation of one's thought is the thought of another; thought is like a brick cemented into a wall. It is a simulacrum of thought if, in his looking back on himself, the being who thinks sees a free brick and not the price this semblance of freedom costs him. ...
>
> Georges Bataille, *Theory of Religion*

I am deeply indebted to my professors at the University of Pennsylvania for their invaluable insights and persistent dedication to my work. Thomas M. Callaghy was the person who first motivated me to toil in field of international political economy. He remains one of the fiercest intellects and warmest personalities I have ever encountered. Ellen Kennedy and Tayyeb Shabbir challenged my arguments from contending perspectives thereby helping me to discover the limits and hidden potential of my own logic. Anne Norton worked tirelessly and imaginatively to make my work rigorous and forceful. Her acuity, courage, compassion, and wit mark her as one of the great minds of our times. Finally, Rudy Sil has provided encouragement, detailed advice, and exceptional mentoring throughout my career.

Research for this project was funded for by the University of Pennsylvania School of Arts and Sciences Dissertation Writing Fellowship; the Queen Elizabeth Visiting Scholar Fellowship at St. Antony's College, Oxford University; and a Dean of Humanities Fellowship at the University of Pennsylvania. I am also grateful to DeAnne Julius and the Bank of England for granting me access to their resources.

Thomas Krantz gave generously of his time and introduced me to a community of policy makers dedicated to the art and science of market regulation. I appreciated my stimulating discussions on the politics and mechanics of international financial markets with Geoffrey R. D. Underhill, Vijay Kelkar, Charles Freeland, Samantha Barrass, Robert B. Herde, Georg Schattney, Jonathan H. Tattersall, Robert Sleeper. I am also grateful to numerous current and former staff at the Bank of England, Bank for International Settlements, Fédération Internationale des Bourses de Valeurs, London Stock Exchange, Deutsche Börse, International Monetary Fund, and World Bank.

Joseph Mink has been influential in this work from its conception to the final chapter. Conrad Barwa reviewed numerous drafts and provided invaluable comments. Their friendship has grounded me intellectually and personally throughout this process. Long discussions with Gurinder S. Tamber helped me to understand the intricacies of international financial markets.

For their collegiality, support, and warm friendship, I am thankful to Jonathan Isacoff, Graham Dodds, Anya Shternshis, Sarah Washbrook, Yoav Alon, Reuben Wong, Neil Ruiz, Jason Kirk, Calvin Chen, Kavita Khory, Jean Allain, and Trevor Parfitt.

I am especially appreciative for the words of encouragement from my community of family and friends in Ohio. Farther afield, the Benedetto family in Lausanne, with whom I first lived as a high-school exchange student, provided me once again with a home away from home while I conducted interviews and research in Europe. My brother and sister-in-law always encouraged me and my nephews brought newfound joys in my life. My work is dedicated to my parents who left everything they had to come to America in order to give their children greater opportunities in life. Their unstinting sacrifices for my education can never be repaid.

Finally, this book could not have been completed without the assistance of Stacey Philbrick Yadav. She read countless drafts with patience and challenged me to become a better writer and a clearer thinker. Her comprehensive knowledge and keen intellect broadened my intellectual horizons. Her love and companionship have enriched my work and my life immeasurably.

Needless to say, all remaining errors are mine.

I Introduction

The history of the contemporary international monetary order is punctuated by financial crises. In recent years, the volatility of exchange rates and asset prices in international financial markets has threatened to shred the economic, political, and social fabric of several countries around the world.[1] Speculative attacks on currencies have imposed costly restrictions on the policy options of sovereign states.[2] Currency assaults and a host of other speculative transactions have been fueled by the development of complex financial instruments and interlinked marketplaces that allow institutions to hedge financial risks and/or speculate for profit. Ironically, this sphere of speculative economic activity has been authorized by governments, rationalized by neo-liberal ideology, and propelled by communications technology. To the extent that a speculative assault may create, intensify, or prolong a loss of confidence in national financial systems and across multiple interconnected markets,[3] the state/market nexus and its ideological apparatus seem to have sown the seeds of their own destruction. Given this apparent catastrophic potential, the real puzzle is: how has this monetary order been able to operate and reproduce itself for so long? How does the monetary order regulate the "risks" it produces and what are the economic, social, and political consequences?

The term "monetary" is not meant to imply a narrow focus on the relationships between national currencies regulated by states, but the entire financial system under which credit is solicited, created, monitored, regulated, allocated, taxed, and used.[4] In fact, exchange rates between currencies are intimately related to the broader financial system. The term "order" indicates only that subjects behave in a certain way because of the *de facto* recognition of the distribution of abstract rights to property and from the particular mode of balancing interests.[5]

A "speculative" financial transaction generally involves:

- The execution of a financial transaction based upon an estimation of the possibility and speed of growth/decline in the market value of an asset or currency (as opposed to the execution of a financial transaction based on evidence of an increase/decrease in productivity); and/or

- The purchase of a financial instrument that does not confer legal claims on the current or future earning from a specific material asset or service; and/or
- The failure to purchase a financial instrument that offsets the exposure of existing assets to probabilistic market dynamics (i.e., insurance).

The paradox is that financial institutions must purchase speculative financial instruments as a form of insurance in order to offset, at least in part, the aggregate effects of speculative financial activities. Speculative financial instruments are commonly labeled as "derivative" financial contracts, because the value of the contract is derived from the prices of underlying contracts, such as equities, bonds, currencies, and commodities. Derivative financial instruments are essentially time-bound contracts (1) to permit the purchase, sale, or exchange of specific financial products such as stocks, bonds, currency, or indexes of other financial products; and/or (2) to offset the effects of a change in value of other financial products. There are several thousand sub-species of derivative contracts that have been articulated, such as financial futures, options, stock indexes, swaps, swap-options, inverse floaters, etc., to produce the specific utility effects demanded by financial institutions. In other words, these financial instruments are sold as mechanisms that are designed to offset the exposure of existing assets to specific risks.

Although speculative financial activity seems to imply a mediated or subordinate relationship with processes of production and trade,[6] speculative activity has moved to center stage in the post-Bretton Woods monetary order. Derivative financial instruments do not represent "exotic," marginal, or super-structural aspects of the international political economy; they are central to the operation of the current monetary order, because they are designed to facilitate exchange in an uncertain and volatile global market. The articulation of these new financial instruments has had the effect of transforming more and more components of finance or financial assets into marketable instruments. Since the early 1980s, there has been an enormous increase in liquidity and in the circulation of financial capital through the marketing of financial instruments rather than lending.[7]

Speculative financial instruments are commonly marketed as sophisticated devices to reduce specified categories of risk, even though the actual aggregate effect of these instruments may be to increase volatility and proliferate risk. The technology of financial risk is related to and draws strength from other positive discourses on risk in society (e.g., health risks, sexual risks, insurable risks, military risks). Building upon an array of risk-management technologies first pioneered by actuarial science, statistics, and probability theory, complex financial instruments have transformed the "risk elements" of any financial contract into separate, manipulable components that can be sold and purchased on the market as a commodity. Interconnected market institutions and sophisticated financial instruments have been developed to disperse risk to those financial intermediaries that will accept risk in exchange for a fee and a potentially large profit margin. Banks, brokerage firms, insurance companies, corporations, governments, and individual investors use derivative financial instruments. Even average home and car buyers participate in derivative contracts when they sign mortgages or loans with fixed or adjustable interest rate charges, since the bank usually purchases a financial instrument to hedge against interest rate changes and it securitizes loans, particularly loans to subprime borrowers (i.e., borrowers with poor credit histories). The exchange of derivative contracts impacts the price of many materials used by ordinary consumers on a daily basis such as petroleum, natural gas, heating oil, and electricity. Where derivative financial instruments are legally recognized as a form of insurance, these contracts allow banks, securities firms, and insurance companies to cut costs associated with the maintenance of sufficient capital reserve holdings and therefore offer more competitive rates for customers. In fact, there is little choice for large financial institutions except to participate in the derivatives market. As Susan Strange observed, "... whereas people who go to the racecourses or bet on the races actually enjoy gambling, the great majority of participants in the speculative financial markets of our times are there involuntarily because they are risk-averse and do *not* want to gamble. They are afraid of uncertainty and they are keen to hedge against it."[8]

Of course, the potential profits from purchasing the risk of other institutions (i.e., speculating on interest rates, foreign exchange rates, or other assets) do represent a highly lucrative mechanism for institutions to increase revenue. For example, in 2006 US commercial banks generated $18.8 billion in trading revenues mainly due to derivatives trading, this represents a 90 percent increase in revenue from 2004, according to the Office of the Comptroller of Currency (OCC). If all derivatives contracts were immediately liquidated, the net current credit exposure of US insured commercial banks would be $185 billion; the notional (i.e., the nominal or face) value of all the derivatives contracts held by US insured commercial banks was $131.5 trillion at the end of 2006 – a figure ten times greater than the US gross domestic product (GDP). The total number of outstanding derivatives contracts increased by 30 percent in 2006 compared to the previous year, indicating an increase in business activity.[9] The top ten investment banks, which hold the overwhelming bulk of all derivatives contracts, increased their trading revenue by 13 percent in the last quarter of 2006, a 45 percent increase from the same period in the previous year.[10] Revenue from trading derivatives encompasses a significant portion of the top US investment bank's gross revenue: JP Morgan Chase earned 9.7 percent of its fourth quarter earnings in 2006; HSBC Bank USA earned 5.1 percent; Citibank 3.9 percent; Bank of America 1.9 percent; and Wachovia 0.3 percent.[11]

At the same time, derivatives trading is also responsible for some of the most spectacular losses in the post-Bretton Woods era (see Table 1.1).

Even though current profit and loss levels may be anomalous, it is apparent that derivatives are growing in importance.

Table 1.1 Dramatic losses from derivatives trading activity

Company	*Estimated Financial Loss*	*Year*	*Activity*
Air Products	$113 million	1994	Leverage and currency swaps
Allied Irish Bank	$691 million	2002	Equity derivatives and currency options
Amaranth Advisors LLC	$6,000 million	2006	Energy derivatives
Askin Capital Management	$600 million	1994	Mortgage derivatives
Bank of Montreal	$680 million	2007	Energy derivatives
Baring Brothers	$1,241 million	1995	Options
Cargill (Minnetonka Fund)	$100 million	1994	Mortgage derivatives
China Aviation Oil	$550 million	2004	Energy derivatives
Codelco Chile	$200 million	1994	Copper and precious metals futures and forwards
Daiwa Bank	$1,100 million	1995	Bonds, futures, and basis trades
Glaxo Holdings PLC	$150 million	1994	Mortgage derivatives
Kidder, Peabody & Co.	$350 million	1994	Stripped government bonds
Long-Term Capital Management	$4,000 million	1998	Currency and interest rate derivatives
Metallgesellschaft	$1,340 million	1994	Energy derivatives
National Australia Bank	$360 million	2004	Currency options
Orange County, CA	$2,000 million	1994	Reverse repos and leveraged structured notes
Proctor & Gamble	$157 million	1994	Leveraged German mark and US dollar spread

Source: Adapted and updated from Ed McCarthy, “Derivatives Revisited,” *Journal of Accountancy* 189, no. 5 (2000): 35.

There is no end in sight for the expansion of this multi-trillion dollar market. This lucrative business supports and is supported by the perpetual discovery of new risk, in the words of one trade journal: "... the creation of new risk always seems to be racing just one step ahead of the abilities of banks to control it."[12] Market participants and financial media pundits are well aware that if existing risks are tamed, new risks will need to be discovered or invented. Edgar Meister, a representative of the German Bundesbank on the Basel Committee for Banking Supervision writes:

> Once the transition period is over, market opportunities will decrease, but the security of the new products will increase in practice and with experience. Product innovation will then be the market solution to develop further business, which, in line with basic marketing ideas, will open up new opportunities for some time owing to the imperfection of the new market segments. However, this process often leads to new problems and risks.[13]

Speculation occurs even in the absence of voluntary participation in derivatives markets. Where no action is taken to counter or hedge a known category of risk, the financial firm engages *de facto* in "speculation" on its exposed assets. Of course, risk management experts of a financial firm may deliberately assume that exchange rates or interest rates will remain the same or move in their favor in the near future and therefore consciously choose to forgo the use of particular risk-management instruments.[14] Financial firms may choose to speculate passively because there is a cost, in terms of premiums and commissions, associated with hedging all open exposures.

The institutionalization of risk management and diversification strategies also seems to encourage market institutions to engage unwittingly in higher-risk activities. Peter L. Bernstein writes:

> The introduction of portfolio insurance in the late 1970s encouraged a higher level of equity exposure than had prevailed before. In the same fashion, conservative institutional investors tend to use broad diversification to justify higher exposure to risk in untested areas – but diversification is not a guarantee against loss, only against losing everything at once.[15]

In essence, the struggle to offset or exploit risk has become unavoidable.

There appears to be a pattern to the all-encompassing spirals of speculation and insurance characteristic of this monetary order. The post-Bretton Woods monetary order operates and reproduces itself through an intertwined and ever-expanding technology of risk. The technology of risk simultaneously increases the opportunities for speculative financial activity and provides remedies at the various sites of financial vulnerability revealed by each speculation-induced crisis. The insurance functions of risk are developed to match each additional speculative opportunity, and speculative instruments are developed to transgress each insurance function. Volatility must be perpetually generated and countered. Financial instruments designed to manage risk would not have any value or use in the absence of volatility and uncertainty. Financial volatility without dampening mechanisms would rattle the monetary order apart.

The result of the unending search to discover the sources of risk is that financial institutions have come to be understood as risk-bearing entities; they are considered to be fabricated with risk. For example, Edward Furash writes,

> "... risk is often unconsciously built into the way the business is run. So it may be assumed that the business is running well, its risks are properly controlled. However, this assumption is wrong. Unanticipated risk is what is usually deadly. And in many circumstances, the true risk inherent in the business is rarely expressed, understood, or measured."[16]

Risk continues to appear where it is least expected leading practitioners to believe that risk is the essence of the firm. Each of the innumerable interactions within the firm, with clients, with regulators, and between firms appears to be a source of risk.

While risk is productive and profitable when disentangled and commodified, by the late 1980s and early 1990s the "production of risk" began to be perceived as a danger to the entire financial system. As one financial magazine noted in the context of the release of an industry think-tank's report on the derivatives market:

> The report, originally commissioned in August 1992, was prompted by the debate which had been raging over whether the various derivative markets ... were in control of their various products. Or are they in the worst case creating a Frankenstein's monster over which they may lose control, with the consequent systemic risk this represents to all financial markets?[17]

Press reports reveal that even senior executives in financial firms began to see derivatives as a potential source of a financial disaster.

> Derivatives are "a time bomb that could explode just like the LDC crisis did, threatening the world financial system," warned Royal Bank of Canada chairman Allan Taylor at the International Monetary Conference in May. And Lazard Frèeres & Co. senior partner Felix Rohatyn was quoted in this magazine's 25th Anniversary issue in July as worrying that "26-year-olds with computers are creating financial hydrogen bombs."[18]

Regulatory officials believed that derivative contracts posed a threat to the international financial system because,

> ... derivatives have been a major factor in tightening linkages among markets and potentially altering the transmission of economic and financial shocks. If a firm that was very active in these markets came under extreme financial stress, regardless of the source of its difficulties, the unwinding of its outstanding derivatives positions and related positions in other financial markets could pose significant challenges both to the firm and to regulatory authorities seeking to contain the effects of its difficulties.[19]

In other words, the complexity, value, and fixed temporal nature of derivative contracts make it difficult to unwind positions quickly during a crisis. As most derivatives contracts are traded between banking institutions, the unexpected termination of a derivative contract or default of a counter-party would theoretically transmit losses to other interlinked counter-parties setting off a ripple effect across the banking system. The danger perceived by regulatory officials was that this complex web of interdependence was not visible. As Alexandre Lamfalussy, the General Manager of the Bank for International Settlements, conceded:

> "We do not know the web of interconnections between banks that has been established through derivatives," [...] "The market is losing transparency, and we do not know who is dependent on whom anymore. Now we will only know after the fact, and by then it could be too late." [...] "At least with the LDC crisis we had an indication of the order of magnitude (of the problem). You had a photograph at any one time of the relationships."[20]

States believed that transparency in derivative financial transactions would increase their ability to monitor and regulate the invisible ties that bind market participants to one another.

Of course, some market participants mocked the obsession of state regulators with systemic risk, Karen Shaw Petrou, President ISD/SHAW Inc., testified to the US Congress:

> A "Joint Forum" of financial regulators is laboring quietly in the vineyards of "conglomerate" [i.e., banking plus securities] regulation, attempting to define which aspects of a financial services firm raise public policy risks and which do not. Its tendency, like those of the regulators that compose it, is to find that virtually everything creates risk pretty much all of the time, warranting comprehensive regulation that would be anathema to most U.S. financial services firms and to the non-bank parents of some of these companies as well.[21]

Whether or not the threat of systemic risk was overplayed as latter-day regulators and financial institutions would contend, the perception of a systemic threat attributed to derivative financial contracts in the late 1980s required the establishment of "external" (i.e., state) and "internal" (i.e., intra-firm) monitoring, regulating, punishing, and correcting mechanisms.[22]

The justification for external or state regulation was not merely dependent upon exogenous public pressure; there were clearly endogenous reasons to explain the necessity for regulating markets:

> Whatever the social costs and benefits of an externally imposed system of regulation may be, public revulsion at the effects and outcomes of failures in unregulated financial systems can force the establishment of systems of deposit insurance and external regulation, no matter what the reservations of the authorities may be. Those who are invested with the responsibility for supervision are often aware of the poison in the chalice.
>
> But the case for external regulation (in addition to, and partly in place of, private self-regulation) does not rest just on surrender to public pressure; and if it did, such pressure should be resisted. Instead, the case depends on circumstances in which the private sector, left to itself, produces market failures, or at least suboptimal outcomes, which are arguably worse than public sector regulation, even with all the biases and failings that such regulations may entail.[23]

From the perspective of the globalization of financial markets, there are also geopolitical reasons to regulate "externally" the derivatives markets. As Howard Davies, head of Britain's Financial Services Authority (FSA), stated bluntly in the wake of revelations that Western finanacial institutions (i.e., hedge funds) were responsible for some of the currency assaults during the Asian financial crisis: "If you cannot give these open economies some kind of assurance that they will not be subject to speculative attack, then they will close up."[24]

However, the external monitoring and supervision of financial institutions would never be sufficient to prevent certain types of crises such as fraud. Dr. Charles A. E. Goodhart, a member of the Monetary Policy Committee at the Bank of England, writes that important lessons were learned in the wake of the collapse of Britain's oldest merchant bank, Barings Bank, from the fraudulent activities of a single derivatives trader at a remote subsidiary. Goodhart argues that supervisors and practitioners realized that the level of *external* regulation required to prevent another case of fraud would have had to be so pervasive, so intrusive, and so expensive as to be practically impossible. Goodhart surmised, "The Barings failure arose from poor internal monitoring and supervision, not from a failure of regulation." Future solutions to prevent a recurrence of the Barings scandal would necessarily require the establishment of *internal* monitoring and supervision to supplement external regulation.[25]

Of course, even before the collapse of Barings in 1995, some regulatory officials had abrasively demanded that financial institutions regulate themselves. For example, David Mullins Jr., Vice Chairman of the US Federal

Reserve Board of Governors, argued that the derivatives industry needed to regulate itself through a legally constituted Self-Regulatory Organization (SRO).

> "The swaps dealers are a big adult market now," he says. "They have responsibilities they can't ignore. Either they create an SRO with teeth and submit to its discipline, or, if there are problems, they might not like the alternatives that could be produced for them here in Washington. I'm not especially impressed by the ability of the regulators and Congress to design optimum rules for new and evolving financial markets."[26]

Given the potential for heavy-handed regulation, it is not surprising that the threats of regulatory officials have been internalized and reproduced by market participants in their public discourse. John Medlin, Chairman of the Wachovia Corporation, stated at the Conference on Capital Federal Financial Institutions Examination Council in Washington, D.C.:

> More freedom brings more risk and requires more self-discipline. Bank managements should never forget that their institutions serve a vital public utility-like function in our economic system. A banking charter gives special privileges and imposes sacred responsibilities. Banks are supposed to inspire confidence and not cause anxiety during times of stress. This requires careful risk management and healthy liquidity and capital. ... Services and systems change, but sound banking fundamentals remain the same. They must be firmly embedded in a bank's culture to survive transient fads and fashions. Banks should be managed as if there were no regulators, no discount windows, and no deposit insurance.[27]

In essence, Medlin argues that it should not matter whether or not the firm is being watched by its regulator. The firm should constrain its own behavior for the greater good. The neo-classical rhetoric in which the pursuit of private vice endogenously leads to public virtue has been temporarily discarded. In smaller subsidiaries of large banks, the disciplinary process is purportedly even more rigorous. As Anil Narang, co-chief executive office of Swapco, a standalone triple-A rated derivatives subsidiary of Salmon Brothers, stated "our regulators are by default the ratings agencies, and the discipline we have is far greater than any regulator would ever want."[28] Although the specific claim of market participants needs to be taken with skepticism, it is apparent that financial institutions have implemented self-monitoring and self-regulating mechanisms. However, there is little evidence to show that these mechanisms have altered actual attitudes toward prudential financial market activity.

It is worth noting that the regulation of risk focused upon risk to individual institutions separately rather than the financial system as a whole.[29] The structure of regulation reinforces the subject position of market institutions. However, the self-regulating financial institution occupies an ambiguous position as it is both an object of risk technology and as a subject that knows how to use that technology.[30] Firms are caught up in a situation in which they subject themselves to discipline.

Mirroring the preoccupation with risk amongst market institutions, regulatory authorities have begun moving towards "risk based approaches" to financial regulation whereby supervisory resources are devoted to those divisions of a bank with a high-risk profile, as opposed to a comprehensive examination of the entire financial institution. In the UK, for example, the Financial Services Authority has explained that this new "style" of regulation will involve a series of consultations or "risk assessments":

> A risk assessment will involve the commitment of resources by both the supervisors and a bank's management. In particular, the supervisors need to spend time on-site discussing the issues with senior bank management. The time taken to perform this work will vary from bank to bank depending on the size and complexity of the institution. However, following a risk assessment, the supervisor will be better placed to decide on the intensity of the future supervision having obtained a better understanding of a bank's risk profile. The intensity of supervision and the amount and focus of supervisory action will increase in line with the perceived risk profile of a bank. One advantage this has for banks is that the cost of supervision, in terms of management time or through direct costs (e.g. reporting accountants' fees), should be more directly related to its risk.[31]

Similarly, the US Federal Reserve System has adopted "risk-focused supervision" programs for large, complex banking organizations (LCBO) and for community banks. After a risk assessment and the development of a supervisory plan, examination procedures are tailored to the institution's risk profile.[32] This regulatory shift represents an economizing of resources on the part of state regulatory officials. The cost of compliance with bureaucratic regulatory requirements is also reduced for market institutions. In the context of rapid proliferation of risk technology, the systemic benefit from this form of economic regulation is less clear.

The internalization and proliferation of the discourse on risk should not be read as a monolithic project. Power excites resistance. Power operates as a mechanism that elicits those peculiarities over which it keeps watch. Risk spreads to the power that searches for it; power reifies the risk that it incites. On the one hand, there is risk that is generated by exercising a power that questions, monitors, watches, searches out, and brings to light; on the other hand there is risk that emerges from having to evade this power, flee from it, fool it, or transgress it.[33]

Efforts by intergovernmental and nongovernmental organizations to devise uniform strategies to contain risk have perversely led to the proliferation of risk at the heterogeneous sites of application. John Medlin writes,

> Banks are not homogeneous. Their business exposures and risk management vary widely. These differences are not taken into account sufficiently under the present capital rules, which have only modest and largely quantitative risk-based features. The revolution in financial services is widening differences among banking organizations. This makes the "cookie cutter" capital regulation scheme of the past even more unrealistic.[34]

The *Economist* adds, "The trouble with the present Basel Accord is that it rewards risky lending, because it requires banks to put aside the same amount of capital against loans to shaky borrowers as against loans to more robust credits."[35]

Additionally, as regulatory officials have long understood, bringing a class of institutions under the regulatory umbrella may either (1) drive that institution to relocate in another jurisdiction; or (2) mislead investors into thinking that these institutions had a regulatory stamp of approval; or (3) lead to compliance that adheres to the letter of the law but not its spirit. In other words, the expansion of regulation inevitably incites resistance and legitimates the perverse. John Medlin states, "the federal safety net is both a blessing and a curse. It prevents financial panic, but it also weakens market discipline, breeds unsound management, and protects uneconomic institutions."[36] Alternatively, note this observation:

> In France, [the European Community's Capital Adequacy Directive (CAD)] has been implemented for over a year, yet the banks still have so many logistical problems that, instead of a daily calculation and control of market risk, CAD regulations consist of a frenzied and last-minute effort at the end of each month (that is to say only once a month) to manually fill out the statutory statements.[37]

Despite the resistance, contradictions, and transgressions generated by the discourse on risk, it is clear that risk has become *the* lens through which the market is understood:[38]

> As far as banks, other financial market players, central banks, and banking supervisors are concerned, it has long become a matter of course that we think more in terms of risk categories than types of business.[39]

How did this matrix of power/knowledge come to be? How did this discourse on risk take shape? How did this discourse acquire such a hold on the state and market?

That phenomenon which is conjured by the discourse on "risk" has an ancient pedigree that has, in its successive forms, evolution, and dissemination, spawned innumerable games of chance, sermons on morality, searches for moral certainty, sciences of probability, and institutions of insurance.[40] In the post-Bretton Woods monetary order, power has intertwined itself once again around risk to generate a regime of truth.[41] Before we examine the ways in which risk produces its truth and the consequences for the international political economy, let us look at some of the surfaces on which the discourse inscribes itself.

The next chapter, "Surfaces of Inscription," traces the field of relations that was reorganized, through a series of unintended and localized events, to permit the contemporary discourse on risk as a possible form of knowledge. In particular, the collapse of the Bretton Woods system of segregated financial markets and the standardization of balance sheets allowed for the rapid transmission of profits and losses across an intensive global network. Efforts to manage subsequent risks from this networked environment led to the creation of financial instruments to transfer or offset risk that occurred "off" the balance sheet. These risk management instruments simultaneously revealed new ways to transfer assets to remote sites outside the state's regulatory gaze. However, the process of financial globalization elaborated by the discourse on risk has not resulted in a uniform distribution of market infrastructure or capital. In fact, official market activity remains intensely focused around three metropolises: New York, London, and Tokyo. Nevertheless, there is a set of "parallel" financial markets often found at the margins of the international arena or as doppelgangers within the metropolis that act as sites of regulatory transgression and financial innovation. The discourse on risk colonizes, articulates, expands, and exploits these spaces of official and unofficial financial activity in the contemporary monetary order.[42]

The third chapter, "Theory of Risk," seeks to explicate the nebulous rules of formation that govern the discourse on risk. The discursive rules of formation must not be thought to exist outside the "non-discursive regime" of institutions, political events, cultural perspectives, and economic processes; rather these rules emerge from within specific institutions, events, perspectives, and economic formations.[43] The technology of risk is malleable and manipulable; it is not an abstract, objective, or scientific discourse. Risk has not been captured, controlled, or rendered docile. In fact, the categories of risk have proliferated and recombined in unexpected ways. Furthermore, volatility has persisted even amongst those actors who actively employ risk instruments to hedge their positions. Thus, the ever-expanding technology of risk has increasingly involved state as well as market participants in the process of developing, implementing, scrutinizing, authorizing, legalizing, and underwriting new techniques of risk assessment and management.

The fourth chapter, "Theory of Regulation," explores the dynamics of the strategic relations amongst the subjects articulated by the technology of risk: state, market, and conglomerate (i.e., state/market) institutions. The chapter analyzes the social facts, norms, and policies that guide regulatory activity in the contemporary financial system. As market participants circumvent prudential regulatory policies, states respond through the articulation of new modes of surveillance and governance. The cunning behavior of market participants results in the expansion of the regulatory gaze across the global stage as market participants engage in regulatory arbitrage between sovereign jurisdictions.

The fifth chapter, "Regulating Risk," synthesizes and builds upon the previous chapters on the theory of risk and the theory of regulation through a historical narrative. By examining the evolution of international capital adequacy rules in the transnational banking sector since the collapse of the Bretton Woods system, the chapter illustrates the productive tension whereby the technology of risk articulates increasingly precise understandings of risk, while simultaneously revealing loopholes through which financial institutions are able to evade regulatory oversight and increase profit.

The sixth chapter, "The Political Arena," examines the political and social context that the technology of risk impacts and the attempt to transcend the political and social volatility via the technology of political risk insurance. Through a brief examination of the costs of the Asian financial crisis, the chapter illustrates some of the long-term asymmetric social and economic consequences of short-term, speculation-induced financial panics in emerging market economies. The chapter then examines the development of political risk insurance as a technology designed to overcome the disruptive social and political effects generated, at least in part, by the volatility of the monetary order. The capitalist and monetarist norms that guide the development of risk technology skew the design of this technique to serve the interests of foreign investors. Political risk insurance claims to provide a market solution to encourage the development of impoverished and "risky" areas of the world. However, it may actually operate to intensify disciplinary pressure on sovereign states and subjects in the emerging economies and developing countries.

The final chapter, "Conclusion," argues that the technology of risk is enmeshed in an inexhaustible spiral of limit and transgression with serious economic, political, and social ramifications for the most vulnerable segments of the global economy. Although risk technology has expanded along several fronts, the technology has failed to capture or comprehend risk. Ultimately, the failure of this technology is related to a failure to address the moral and ethical roots of economic activity in a liberal capitalist system. A technology of risk that fosters stability and promotes economic development must redress the chasm between regulatory compliance and actual belief in the value of prudential behavior.

2 Surfaces of inscription

Risk has become the lens through which the market is understood. Despite the long history of risk and its related discourses in gambling, religion, mathematics, and probability, the prominence of risk in the contemporary monetary order is the product of a series of strategic responses to unanticipated events rather than a continuous process of scientific or mathematical progress. These unintended events, since the collapse of the post-war monetary order, have had the effect of clearing and reorganizing financial space. The reintegration of financial markets in a period of intense political and economic turmoil created economically unmanageable volatility. The concept of "risk management" first appeared in this monetary order as a market-oriented solution to the problem of volatility in time-lagged and conditional transnational financial arrangements (e.g., contracts for imported goods denominated in foreign currencies). The management of risk focused upon the micro-foundations of the emerging monetary order, the balance sheet, as the site where risk emerged within the firm. The techniques developed to transfer and exploit the risk on and off the balance sheet have rewritten the map of the monetary order as market participants learned to exploit these techniques to avoid regulation and engage in speculation. Like the manipulation of a complex genetic code, the manipulation of the risks surrounding the firm's balance sheet has resulted in the creation and growth of a new monetary order. This chapter provides a rough map of this monetary order that is unfolding itself across a multidimensional space.

The unintended order

The development of the post-Bretton Woods monetary order is not the product of intergovernmental agreements or treaties; it evolved from the repeated failure of international agreements to alter the trajectory of the monetary order in the 1960s and 1970s. The proximate cause of the collapse was the result of a currency assault on the US. The US terminated the central component of the Bretton Woods monetary order, i.e., the gold – dollar exchange, on 15 August 1971. The US became the subject of speculative assaults on its gold reserves after its current account fell into deficit for the first time since 1893 and market participants gambled that the US would have to devalue its currency to boost exports. The estimated hundreds of billions of dollars spent on the Vietnam War as well as the domestic "War on Poverty" had devalued the dollar *de facto*, but the US was unwilling to allow the conventions of the monetary order to restrict its domestic or foreign policy objectives.[1] By "closing the gold window," the US sought to shift the burden of adjustment to other countries in the monetary order. Speculators sold dollars in unprecedented proportions in exchange for German marks, Japanese yen, and other currencies that the speculators expected would be revalued against the dollar.[2] The old order collapsed as speculative capital flows inundated the German and Japanese central banks. The logic of the monetary order required these countries to choose between accepting rapid inflation in the domestic money supply (as the central banks purchased dollars for marks or yen); implementing weak and ineffective unilateral controls on capital flows; or floating their currencies relative to the US dollar. The Germans and Japanese adopted the least politically costly option, i.e., floating the value of their currencies relative to the dollar.

Nevertheless, it is likely that the Bretton Woods system would have collapsed under its own weight even without the specific assault on the dollar in 1971. As Gordon Thiessen, Governor of the Bank of Canada, stated:

> This system, which had been viable, although prone to periodic crises, throughout the 1950s and 1960s, was clearly unable to cope in a world of liberalized trade and international capital mobility. The Bretton Woods system, while laudable in concept, proved to be flawed in practice.
>
> The main problem was that the imbalances that the system was supposed to address, through discrete changes in the parity value of the affected currencies vis-à-vis the US dollar and gold, proved to be much larger and more intractable than the architects of the system had ever envisaged. Moreover, countries were reluctant to adjust their currencies, even when the problems were shown to be fundamental. Thus, authorities would often subvert domestic economic objectives, such as price stability, economic growth and full employment, in order to protect outdated parities. As a result, the system was in disequilibrium more often than not. And its adjustable nature did not prove flexible enough to help countries deal with the shocks that regularly hit the international financial system.[3]

Whereas the Bretton Woods system was the product of a specific set of international agreements, the new monetary order is not the product of any specific international treaty. A floating exchange rate system amongst major reserve currencies along with the liberalization of capital and commodity flows forms the core components of the post-Bretton Woods monetary order.[4] As in the pre-war monetary order, strategies of accumulation are no longer confined to the "natural" space of the nation state. A revitalized economic orthodoxy has successfully fractured and marginalized the post-war emphasis on national sovereignty, participatory democracy, social stability, and social justice.[5] The subordination of finance to production has been inverted. In other words, the old order has been dismantled and reassembled in accordance with an "orthodox" vision of political economy.

The balance sheet

In the absence of a formal agreement by states, the contemporary monetary order is assembled and interlinked through the balance sheet of each individual financial firm within the international financial system. Balance sheets are the micro-foundations of the monetary order. The balance sheet is a document associated with an (individual or) organization that literally re-presents a moment in the financial gestalt of that entity. The harmonization or standardization of legal, regulatory, and accounting practices associated with the structure of the balance sheet permits the extension and interconnection of separate financial institutions and marketplaces across time zones and around the clock. Harmonized or standardized balance sheets are the surface against which financial contracts become legible and mobile. The harmonization or standardization of the format of balance sheets facilitates the consensual, rapid, and accurate interpretation of meaning and insures the integrity of the information recorded. Of course, this conduit that facilitates the transmission of rapid profits between institutions may also transmit rapid losses if a party to a financial contract defaults.

The balance sheet is the site where the signs of the solvency and creditworthiness of the firm becomes legible to the firm itself as well as to its investors, clients, and regulators. The balance sheet is also the site where the ephemeral, digitized electronic flows of capital are made lasting and material. The balance sheet contributes to the effect of a discreet firm from an overlapping, ambiguous, and shifting process of production (i.e., the social division of labor). The balance sheet is the site where the dispersed "private" activities of the firm are retroactively centralized and rendered accountable to the "public." Knowledge about the balance sheet becomes the basis of relations with the firm to itself and to other subjects. For investors and competitors the balance sheet is a critical component in understanding the creditworthiness of the firm. The balance sheet is also the site of intense activity by states because the balance sheet is useful for taxation as well as the regulation of the pace and character of market activity. In fact, the definitions of capital and financial risk used to set international regulatory policies emanate from an analysis of the balance sheet rather than an examination of the total business risk.[6]

Each age of the "globalization" of capital has been grounded upon the standardization of balance sheets. In the first half of the fourteenth century, Italian merchants created a mechanism known as "bills of exchange" whereby the balance sheets of firms could be cleared without face-to-face contact or the material exchange of coins.[7] The double-entry bookkeeping system, with its emphasis on numeracy (or the quantification of qualitative phenomena) and precision in data entry (as opposed to accuracy) functioned to produce a visible sign of the merchant's honesty, thereby creating the possibility of credit amongst otherwise anonymous merchants.[8] To this day, the standardized balance sheet remains a critical component for the expansion and intensification of financial space because the balance sheet is intimately related to the production of the signs of trustworthiness and creditworthiness between institutions.

The current monetary order results not only from the standardization of balance sheets, but also from an intense scrutiny of the activities that transpire "off" the balance sheet in an effort to develop mechanisms to dampen financial volatility. The birth of the new monetary order occurred during a period of intense political and economic turmoil. In particular, the crisis in the Middle East and the subsequent oil price shocks created great volatility in the foreign exchange markets. The transmission of volatility between integrating markets created economically (and politically) unmanageable volatility. Economists and market participants focused upon the firm's balance sheet as the site where volatility circulated and surfaced. They observed that the transactions that appear on the balance sheet of the firm did not provide a comprehensive picture of the activities of a firm. In fact, those financial transactions that could not be made to "fit" on the balance sheet could undermine the solvency of the firm. For example, conditional financial transactions (e.g., confirmed credit lines, futures, options, etc.) are contractual arrangements that are activated at the initiative of the customer or "counterparty." These contracts are considered "off-balance sheet" activities because the outflow of money occurs conditionally upon the exercise of the contractual option by the counterparty. The corresponding outstanding balances appear in the balance sheet only after the financial instrument is exercised.[9] Similarly, time-lagged financial contracts between transnational firms (e.g., import or export firms) expose the balance sheet to fluctuations in the value of foreign exchange rates until the contract is executed. The extension and use of conditional and time-lagged contracts increases the assets or liabilities of a firm without necessitating an immediate record of that transaction on the balance sheet. The first rudimentary methods of financial risk management emerged as techniques to purchase offsetting contracts (i.e., as a form of insurance) or to commodify and sell the volatile elements of time lagged and conditional financial arrangements. Drawing upon the model of futures and options markets for agricultural products and other physical commodities, markets were developed for the volatile financial components of contractual arrangements.

The detailed examination of off-balance-sheet activities coincidentally also revealed a mechanism to transfer and avoid regulatory scrutiny as off-balance-sheet transactions occurred without necessitating an adjustment of the main balance sheet. The emergence of a series of parallel, lightly regulated, offshore markets during the post-war order, provided the ideal location to which capital could be transferred. Thus, financial innovation in the post-Bretton Woods era has continued to focus on off-balance-sheet transactions as mechanisms to avoid regulatory scrutiny, enhance speculative profit, and hedge risks. In fact, the turn toward the derivatives trade and other off-balance-sheet transactions "... has made the use of occasional (e. g. monthly) balance sheet data less reliable as a guide to the bank's state of health (over the next few succeeding weeks)."[10] As states expand their gaze to include off-balance-sheet activity and offshore markets, market participants have developed newer, more complex, off-balance-sheet financial instruments and linkages with alternative/virtual sites of financial market activity.

As more and more assets of the bank become tradable and as banks surge towards the once taboo fruits of the securities sector, international regulatory strategies have divided the balance sheet of a bank into a "banking book" and a "trading book." The banking book, which still constitutes the greater component of most large banks, holds non-traded assets such as loans.[11] The trading book records the tradable assets of the bank such as equity and derivatives contracts. The trading book is the site of the most intense regulatory activity and debate as it is also the major source and destination of speculative financial activity in the monetary order. This partition of the firm's activities is artificial and problematic. In France, for example, the dyadic relationship between the banking and trading book opened interesting loopholes where the definition of the trading book allowed some banks to escape all capital requirements by transferring trading book positions to the banking book by the end of each business day. As capital requirements were calculated at the end of the day, banks also learned to take advantage of interlinked markets and time differences to transfer their positions to affiliates around the world, cleverly avoiding the close of business in each country in a global race with the sunset.[12] Attempts to stabilize and monitor the fluid activities of the firm have consistently met with nominal compliance, resistance, and transgression.

The use of on- and off-balance-sheet activities to avoid regulatory oversight has resulted in a dramatic expansion of the monetary order, both in terms of the volume of activity and in terms of the spaces of financial activity. Market participants have extended branch operations into other jurisdictions throughout the "global" marketplace to avoid taxation and exploit arbitrage and speculative opportunities. Branch operations in alternative jurisdictions allow banks and other financial institutions to transfer assets and liabilities from the parent institution's balance sheet in order to improve profits, reduce taxes, and/or facilitate nominal compliance with prudential regulations. Moreover, a particular series of over-the-counter (OTC) markets, which are not located at any one particular site, have emerged as spaces for substantively unregulated derivatives trading. As new linkages are formed to exploit off-balance-sheet opportunities, the discourse on risk has inscribed itself across the globe and within the virtual.

The globe

The "global" marketplace is marked by a spatial concentration of the major markets and institutions. The majority of *officially regulated and monitored* financial market activity occurs in the developed countries. In addition, the overwhelming majority of major financial institutions are headquartered in the developed countries. For example, the top 25 banks in the world are almost exclusively headquartered in Western Europe, Japan, and the US.[13] At the same time, however, there is a set of "parallel" financial markets at the margins of the international arena that often act as sites of regulatory transgression and financial innovation. The minor sites are linked to the major sites through the branches, subsidiaries, and affiliates of the major banks and financial institutions. The aggregate financial activity from the marginal sites is extremely large and very influential upon the activity in the major markets and vice versa. Arbitrage between markets tightens the links and narrows the price differentials between markets in periods of financial stability; in periods of financial crisis, capital flight up the hierarchy of markets exacerbates price differentials.[14] Thus, the structural relationship between the major and minor sites is a fertile terrain for the circulation and reproduction of capital and volatility, and hence a major contributing cause and product of the spirals of speculation and insurance embodied in the technology of risk.

There are two main reasons why financial activity is concentrated in the developed countries: the role of states and the role of the "corporate services complex." Despite the rhetoric of liberalization, states in the developed countries are active participants in assisting and implementing the process of market expansion and integration. In fact, this international monetary order was permitted and endorsed by states in the developed countries as well as financial interest groups.[15] Of course, there are often contending oversight and regulatory systems within a state. Through the fractured structures of authority in the contemporary monetary order, states provide the legality essential to the operation of the monetary order. Saskia Sassen argues, "One of the roles of the state *vis-à-vis* today's global economy, unlike earlier phases of the world economy, has been to negotiate the intersection of national law and foreign actors – whether firms, markets, or supranational organizations."[16] Private firms also "contribute" to the regulatory process through the institution of self-regulatory organizations, lobbying groups, and the development of self-regulatory techniques and instruments. The fractured structures of authority and the competition with other sites of financial activity expand the possibility for regulatory transgression and linkages to sites and institutions that may undermine established prudential standards and enhance systemic volatility.

The concentration of financial activity in the developed countries is assisted by the development of the "corporate services complex," or networks of financial, legal, accounting, advertising, and other corporate services that handle the complexities of operating in more than one national system of laws and regulations under conditions of rapid innovation. These services are so complex that many large firms choose to purchase advice from specialized consulting firms rather than developing the services in-house. The contemporary financial firm elaborates itself in relation to this mass of consultants and experts. Sassen argues that "these agglomerations of firms producing central functions for the management and coordination of global economic systems, are disproportionately concentrated in the highly developed countries ... This concentration of functions represents a strategic factor in the organization of the global economy. ..."[17] The development of a corporate services complex in developed countries makes it unlikely that innovations in communications technology will equitably disperse the core sites of financial activity.

The corporate services complex enables financial institutions in the major markets to establish branches and linkages with a series of secondary and tertiary markets located at dispersed sites around the globe. Of course, the actual management and operation of the bank branches usually remains situated in the major market centers. Thus, major markets are generally populated with financial doppelgangers from secondary and tertiary markets that transgress the established rules from within the developed countries. It is, at least in part, through the relationship between the major and the marginal sites that this monetary order functions and reproduces itself.

The following sub-sections examine some of the overlapping instruments, markets, and sites of financial activity at the center and margins of the global monetary order.

Official exchanges

The major financial marketplaces are organized around a set of official exchanges. The network of official exchanges within a developed country is the hub of its broader financial system. Official exchanges work to certify the credit and integrity of its members. Exchanges usually require contracting parties to operate through a clearinghouse that records all transactions. By recording all transactions, exchange officials are aware of the amount traded, the movement of prices for different types of transactions, and the net profit or loss of individual dealers. Exchange officials have the information to warn members or demand increased collateral if they may be potentially over-exposed. In case of default by a contracting party, the clearinghouse collects funds from all members of the exchange to quickly settle accounts. Contracts traded on an official exchange are usually standardized to facilitate trading and rapid settlement. Exchange-traded derivative contracts are also standardized and are subject to the rules imposed by an official exchange.

Foreign exchange markets

A core component of the network of organized exchanges is the foreign exchange market. A country's currency achieves part of its value in relation to the value of other currencies. Foreign exchange markets reflect the value of a currency relative to the supply and demand of market participants (including central banks). The exchange rate of a country's currency in conjunction with its legal code influences the rate of foreign investment in equities, bonds, and private property. In essence, the foreign exchange rate is a factor that encourages or constrains the character of domestic and foreign ownership in the productive assets of a capitalist society. The exchange rate also influences the prospects and rate of exports and imports in goods and services. Misalignments between officially stated or desired exchange rates and market demands create opportunities for arbitrage and speculation as well as the necessity of hedging strategies. Hence, foreign exchange markets play a central role in the circulation of capital and volatility.

The focal points of traditional foreign exchange trading are generally centered around the UK, US, and Japan, which accounted for roughly 58 percent of global foreign exchange trading in 2004, with an average daily turnover of $1.9 trillion in 2004.[18] Secondary foreign exchange markets located in Singapore, Germany, Hong Kong, Australia, and Switzerland together make up another 25 percent of global foreign exchange trading. Tertiary markets in France, Canada, Denmark, Sweden, and Russia make up much of the remainder. Secondary and tertiary foreign exchange markets facilitate 24-hour trading through their location in important time zones and at regional sites that are linked to a conglomeration of other financial services. Banks in all of these cities belong to one market in that they trade with each other using either the Reuters or EBS system. Market participants view the

Table 2.1 Foreign exchange markets by percent of global foreign exchange average daily turnover and region (2005)

	Africa	*Australia and Asia*	*Europe*	*Middle East*	*North and South America*
Major FX Markets (Total 58%)	–	Japan	United Kingdom	–	United States of America
Secondary FX Markets (Total 25%)	–	Hong Kong Singapore Australia	Germany Switzerland	–	–
Tertiary FX Markets (Total 9%)	–	–	Denmark France Sweden Russia	–	Canada

Source: Adapted from Bank for International Settlements, "Triennial Central Bank Survey." (2005), 12–Table B.6.

same price and they exchange the same standardized legal contracts.[19] Almost three-quarters of foreign exchange trading is between banks. The most heavily traded currency in the foreign exchange markets is the US dollar, which is the principal official reserve asset for most central banks. The dollar is also demanded for the purchase of most raw materials, especially oil, on international markets.[20]

Although the major markets for foreign exchange trading exhibit a strong spatial concentration in a few countries, these core markets are tightly interlinked with a variety of official financial derivatives markets, a dispersed set of offshore financial centers, and national currency markets in emerging economies.[21]

Financial derivatives markets

The legal, institutional, and physical terrain for trading derivative financial instruments began in the early 1970s as a series of markets derived from the major currency exchanges. In 1972, the International Monetary Market (IMM) was established at the Chicago Mercantile Exchange (CME). The IMM allowed financial futures contracts on foreign currencies to be exchanged. A financial futures contract is a contract in which two parties agree to buy and sell a certain amount of an underlying financial asset at a pre-specified price and time in the future.[22] Thus, market participants could hedge against or speculate upon the volatility of international currency rates in the wake of the fixed exchange rate era. It took time for this new market to become utilized, but volume picked up by the late seventies as rising inflation and highly volatile foreign exchange rates increased the necessity to hedge or "insure" large financial positions with futures contracts.[23] The establishment of the IMM marked the beginning of a market for financial futures with cash settlements instead of delivering an underlying commodity as the forerunners (i.e., commodity futures exchanges) had done for centuries.

A year later, the Chicago Board of Trade (CBOT) established the Chicago Board of Options Exchange (CBOE). Options are similar to futures contracts except that an options contract gives its holder the right but not the obligation to purchase the underlying asset. Thus if the price of the underlying asset drops below an agreed price, the holder of the option can simply give up the right to exercise the option because it would result in a loss. If the price of the underlying asset rises above an agreed price, the holder of the option will exercise his right to gain the difference between the market price of the underlying asset and the agreed price.[24]

Another key development was the creation of financial contracts based on a composite of other financial contracts, this allowed financial institutions to hedge against or speculate upon aggregate stock price movements as a proxy for the effect of interest rates changes. The Kansas City Board of Trade (KCBT) created a futures contract based on an index of the stock exchange in February 1982. A few months later the CME started futures trading on the Standard & Poor's 500 Stock Index, and the New York Futures Exchange (NYFE) started trading futures on the New York Stock Exchange Composite Index.[25]

Following the initiative of these exchanges, 42 major futures and options exchanges have been established around the world. Of course, the rhetoric of globalization masks the extent of spatial concentration; the US hosts 13 of the 42 major futures and options exchanges.[26] Nevertheless, a diffuse series of minor exchanges are linked to the major derivatives markets. These minor sites are often important sources of financial activity and innovation as they attempt to poach business from the major financial centers.

For example, the Singapore International Monetary Exchange (SIMEX) was created in 1984 as an offshoot of the Chicago Mercantile Exchange (CME).[27] The CME and SIMEX were linked by a "mutual offset link" that allowed a contract bought on one exchange to be closed on another. This arrangement was useful as it significantly extended the trading hours for customers in Chicago. Singaporean officials welcomed the idea because they wanted their country to become the Asian center for financial futures trading.

SIMEX initially acquired customers by exploiting the Japanese Ministry of Finance's reluctance to permit derivative trading. SIMEX offered a futures contract based on the Nikkei 225 stock average. The Nikkei stock average is the most widely monitored index of stock market activity in Japan, as the stock average is considered representative of Japan's industrial structure. The 225 components of the index are among the most actively traded issues on the Tokyo Stock Exchange. The Nikkei 225 futures contract offered by SIMEX allowed cautious investors to hedge themselves against corrections in the Japanese stock market. The contract offered by SIMEX forced the hand of the Japanese Ministry of Finance, which permitted the Osaka Stock Exchange (OSE) to trade its own Nikkei 225 futures contract in 1988. Business quickly went to the OSE, because large Japanese pension funds preferred to deal on a familiar market.[28]

During the collapse of the bull market in 1990, the Japanese government attempted to prop up the value of the stock market by buying Nikkei 225 futures contracts from the OSE. These "price keeping operations" by the Japanese government failed because the weight of the selling in the Nikkei was too great. However, as an unintended effect, the government's large purchases of Nikkei 225 futures contracts increased the price of the futures contracts. Each time the Japanese government attempted to indirectly intervene in the stock market, the price of the Nikkei futures sold in Osaka would rise above fair market value. This presented a lucrative opportunity for those financial firms (e.g., Salomon Brothers and Morgan Stanley) that had the capability to arbitrage the razor thin differences between futures and "cash" (i.e., equities) markets. These firms sold futures and bought shares of stock on the Tokyo Stock Exchange each time the Japanese government intervened in the market. Government officials in Japan interpreted this activity as unhelpful exploitation by foreign speculators that need to be stopped as quickly as possible. Thus, the Japanese government imposed controls on the OSE in order to prevent this speculative activity. Specifically, the Japanese government increased the broking commissions on futures and options trading at the OSE, curtailed the trading hours, and introduced rules to make arbitrage traders produce daily reports on their share trading activities. These actions by the Japanese government made SIMEX a competitive market once again.

The arbitrage opportunities afforded by SIMEX led to a number of complex financial innovations and strategies in the 1990s.[29] In fact, it was the poorly understood and blatantly fraudulent derivatives trading activities of a manager at Barings Futures (Singapore), a poorly supervised subsidiary of the London based Barings Group, at SIMEX that resulted in the collapse of the oldest merchant bank in Britain. However, the collapse of Barings did not lead to a reduction in derivatives trading. In fact, there was a growth in derivative trading during 1995.[30]

Offshore financial centers

A significant amount of cross-border financial activity in the contemporary monetary order is conducted through the (legally indistinguishable) branches or subsidiaries of major banks that are registered in the substantively unregulated "offshore" financial centers. These branches allow banks to upload and download assets and liabilities from the parent banks in order to improve profits or facilitate nominal compliance with prudential regulations. Offshore financial centers also provide a set of parallel financial markets and foreign exchange markets that compete with onshore markets and currency exchanges. The International Monetary Fund (IMF) characterized the use of offshore banking as a "pervasive activity" with respect to both the number of offshore centers and the volume of transactions. Offshore financial centers exist in 69 countries and the cross-border assets of offshore centers grew at an average annual rate of 6.4 percent from US$3.5 trillion to US$4.8 trillion in five years from 1992 to 1997. In 1997, the share of cross-border assets from offshore financial centers represented 54.2 percent of all cross-border assets.[31]

A brief history of offshore markets

Offshore financial markets first began to grow, during the Bretton Woods regime in the late 1950s and 1960s as states in developed countries attempted to channel capital flows toward national priorities. For instance, one of the first off-shore markets, the "Euromarkets," began during the 1957 sterling crisis when the British government prohibited London-based banks from financing third-country trade in the pound, and encouraged the use of dollars for this purpose, thereby attracting dollars for deposits and lending instead of pounds.[32] As the British economy was recovering from the Second World War, the British government wanted to promote exports by only paying for imports in pounds; this "export-forcing" scheme required that all pounds be used for promoting exports rather than financing third-party trade. As large amounts of dollars began to circulate outside the US, a market emerged to trade and arbitrage these dollars for other currencies.

In a similar fashion, the "Eurobond" market took off after 1963 when the US imposed a tax, i.e. the Interest Equalization Tax, to discourage US firms from buying bonds in foreign companies unless the investment was financed abroad. The legislation also made it difficult for foreign firms to issue bonds in the US. US firms circumvented this legislation using offshore branches to issue "Eurobonds." Eurobonds were like any other bonds issued by companies as a means of borrowing money, i.e., pieces of paper that promised to pay the bearer an amount of money plus interest payments on the debt. However, instead of being bought and sold in a single country, these bonds were issued offshore by companies and held by investors who did not want to pay a capital gains tax on their investment in their own country. The bonds were issued in dollars by companies of various nationalities and sold through London merchant banks.[33] Syndicated bond issues outside the US rose from US$135 million in 1963 to US$696 million in 1964.[34]

In February 1965, the US Federal Reserve instituted a "Voluntary Foreign Credit Restraint Program" to curb borrowing by foreign firms and governments in US markets. The Federal Reserve also instituted a "Foreign Direct Investment Program" in order to limit the amount of capital US firms could transfer abroad. The intention of these acts was to stimulate investment in domestic industry and prevent upward pressure on the dollar. However, the effect was the expansion of the offshore or "Eurodollar" market as private capital surreptitiously circumvented official controls. From 1964 to 1973, the number of foreign branches of US banks grew form 181 to 699, of which 181 were in Caribbean countries and 156 in Europe. From 1963 to 1970, the total overseas assets of US banks increased from US$7 billion to US$53 billion.[35] In addition, as American corporations established linkages abroad, their banks followed to continue to serve their customers.[36] Another factor in the development of the Eurodollar market was the Cold War. The Soviet Union and East European countries were fearful that their dollar denominated holdings could be frozen by the United States. Therefore, these countries invested most of their dollar holdings in British banks in London.[37]

Although the offshore Euromarkets emerged from unforeseen regulatory loopholes, the markets flourished because of official state support as well as intentional neglect. The Bank of England supported the Euromarkets as a part of its desire to promote London as an international financial center. Helleiner argues that the British government and the Bank of England in particular,

> . . . remained strongly committed to promoting London's role as an international financial center long after Britain's days of financial predominance were over. Because British capital controls were required on the international use of sterling to defend the country's weak balance of payments in the 1950s and 1960s, British officials recognized that London's internationalism could best survive by allowing bankers to operate in foreign currencies, especially the dollar. Once the market emerged, they actively supported its growth.[38]

Notably, the US did not act to prevent American banks and firms from operating in the Euromarkets although it could have done so. US regulations were not applied to foreign branches of US banks, thereby providing a perverse incentive for US banks to establish branches in offshore financial centers. Helleiner argues that once the offshore markets were a *fait accompli*, the US recognized that Euromarkets would make dollar holdings more attractive to investors and foreign central banks at a time of growing US balance-of-payments problems. A liberal international order would help finance growing US deficits and preserve America's central financial position in the world.[39]

In 1980, after the collapse of the Bretton Woods system, the US modified its regulatory structure to attempt to bring back the banking business lost to the offshore markets. The government removed regulations that had imposed cash reserve requirements on demand deposits, and capped interest rates on time deposits (i.e., Regulation Q of 1977 and Regulation D of 1979). Additionally, US and foreign banks were allowed to invest in newly established International Banking Facility (IBFs) located in New York and a few other cities. The IBFs acted as an "offshore" market located within the territory of the US and under the supervision of the Federal Reserve System. However, US citizens were not permitted to use or conduct business with banks in the IBF and foreign citizens were required to adhere to a minimum deposit/withdrawal limit of $100,000 and a 48-hour minimum maturity period. Banks that operated in the IBF were not permitted to issue negotiable instruments. The IBFs attracted some wholesale banking business, but many large banks continued to maintain a presence in the offshore markets. Many foreign bankers feared the continuity and consistency of US banking regulations from one administration to the next and preferred the less inhibiting regulatory climate in the offshore centers.[40]

Despite the limited success, 395 IBFs were established in the territorial US within the first year. US-based banks which preferred the idea of a centralized administration of assets and liabilities took advantage of the new regulations.

Matching the US initiatives, Japan relaxed or removed many restrictions on foreign exchange trading in 1980, thereby giving a huge boost to its eight-year-old Tokyo Dollar Call Market. However, non-residents were not allowed to participate in the market, as the Tokyo Dollar Call Market. In 1986, Japan created a new "offshore" foreign exchange market that permitted non-residents to participate in order to promote the status of the yen as an international reserve currency. The Japanese Offshore Market (JOM) was modeled on the IBFs established in the US.

Offshore financial centers also multiplied around the world as banks, commercial enterprises, and criminal networks in the developed countries engaged in fierce "arbitrage" between offshore centers with the intention of maximizing profit and minimizing supervisory standards.[41] As these offshore financial centers have mushroomed in recent years, a new vulnerability to the monetary order has been revealed. The developed countries and the intergovernmental financial supervisory organization have taken a great interest in demanding stricter regulatory enforcement from the host offshore centers, an ironic demand given the historic rationale for the creation of these financial centers.

Location and functions

The primary markets have not displaced offshore financial centers. A series of secondary or regionally dominant offshore financial centers (see Table 2.2 below for examples) serve to intermediate funds in and out of their region. Secondary markets in Asia increased their turnover from 1987 to 1997, but secondary offshore centers in the Middle East and Latin America remained static or declined in the same time period.[42]

A series of tertiary or "brass plate" offshore markets (see Table 2.2 below for examples) also dot the globe. These offshore financial centers do not engage in regional intermediation, but rather serve as registries for branches of major banks and other financial institutions. As noted above, tertiary offshore markets located in small island nations were often chosen as hosts by large banks and corporations because these small countries cannot possibly devote the same amount of financial and human resources to monitor the activity of the financial institutions registered in their jurisdictions.[43] As the actual management of these offshore firms is usually located in one of the major financial centers, it is difficult for a small staff to monitor properly the institution's activities. Thus, banks use the lax regulatory climate of tertiary offshore financial centers to add and remove liabilities from parent banks through intra-bank transfers. These bank branches benefit by being exempt from disclosure rules, except to the extent that they conduct business on regulated financial exchanges in major markets. Tertiary offshore sites are also useful for investors seeking anonymity in their financial transactions. Thus, offshore sites are commonly used for regulatory and tax transgression as well as money laundering and other dubious purposes.

Host countries benefit from offshore financial centers by gaining access to international capital markets and/or an element of competition to domestic markets. Some host countries may also use their offshore financial centers to attract a well-educated workforce to their remote locations.

Secondary and tertiary offshore centers compete for business with one another as well as the major financial centers. Economists argue that the competition from offshore centers help produce lower prices for financial products. However, regulatory officials in the developed countries tend to view offshore financial centers as sources of financial crisis in the international financial system. In fact, the IMF argued that offshore banking played a role in the 1997–98 Asian Financial Crisis and the crises in Latin

Table 2.2 Offshore financial markets by location and function (1999)

	Africa	*Australia and Asia*	*Europe*	*Middle East*	*North and South America*
Major Offshore Markets		Japan*	United Kingdom*		United States of America*
Secondary Offshore Markets		Hong Kong Singapore*	Luxembourg	Bahrain Lebanon	Panama
Tertiary Offshore Markets	Djibouti Liberia Mauritius Seychelles Tangier	Australia Cook Islands Guam Macau Malaysia* Marianas Marshall Islands Micronesia Nauru Niue Philippines Thailand* Vanuatu, Western Samoa	Austria Andorra Campione Cyprus Gibraltar Guernsey Hungary Ireland* Sark Isle of Man Jersey Liechtenstein Luxembourg Malta Madeira Monaco Netherlands Russia Switzerland	Dubai Israel Kuwait Oman	Antigua Anguilla Aruba Bahamas Barbados Belize Bermuda British Virgin Islands Cayman Islands Costa Rica Dominica Grenada Montserrat Netherlands Antilles St. Kitts and Nevis St. Lucia Puerto Rico St. Vincent and the Grenadines Turks and Caicos Islands Uruguay

Source: Adapted from International Monetary Fund, "Offshore Banking: An Analysis of Micro- and Macro-Prudential Issues," Working Paper, (Washington, D.C.: International Monetary Fund, 1999), 11–Table 2.

Note:
* Offshore financial center is a separate entity within a single territory.

America in 1998.[44] Officials in developing countries view offshore financial centers as a drain on tax revenue. A policy paper released by Oxfam estimates that developing countries lose at least $50 billion in revenue because of the existence of and competition amongst offshore tax havens. Fifty billion dollars is a figure roughly equivalent to the level of aid flows to the developing countries, or six times the cost of achieving universal primary education in the developing world.[45]

Offshore banks and financial institutions engage in three main activities: (1) offshore currency (i.e., Eurocurrency) loans and deposits, (2) the underwriting of offshore bonds (i.e., eurobonds), and (3) the over-the-counter (OTC) trade in financial derivatives.

Offshore currency markets compete with "onshore" foreign exchange markets in a variety of countries by offering similar instruments within a simplified (i.e., minimalist) regulation and taxation structure. Currencies do not change hands in the offshore markets, but these markets are tightly integrated with the international foreign exchange markets as well as the national markets. The linkage is evident in the interest rate relationships or the relative availability of funds among the different markets. An offshore deposit trader will typically use the foreign exchange (spot and forward) markets to hedge the exchange rate risk associated with an offshore currency funding.[46]

Of course, the competition between "onshore" and "offshore" is not always "efficient" in the delivery of the best price or rate of return for investors and borrowers; offshore competition may lead to speculative assaults and dramatic volatility in the substantive exchange rate as well as a loss of policy autonomy in fixed exchange rate systems. For example, several Asian emerging market economies considered the offshore currency markets to be a source of volatility and speculation during the Asian financial crisis of 1997–98. Thailand, Korea, Malaysia, Singapore, and Indonesia imposed a series of capital controls to limit offshore trading in their currencies.[47] As offshore banks usually need to clear transactions with domestic banks, states have the ability to restrict such transfers. However, an offshore market may still emerge in the form of a non-deliverable forward market, where it is possible to undertake transactions without having access to the currency itself.[48]

A significant portion of international money market instruments (i.e., bonds and notes) is currently issued in offshore financial centers. From 1992 to 1997, the outstanding amount of international money market instruments issued in offshore financial centers grew at an average annual rate of 20.2 percent. At the end of 1997, the instruments stood at US$746.1 billion, or 21.1 percent of the total international money market instruments.[49]

Data is not readily available on the extent of OTC derivatives trading originating in offshore centers; however, it is known that the prominence of the interbank market in offshore banking suggests that a large part of the growth in OTC trading of derivatives involves offshore banks.[50] From 1987 to 1996, the total notional value of interbank currency and interest rate swaps grew at an average annual rate of 31.8 percent and 54.3 percent, respectively. At the end of 1996, the notional value of interbank currency and interest rate swaps stood at US$3.1 trillion and US$10.3 trillion, or 27.2 percent and 53.5 percent of total interest rates and currency swaps, respectively.[51]

The major "onshore" OTC derivatives markets in terms of turnover are London, New York, Paris, and Frankfurt.[52] The trade in over-the-counter derivatives from both onshore and offshore sites constitutes a massive and generally unregulated market that is directly tied to the financial activities on official foreign exchange and derivatives markets. The next section investigates this invisible market.

The phantom market

A virtual terrain for the circulation of capital and volatility is the OTC derivatives market. Market participants are able to avoid regulation and taxation through participation in or selective linkages with the OTC markets. States are aware of these markets but choose not to monitor or regulate them for fear of driving business to rival sites of financial activity. These "invisible" sites of speculative financial activity are intimately linked to the "visible" sites of financial activity at official financial exchanges. In fact, the price of contracts traded outside of official exchanges is usually derived from the price of contracts on the exchange.[53] Linkages to institutions within these unmonitored realms allow commercial banks to engage by proxy in highly leveraged and speculative activities that are prohibited or discouraged by official rules and norms. Direct or indirect participation in the OTC markets offers highly lucrative rates of return on an investment, but may also rapidly transmit large losses. Thus, the shadowy realms that appear to occupy the periphery of the state's gaze are productive and integral to the operation of the monetary order.

It is difficult to estimate the worldwide total trade in derivative financial instruments and the share of that activity that occurs over the counter. Most national accounting systems do not require financial institutions to reveal their OTC derivative dealings and whether these activities add up to a net asset or liability to the enterprise.[54] In most countries, including the US, no single agency oversees derivatives.[55] An estimate of the aggregate value of international exchange and OTC derivatives activity is provided in Tables 2.3 and 2.4. The tables are derived in part from a triennial voluntary survey of 52 central banks and 1,200 market participants conducted by the Bank for International Settlements (BIS) since 1989 (OTC transactions were only added to the survey in 1995). The total estimated *daily* global turnover in the OTC derivatives markets (i.e., foreign exchange and interest rate derivatives) rose from $880 billion in 1995 to $2,410 billion in 2004.[56]

Tables 2.3 and 2.4 illustrate that only 29 percent of these derivative financial instruments appear to be traded at an official exchange whereas 71 percent of derivative financial instruments are traded OTC. Financial activity

Table 2.3 Estimate of international financial derivative activity (notional amount outstanding, end-March 1995 and end-December 1999, US$ billion)

	Interest Rate		*Equity*		*Foreign Exchange*		*Commodity*	
	ET	OTC	ET	OTC	ET	OTC	ET	OTC
Global 1995	$15,674	$26,645	$645	$599	$120	$13,153	$142	$317
Global 1999	$11,669	$60,091	$1,793	$1,809	$59	$14,344	n/a	$548

Sources: Adapted from David Lynch (1997) "Growth in Asia-Pacific Markets," in *Derivatives: The Risks that Remain*, Elizabeth Sheedy and Sheelagh McCracken, eds., New South Wales, AU: Allen Unwin/Macquarie Series in Applied Finance, 17, Table 1.3. Lynch's data was derived from material released by monetary authorities that participated in the Bank for International Settlements (BIS) global survey of derivatives. See also IMF 2000, 28, Table 2.5; 30. Table 2.7. Note that $11,488 billion of OTC activity in December 1999 was listed as "Other."

Notes:
ET stands for "exchange traded" and OTC stands for "over-the-counter." Exchange traded excludes convertible and warrant bonds.

Table 2.4 Estimate of total international financial derivative activity (notional amount outstanding, end-March 1995 and end-December 1999, US$ billion)

	Total ET	*Total OTC*	*Total*
03/1995	$16,581	$40,714	$57,295
12/1999	$13,522	$88,000	$102,000

Sources: Adapted from David Lynch (1997) "Growth in Asia-Pacific Markets," in *Derivatives: The Risks that Remain*, Elizabeth Sheedy and Sheelagh McCracken, eds., New South Wales, AU: Allen Unwin/Macquarie Series in Applied Finance, 17, Table 1.3. Lynch's data was derived from material released by monetary authorities that participated in the Bank for International Settlements (BIS) global survey of derivatives. See also IMF 2000, 27. The IMF Data is derived from the Bank for International Settlements (BIS).

Notes:
ET stands for "exchange traded" and OTC stands for "over-the-counter." Exchange traded excludes convertible and warrant bonds.

conducted OTC does not have the benefits of a clearinghouse. A party to an OTC transaction is unaware of the exposure of their counterparty. The price of an OTC contract is generally inferred by looking at similar contracts on official exchanges. Thus, the majority of speculative financial activity (i.e., OTC) occurs in an opaque and unregulated environment.

A variety of institutions use these complex financial instruments. Overall, the largest market participants are US banks and trust companies. JP Morgan Chase, Bank of America, Citibank, Wachovia, and HSBC Bank USA are the major players. In the US, the five largest dealers hold 97 percent of all contracts and the top 25 banks account for 99.7 percent of all outstanding derivatives contracts. These banks conduct almost all of their trade outside of regulated exchanges (see Table 2.5).[57] Non-financial corporations are the major users of derivative instruments known as currency swaps. These corporations are usually multinational corporations that borrow and conduct business in a variety of currencies. Financial institutions are the major users of interest rate swaps, which are instruments designed to hedge fluctuations in interest bearing paper. Corporations accounted for only a bit more than a third, and governments a tenth of trading in interest rate swaps.[58]

Even institutions that do not participate directly in exchange traded or OTC derivative transactions may be connected to such activities through their lending practices. For example, after the dramatic debacle of the US-based hedge fund, Long-Term Capital Management (LTCM), the Basel Committee on Banking Supervision found "alarming" interrelationships between banks and hedge funds or "highly leveraged institutions" (HLIs). These institutions were characterized by the Committee as (1) subject to little or no direct regulatory oversight, as a significant proportion operate through offshore financial centers; (2) subject to limited disclosure requirements; and (3) taking on significant leverage (i.e., margin borrowing) in financial transactions. The Basel Committee report stated that most banks did have collateral for their loans to the HLIs, but the amount of collateral was not sufficient for crisis situations:

> However, in the event of default or disorderly liquidation, banks may have been further exposed to losses resulting from the liquidation of collateral and the rebalancing of portfolios under adverse market conditions. With regard to LTCM, these potential *secondary exposures* were significant, given the prevalent market volatility and the potential for a major adjustment in prices once the liquidation process commenced. (Nevertheless the potential losses would have been manageable at the individual counterparty level.) Furthermore, the limited transparency of LTCM prevented creditors from obtaining a complete picture of its investment positions, and consequently limited their ability to gauge such secondary exposures.[59]

Table 2.5 Notional amount of derivatives contracts of the five commercial banks and trust companies with the most derivatives contracts (31 December 2006, US $ million)

	Total Assets	*Total Derivatives*	*% Traded OTC*
JP Morgan Chase Bank	$1,179,390	$65,347,339	91.3
Bank of America	$1,196,124	$26,674,360	95.7
Citibank National	$1,019,497	$25,403,637	98.7
Wachovia Bank National	$518,123	$5,491,931	67.5
HSBC Bank USA National	$165,673	$4,464,969	95.9

Source: Adapted from "OCC's Report on Bank Derivatives Activities, Fourth Quarter 2006," (2007), 25, Table 3.

Exchange and OTC derivatives markets have experienced rapid growth and innovation in recent years. This growth in financial activity can be illustrated even if one's scope is restricted to those financial derivative transactions carried out on an official exchange. Table 2.6 illustrates the range of derivative contracts offered at the Chicago Board of Trade (CBOT), and Table 2.7 illustrates the annual volume of financial futures and options at the CBOT from 1975–2000. The term volume refers to the number of contracts traded in a market over a year. The range of derivative contracts offered at the CBOT has steadily increased, although many instruments

Table 2.6 Types of futures and options instruments offered/traded at CBOT (1975–2000) – numbers in parenthesis indicate number of actively traded types of contracts.

	Financial Futures	*Financial Options*	*Stock Index Futures*	*Stock Index Options*	*Insurance Futures*	*Insurance Options*	*Combined Total*
1975	1	–	–	–	–	–	1
1976	1	–	–	–	–	–	1
1977	3	–	–	–	–	–	3
1978	4	–	–	–	–	–	4
1979	6	–	–	–	–	–	6
1980	6	–	–	–	–	–	6
1981	7 (6)	–	–	–	–	–	7 (6)
1982	8 (4)	1	–	–	–	–	9 (5)
1983	9 (4)	1	–	–	–	–	10 (5)
1984	10 (4)	1	1	–	–	–	12 (6)
1985	11 (4)	2	3	–	–	–	16 (9)
1986	12 (5)	2	3	–	–	–	17 (10)
1987	13 (5)	3	4 (2)	–	–	–	20 (10)
1988	15 (6)	3	5 (2)	–	–	–	23 (11)
1989	16 (6)	4	5 (2)	–	–	–	25 (12)
1990	8	6	2	1 (0)	–	–	17 (16)
1991	11 (10)	8 (7)	2 (1)	2 (1)	–	–	23 (19)
1992	11 (8)	9 (7)	2 (1)	2 (1)	2	2	28 (21)
1993	10 (7)	7 (5)	2	2	5 (3)	5 (2)	31 (21)
1994	9 (7)	12 (10)	1 (0)	1 (0)	5 (1)	5 (4)	33 (22)
1995	9 (6)	12 (9)	–*	–*	5 (0)	5 (2)	31 (17)
1996	11 (8)	14 (4)	–*	–*	4 (0)	4 (1)	33 (13)
1997	10 (9)	13 (11)	1	1	–	–	25 (22)
1998	7 (6)	10 (8)	1	1	–	–	19 (16)
1999	7 (6)	10 (8)	1	1	–	–	19 (16)
2000							

Source: Adapted from Chicago Board of Trade (2000) *Annual Volume Data 1920–1999*, Chicago, IL: Chicago Board of Trade.

Notes:
The CBOT lost the right to sell the Major Market Index in 1994. The Major Market Index is a 20-stock high capitalization index created in 1983 and licensed by the American Stock Exchange. The Chicago Mercantile Exchange (CME) won the right to sell the Major Market Index.

have been phased out due to inactive trading. Similarly, trading volume has also increased steadily. The majority of derivatives activities at CBOT still consist of financial futures and options rather than stock index futures and options or insurance futures and options contracts.

These tables graphically illustrate a familiar "Darwinian" narrative. As particular species of financial derivatives succeed in the marketplace, variations of the successful instrument are offered on the market. Many more financial products are invented and offered than are likely to succeed. In many cases, the ratio of contracts offered to actually traded contracts was two to one. Through a process of dispersed selection, a few products seem

Table 2.7 CBOT annual volume for futures and options (1975–2000)

	Financial Futures	*Financial Options*	*Stock Index Futures*	*Stock Index Options*	*Insurance Futures*	*Insurance Options*	*Combined Total*
1975	20,125	–	–	–	–	–	20,125
1976	128,532	–	–	–	–	–	128,532
1977	458,075	–	–	–	–	–	458,075
1978	1,531,154	–	–	–	–	–	1,531,154
1979	3,560,653	–	–	–	–	–	3,560,653
1980	8,844,585	–	–	–	–	–	8,844,585
1981	16,362,737	–	–	–	–	–	16,362,737
1982	19,822,028	118,772	–	–	–	–	19,940,800
1983	22,058,709	1,664,492	–	–	–	–	23,723,201
1984	32,525,207	6,635,819	1,514,737	–	–	–	40,675,763
1985	43,727,876	12,078,408	2,624,062	–	–	–	58,430,346
1986	57,963,696	18,315,031	1,778,951	–	–	–	78,057,678
1987	73,726,546	23,260,886	2,631,062	–	–	–	99,618,494
1988	77,309,257	20,692,839	1,231,371	–	–	–	99,233,467
1989	79,355,659	22,054,370	1,100,495	–	–	–	102,510,524
1990	84,995,167	28,444,924	951,555	0	–	–	114,391,646
1991	78,578,593	23,014,276	702,927	3,059	–	–	102,298,855
1992	89,121,811	23,533,861	360,879	2,215	212	50	113,019,028
1993	105,989,406	30,333,411	156,964	1,420	9,456	6,584	136,497,241
1994	139,483,486	37,534,091	*–	*–	4	9,420	177,027,001
1995	124,016,379	36,283,780	–	–	0	3,324	160,303,483
1996	120,268,387	36,725,763	–	–	0	66	156,994,216
1997	140,391,980	39,311,358	755,476	156,132	–	–	180,614,946
1998	165,960,763	52,609,469	3,567,512	245,398	–	–	222,383,142
1999	143,941,513	47,054,651	3,896,086	229,560	–	–	195,121,810
2000							

Source: Adapted from Chicago Board of Trade (2000) *Annual Volume Data 1920–1999*, Chicago, IL: Chicago Board of Trade.

Notes:
* The CBOT lost the right to sell the Major Market Index in 1994. The Major Market Index is a 20-stock high capitalization index created in 1983 and licensed by the American Stock Exchange. The Chicago Mercantile Exchange (CME) won the right to sell the Major Market Index.

to succeed and open the possibility of new variations. Of course, these tables mask the dynamic and productive tension between the technology of risk and the strategic relations between states and financial institutions that propels the drive for innovation and expansion of the monetary order.

Emerging economies and developing countries

Another terrain for the circulation of capital and volatility has been the emerging economies. Investment and disinvestment in the emerging market countries are integral to the perpetual evolution of risk technology. First, the technology of risk has played an important role in justifying investment in emerging markets as part of a strategy of risk management through portfolio diversification. Second, the periodic occurrence of financial crises in these markets serves to validate the need to use hedging techniques and instruments. Third, financial firms often learn to develop new risk-management techniques and instruments through unanticipated failures of existing techniques during serious financial crises.

In fact, the evolving technology of risk may also contribute to the recurrence of financial crises in some emerging markets. The herd-like behavior of institutional investors who seek to rebalance portfolio investments rapidly after an unfavorable market signal can often create or increase the severity of a financial crisis in the emerging markets (see Chapter VI). In addition, as there is a strong correlation between emerging financial markets and US markets as well as between emerging markets and international oil prices, the signals that induce herd-like behavior amongst institutional investors may be unrelated to the "fundamentals" of an emerging market economy.[60] There is a strong hierarchy amongst financial markets that becomes readily apparent during a financial crisis as investors "climb up the ladder" of financial assets from equities to bonds, from local currency to dollar denominated debt, from private to public debt, and from emerging markets to mature markets in developed countries.[61] The empirical evidence for the hierarchy of economic markets is recorded by the spread between emerging market bond indices (e.g., EMBI or EMBI+) and a variety of rival investment instruments such as US Treasury bills during periods of financial stability and crisis.[62] Hence, the techniques of risk management and the hierarchical position of the emerging markets condemn these countries to witness recurrent financial stampedes in and out of their markets even though they have little influence over either the regulation of transnational financial market participants or the causes of herd behavior.

Although there is an expanding network of regional banking centers in the developing world, sovereign borrowers from developing countries have been marginal players in international financial markets since the debt crisis of 1982. As one blunt author, Dimitris Chorafas, stated, "The eight hundred million people of India, the billion people of China and most of the population of Africa as well as Latin America are by now below the red line. They might be eligible for . . . short-term loans for trading deals, or . . . for advice in return for a fee, but they are too unreliable or too incomprehensible to be worth the commercial risk of longer term loans."[63] While Chorafas conflates emerging economies and developing countries, his statement certainly reveals the dismissive attitude of financial market participants towards the developing countries. The marginalized developing countries are unable to speak for themselves in international finance; their needs are inferred or re-presented by others. The developing countries, which are often saddled with massive debt and poor credit ratings, have little access to international financial markets and must rely heavily on financial assistance from developed countries and intergovernmental organizations. To the extent that capital does flow to the developing countries, financial institutions are likely to demand high yields, a rapid rate of return on their investment, and the ability to withdraw their capital investment quickly.

Conclusion

The surfaces on which the discourse on risk inscribes itself is constantly shifting. A map of the monetary order can only be provisional, like a map drawn in the sand. The techniques and sites of financial activity that initially provided the surfaces for the proliferation of the discourse on risk have already been reconfigured by the discovery of new techniques and sites. From its genomic micro-foundations in the firm's balance sheet, the order has expanded and interconnected many fronts along a multi-dimensional space. However, there is certainly a spatial concentration and a hierarchy between the sites of financial activity, which is clearly manifest in the spatial flow of capital during periods of economic crisis and periods of relative economic stability. For the most part, the technology of risk reinforces the hierarchy amongst developed, emerging, and developing countries as the developed markets are considered inherently safer investments (despite the history of financial crises in the developed countries). Consequently, it is not surprising that foreign investors in the emerging markets demand quick returns, large profits, and the removal of all impediments to capital investment repatriation. It is important to keep in mind that the language of risk is spoken in the dialect common to this hierarchical spatial concentration. In other words, the technology of risk emerges from a particular place and through a limited perspective.

The next chapter, "Theory of Risk," critically examines the internal logic of the technology of risk assessment and management. Despite surface appearances, the technology of risk is not an abstract or objective discourse. The categories of risk are socially constructed and the techniques of risk management carry important economic, political, and social implications. The internal logic of risk technology elaborates and activates a set of roles and relationships between creditors and debtors, as well as regulators and market participants. The technology also influences the pace and character of financial entry and exit strategies in international markets. Hence, charting the internal logic of risk technology is a critical aspect of understanding when and how the fluid map of the contemporary monetary order will change.

3 Theory of risk

> And some writers have endeavored to classify panics according to the nature of the particular accidents producing them. But little, however, is, I believe, to be gained by such classifications. There is little difference in the effect of one accident and another upon our credit system. We must be prepared for all of them, and we must prepare for all of them in the same way – by keeping a large cash reserve.[1]
>
> Walter Bagehot, 1873

> More and more, the bank is a 'risk machine'. It takes risks, it transforms them, it embeds them in banking products and services. In this context, those banking institutions which actively manage their risks have a decisive competitive advantage. They take risks more consciously, they anticipate adverse changes, they protect themselves from unexpected events, they gain the expertise to price risks. The competitors who lack such abilities may gain business in the short run, simply because of inadequate risk-taking decisions or because they do not price risks to clients. But they will lose ground with time, when those risks turn into losses.[2]
>
> Joël Bessis, 1998

The conception of financial risk has undergone a dramatic transformation since the collapse of the Bretton Woods monetary order. The end of the gold-dollar exchange rate arrangement, oil-crisis induced inflation, deregulation of financial market segmentation, and increased competition from international financial conglomerates in the 1970s and 1980s enhanced uncertainty and market volatility.[3] The necessity for financial institutions to increase revenue, reduce costs, and manage financial risk without a direct reliance on the outmoded intergovernmental mechanisms and institutions associated with the Bretton Woods regime (e.g., a fixed exchange rate, controls on capital movements, and the International Monetary Fund) has incited a discursive explosion over the conception of risk.[4] A generalized and vague recognition of financial risk has become the object of a dense network of power, knowledge, and authority.

The assessment and management of risk has become a technology.[5] In other words, the rational process of financial risk-assessment and management, expressed in positivist discourse, involves an expertise with reproducible and quantifiable "facts." Risk assessment appears as an abstract, rational, and mechanical technology designed to be integrated with financial institutions and legal codes. The mathematical models and computer programs created for the detection, simulation, prediction, and management of risk are the legal, intellectual property of financial firms underwritten by the legality of the state. A new class of experts creates and deploys these models and programs to discover, classify, manage, exploit, and transfer the sources of risk within financial firms and markets. A body of state authorities serves to scrutinize, certify, and legitimate the work of the risk experts.

Despite the political and scientific authority accorded to this new technology, risk has not been captured, controlled, or rendered docile. Risk is neither a single concept, formed once and for all, nor is risk a vast and obscure realm that knowledge will gradually map. Risk must not be thought of as either a dense singularity or a ubiquitous phenomenon that is disobedient to a loquacious power that exhausts itself trying to subdue it and often fails to control it entirely.[6] Risk is a transfer point for relations of power across a dense network of state and market institutions. Risk is endowed with instrumentality; it is useful and productive for a number of maneuvers and strategies to order, divide, and interconnect economies, states, markets, firms, populations, and individuals. Thus, a mapping of the concept of risk is a critical component in understanding the configuration of international finance within the current international political economy.

Technology

The technology of risk is more than an area of consensual knowledge that permits cooperation amongst an elite community of academics, market institutions, and policy makers. The discourse on risk involves a general terrain of thought that permits the interplay of simultaneous and occasionally contradictory opinions and tactics. The technology of risk is not a unified approach or cumulative science with objectively fixed categorical designations and methodologies. Even where rigorous formal models are utilized, subtle variations in the assumptions, definitions, and parameters of risk assessment lead to different estimations of risk. Additionally, the strategies designed to formalize and instrumentally rationalize risk have had perverse and unintended results. Given its contradictions and consequences, how does this technology operate? What are the characteristics of this new technology of risk? What is permitted or rendered productive by this discursive order? What is prohibited or silenced?

Risk assessment and management is a technology based upon an art of constructing, segregating, combining, and proliferating categories. The vast categories of the sources of risk that have been elaborated do not represent the comprehensive application of the technology of risk. The categories of risk are always only a possible instantiation of risk.[7] Risk materializes wherever experts manage to locate a particular class of risk. Of course, the risk assessment expert does not merely passively register risk and devise instruments against it; he also actively produces risks. He makes a class of risk appear "... where each person had hitherto felt obliged to submit resignedly to the blows of fortune."[8] Experts only construct risk categories that are deemed necessary, useful, permissible, and profitable to their employers.

The constructed categories of risk are not objective. The categorical constructs hide important interconnections between categories that may not be self-evident, particularly in periods of stable market activity. Hence, there are limits to the ability of risk technology to manage financial risk. For example, there is an interrelationship between *market risk*, *foreign exchange risk*, and *credit risk*. Market risk is the risk of financial loss to a bank or financial firm due to adverse price movements in financial markets. Foreign exchange risk is the risk of financial loss due to adverse changes in currency exchange markets. Credit risk is the risk of financial loss due to the default of a borrower or a decline in the borrower's credit quality. Foreign exchange risk is related as a subset of the parameters measured by market risk. An increase in exchange rate volatility influences the general perception of market risk. Furthermore, exchange rate volatility can damage the ability of exporters and importers to service their debts (i.e., create credit risk). There is also an interaction between credit risk and market risk where debt instruments cannot be readily liquidated at a discount when the credit standing of a borrower declines. For example, over-the-counter risk management instruments (e.g., financial derivatives, currency swaps, and options) are difficult to liquidate because of the tailored (non-standardized) nature of some of these instruments. Therefore, the credit risk changes constantly with market movements during the entire residual life of the instrument. There is also a credit risk since the bank exchanges flows of funds with a counterparty that might default.[9] Thus, risk is difficult to isolate and manage along narrow categorical designations.

Recent financial crises confirm that there are significant problems with the conceptualization of the categories of risk. The boundaries between categories of financial risk do not appear to have any external validity as the causes of financial volatility may be intensely interrelated. As an analysis of the 1997–99 Asian financial crisis by the Institute of International Finance stated,

> These market dynamics created a feedback effect among risk types (e.g., market liquidity and credit risks) of unprecedented strength and proportion. It seems clear that the use of more liquid credit instruments and more sophisticated hedging techniques is blurring the boundary between market and credit risks. This enables firms to underwrite more business and expand economies of scale; but it also exposes both firms and economic systems to hitherto unanticipated levels of volatility.[10]

In certain cases the combination of a global network and advanced financial instruments derived from formal models of risk assessment has led to the creation of new categories of risk in international finance whose exact risk profile is completely unknown such as: *multiple market risk* (arising from price risks of the derivatives market and the market(s) underlying the derivatives), *settlement risk* (arising from delays in the settlement of transactions), *operational risk* (arising from operating systems without adequate controls), *legal risk* (arising from uncertainty about the legality of some derivative contracts) and *aggregation* or *interconnectivity risk* (arising from the sheer complexity of exposure to many markets).[11]

The failure of a technology to reproduce, predict, and manage events is rarely a surprise, the important question is what other ends are served by this failure. The failure of expertise to achieve stated goals is often followed by calls for an increase in the scope of power of experts and their technology. Thus, despite this significant aporia in the constitution of risk categories, a technology continues to develop and expand across a dense network of state and market institutions. The technology of risk employs at least three tactics to assess and manage financial risk.

Transferable risk

The first tactic of the technology of risk is to transfer risk to other sites and institutions. The technology of risk makes possible a range of strategic hedging/speculating combinations shaped to suit their assigned functions and intended utility-effect.[12] Strategic combinatory instruments, such as financial futures, financial options, or financial derivative contracts seek to legally transfer the consequences of particular types/sources of risk by matching risk-averse and risk-appetitive institutions through prior (and often standardized) contractual arrangements. In other words, the technology of risk management reproduces risk as a "thing" that is capable of being "unbundled" or disentangled from its sources and sold on the market to hedge financial activity or speculate for profit. Categories of risk become commodified in so far as their value derives from their resale potential in the market. Notably, strategic combinatory instruments for risk management would not have any value if volatility were absent.

Strategic combinatory instruments function through the creation of a diverse portfolio of intersubstitutable assets. Borrowers, investment categories, economic sectors, and geopolitical regions are rendered intersubstitutable in order to minimize the impact of dramatic loss. The logic of the "diversification effect" is that "[t]he risk of a portfolio is less than the sum of the risk of the individual transactions each considered alone."[13] Ironically, the production and reduction of risk at a single point entails proliferating the number of points at which risk may appear.

Portfolio diversification increases the demand for a wider range of debt instruments and investment opportunities: a wider group of currencies, sectors, companies, and emerging stock markets.[14] The increasing demand for diversification means that investment firms will tend to buy a company's stock (or government bond) not because they know the company well but because they like the sector, region, or country in which that the company is located. The small company, therefore, finds that its access to monies depends on how it is perceived as part of the wider portfolio strategies of the investors.[15] This also implies that during a financial crisis divestment will be carried out across an entire category of investments regardless of the individual merits of a particular company. In a panic, the equity value of a company may be rapidly degraded, forcing other short- and medium-term investors to sell as well. Diversification may also encourage asset managers to deliberately increase the risk exposure of portfolios they run in order to improve performance.[16]

Risk management instruments are traded either privately or on a series of markets that that were constructed in the wake of the collapse of the Bretton Woods system. After the termination of the fixed exchange rate arrangement, currency futures markets were established to hedge risks associated with foreign exchange fluctuations.[17] Trading volume rapidly increased in the late 1970s as the need to hedge against rising inflation and highly volatile foreign exchange rates became apparent.[18] Next, as other active futures markets emerged around the world, a "mutual offset trading system" was devised which allowed a trader to be cleared on one exchange and then transferred to another exchange. Finally, the development of sophisticated financial instruments (e.g., financial derivatives) has allowed financial intermediaries to hedge risks extremely quickly and through complex mechanisms.[19] However, these tools, which are designed to manage risk, are simultaneously linked to a cadre of speculators willing to accept risks in exchange for the possibility of large profits. The post-Bretton Woods monetary order has become a globally networked risk environment, which has come to be constituted through risk, rather than risk being an incidental factor.[20]

Nontransferable risk

The second tactic of risk technology is to reorganize and rationalize the technologies and activities considered to foster risk. Categories of risk that are traced to technical, procedural, and organizational flaws (i.e., "operational risks") within financial firms are not necessarily quantifiable or transferable on the market. However, executives are often willing to reorganize and rationalize the institution in accordance with the recommendations of risk experts. The technology of contemporary risk assessment allows for the operation of a totalizing and individualizing mode of power/knowledge. The management of different types of risk is conducted through the accumulation of information from each individual transaction and every business unit of a firm.[21] The activities of a financial firm are methodically deconstructed and reassembled to compare, discover, and diminish risk in order to achieve business goals.

The deconstruction of risk is an attempt to rationally reconstruct financial behavior. Rationality can be understood as a learned ignorance of particular contingencies.[22] Rational behavior, for example, is constructed through simplified steps (i.e., one step at a time). The rational project is to regenerate activity in a certain manner whereby each step is taken in ignorance of what the next is to be.[23] Risk is tackled through the minute analysis of specific risks and each business unit is treated in isolation of the activity of other business units. This technical knowledge is an exercise of power, although this power is productive rather than merely repressive.

For example, in the banking sector *operational risk* is defined as a major financial risk that emanates from the malfunctioning of the information systems, of reporting systems, and of the internal risk monitoring rules rather than movements in the market. At the *technical level*, this risk occurs when the information system or the risk measures are deficient. At the *organizational level*, the reporting and monitoring of risk and all related rules and policies are integral to minimizing this risk.

The *technical level* of operational risk is composed of a very large number of itemized or *specific risks* such as errors in the recording process of transactions, deficiencies of the information system, or the absence of adequate tools for measuring risks. In some cases where the specific risk described occurs over a specified period of minimal duration, the word "risk" merely notes a process of social interaction and the possibility of errors occurring during that interaction. For example,

> Delivery risk is a deferred risk with a very short time span. It appears only at the time of netting the flows which settle the transaction, and not before, and it lasts only during the lag between flows. The existence and the importance of such risks are highly dependent on the technical systems used to settle transactions, which have various levels of safety embedded in their design.[24]

In this passage, "delivery risk" is a categorical construction that attempts to isolate a moment of social interaction that might have adverse financial results. Delivery risk connotes a discrete stage in a process. It is difficult for any firm to make a complete list of all of the specific risks. In other words, " [a]ny missing information is a source of risk."[25] At the extreme, experts come to believe that the possibility of financial risk surfaces in every social action within a firm and more broadly within the network of state and market institutions. Each financial scandal potentially reveals a new source of risk to the gaze of risk management experts.

The *organizational level* of operational risk is also the composite effect of innumerable *specific risks* generated by the structural organization of the financial firm. Firms are encouraged through official regulations and academic literature to restructure their organizations to combat organizational risk. For example, a basic requirement for the contemporary financial firm is to create a "middle office" by separating the "risk takers" from the "risk controllers." The risk takers are assigned to improve profits and volume of business, whereas risk controllers are in charge of authorizing risk-taker activity through a basic yes – no decision process.[26]

The elaboration of the categories of risk has greatly broadened the scope of risk management activities beyond the bank's balance sheet or the firm's trading book. The goal of risk management is moving beyond managing "already existing risks" within the bank or financial firm to the stage where it can have an impact on the decision-making process:

> Risk management includes the reporting and hedging of risks once decisions are made. But it should be more than that and should influence the decision-making process before decisions are made. The challenge is to capture risks upstream in the decision process, not downstream when decisions have already been made and when risks already exist.[27]

It is implicitly assumed that radical uncertainty in business decisions can be effectively countered through anticipation and probability based analysis.

The technology of risk management is also used to justify the increased and perpetual surveillance of the firm's clients (e.g., borrowers). The development and implementation of "warning systems" and "credit enhancement" techniques, such as covenants and guarantees, function to create increased surveillance over borrowers and financial protection for the lender *after* the decision to lend has been made. Essentially, a legal covenant is an additional agreement by a borrower that restricts the initiative of the borrower. Borrowers are limited from diversification out of the core business. Furthermore, funds are pre-committed to repaying the lender before payments are made to any other parties following a default. Failure to honor the stipulations of a covenant legally triggers pre-emptive action by the lender. Depending on the nature of the specific covenant, the lender may be entitled to prompt repayment of the entire loan if the borrower's credit rating declines (i.e., prior to an actual default on a loan repayment). However, the usual goal of a covenant is to initiate a dialogue between the borrower and the lender before the emergence of a default scenario.[28]

In summary, the rationalization of the sources of risk is a project that appears to limit the scope of freedom for market participants that circulate in and around the firm whilst also providing new opportunities for profit and transgression that increase the scope of freedom.

Universal risk

The third tactic of risk technology is to aggregate and negate risks through the provision of capital reserves. There has been a cultivation of mathematically sophisticated and highly abstract Value-at-Risk (VaR) and Capital-at-Risk (CaR) simulation models. These simulation models differ from the capital reserve policies of the Bretton Woods era in that the simulation models seek to discover the absolute minimum level of capital reserve necessary to prevent default and models are tailored for the investment activities of specific firms. Additionally, these aggregate, abstract, formal simulation models provide a common denominator to measure and translate the levels of risk faced by particular groups or firms. Regulatory policy has focused on the management and certification of these simulation models as a mechanism to regulate the activity of financial firms.

The VaR technique is a simulation model of the maximum amount the portfolio of investments can lose with a given probability in a given time period; similarly the CaR is utilized to estimate the losses for all of the assets of a bank. When the probability of loss exceeds the value at risk, there is the likelihood of default. The VaR approach is considered superior to "traditional measures" of risk, because "it is expressed in [currency] value, it is synthetic, and it is fungible."[29] Nevertheless, the VaR ". . . is not a replacement for such specific measures, but it summarizes them."[30] The VaR approach serves as the basis for calculating CaR, an internal model and proxy for determining capital adequacy. The CaR is calculated for the entire portfolio of a bank and aggregated over all types of quantifiable risk. Both VaR and CaR measure potential losses, however the tolerance level for unexpected losses is much less flexible when the solvency of the entire bank is at stake.[31] The objective and scientific veneer attached to these simulation models only thinly disguises the degree of subjective judgment and political arm-wrestling involved in operating the model.

The VaR technique estimates the value of potential financial losses from the shape of a distribution of market transactions. Risk management experts often *estimate* the shape of the loss distribution. For example, the loss distribution for market risk is generally estimated to be a bell-shaped curve. To arrive at a VaR estimate, one generally assumes that returns are independently distributed over time and identically distributed over time. Critics from the US Federal Reserve have argued that these assumptions make the model analytically tractable but they are not necessarily close to reality.[32] It has been widely recognized for many years that financial markets exhibit significant non-normalities. In particular, asset returns exhibit "fat tails," meaning that more of their probability is to be found at the tail ends of the distribution and less at the center.[33] Fat tails are associated with low probabilities of occurrence of large losses. Additionally there are "portfolio effects" which make losses dependent on several underlying random parameters, instead of one, and upon the diversification of the risk of the portfolio.[34]

Bessis explains that potential losses are categorized by expected loss, unexpected loss, and exceptional loss.[35] The expected loss represents the mean of the distribution of defaults for a portfolio. The expected loss is the statistical average over a portfolio of a large number of loans or transactions. Unexpected losses are those losses that exceed expected losses. Expected losses are usually deducted from revenue, however, capital reserves are necessary to cover unexpected losses. Exceptional losses are a subset of unexpected losses. Exceptional losses are dramatic losses such as those that could eliminate all of the assets of a bank. Exceptional losses are *arbitrarily* separated from unexpected losses because to include them would "drastically increase" the capital reserve requirement.[36] Despite the evidence of dramatic losses (e.g., Barings Bank collapse in 1995, Daiwa Bank's loss of $1 billion in 1995), bankers consider exceptional losses highly unlikely given the diversification strategies of most banks.

The line between unexpected loss and exceptional loss is called the confidence interval or "tolerance level." Some tolerance level has to be specified to assign a value to those losses. The tolerance level is expressed as a percentage, usually between 95 to 99 percent. The lower the tolerance level, the higher the VaR.[37] For example, if the daily VaR were estimated to be $1 million at the 95th percent tolerance level, one would expect to lose no more than $1 million in one day 95 percent of the time. Industry practice had been to use between a 95 to 99 percent tolerance level and a time period (or "holding period") of two days. The Basel Committee on Banking Supervision, a consultative inter-governmental organization of central bankers and finance ministers from the G10 developed countries, favors a conservative 99 percent interval over a two-week (10 business days) holding period.[38]

A third important parameter is the data window, or the period for which the historical distribution is sampled or for which risk-factor returns are computed. Long data windows of several years lead to more precise coverage of the actual return distribution, however long data sets might be available for only a limited number of standard risk factors.[39] The Basel Committee fixed on a data window of one year, which reflects these trade-offs.[40]

In other words, the Basel Committee believes that a longer time horizon reveals greater risks and thus requires greater capital reserves, while financial firms are resistant to setting aside larger reserves that could be used for investment. This seemingly "technical" struggle between regulators and financial firms to determine an appropriate holding period, tolerance level, and data window occurs because all parties recognize the subjective components necessary to operate the model. Moreover, (as it will be shown in Chapter V) financial firms often lobby regulators to negotiate "acceptable" (i.e., minimal) parameters for these risk models.

The Basel Committee cannot make any binding resolutions, only recommendations, which may be subsequently implemented through national legislation by the respective national banking regulatory agency. Over 100 countries have adopted the banking standards recommended by the Basel Committee. The Basel Committee serves to reinforce the conservative judgment of state regulators regarding the assumptions built into the simulation models of market institutions.

Despite the certification of the risk-assessment simulation models by state regulators, the assumptions required in the quantification of risk necessarily distorts the value of VaR and CaR measures.[41] The reliance upon historical data in risk assessment models is deceptive since history is not a series of independent events, but a sequence of interrelated events. The impact of financial innovations and the expansion of market participants can influence the predictive capacity of risk-assessment models. As markets expand, institutions are exposed to a wider number of variables, aggregate effects, and counterparties.[42] Probability theory deals with an abstract and homogenous time that is unable to incorporate the constant flux of the economic environment. Probability theory requires the construction of a hypothetical economy in which the past, present, and future are merged into a single abstract moment. Furthermore, the "small *n*" problem familiar to empirical social scientists is also an obstacle to economists and financial engineers. Peter Bernstein writes, "History provides us with only one sample of the economy and the capital markets, not with thousands of separate and randomly distributed numbers."[43] There are methods to deal with some of these problems; however, there is no comprehensive solution.[44]

These methodological problems draw into question whether a science of risk assessment is at all possible. However, in the absence of an alternative approach, which meets with the positivist preferences of state and market institutions, risk-assessment simulation models have gradually received the official endorsement of states through intergovernmental meetings of the developed countries at the Basel Committee on Banking Supervision.

Conclusion

If the possibility of a science of risk remains dubious, why have firms invested so much effort and capital in the management and manipulation of risk? One might be tempted to argue that risk is merely an ideological or super-structural element as there does not appear to be such a thing as pure risk or "risk-in-itself." However, risk is not simply an ideological projection, although the concept of risk contains ideological elements, risk is a technology that permits and constrains the mode of production in advanced capitalist societies.

First, the knowledge of risk provides opportunities for value creation and profitability despite imperfections in that knowledge. Risk technology creates value that would otherwise have been unrealized or eliminated by chance. By objectifying particular events as risk, meaning is inverted: events that were previously obstacles are transformed into possibilities.[45] The knowledge of risk is integral to the operation of international finance because risk is a factor in the justification of profit. By labeling particular activities, individuals, and classes of borrowers as "risky," high margin loans can be developed by banks to increase earnings and exploit opportunities. In periods of stable market activity, risk-assessment techniques can allow firms to achieve superior risk-return ratios to rival firms. Knowledge of risk also allows banks to price risks with relative accuracy in periods of normal (i.e., familiar) market activity.

Second, the commodification of risk serves as a mechanism for the private protection of accumulated capital. In the Bretton Woods monetary order (1945–71) the task of private wealth protection was assigned to states and taxpayers. Since the collapse of the Bretton Woods system, market institutions have wagered that they could simultaneously secure their accumulated capital and enhance profits. The official endorsement of private,

Table 3.1 IFCI – International Financial Risk Institute's glossary of financial risks

Absolute Market Risk	Foreign Exchange Risk	Pre-Settlement Credit Risk
Absolute Risk	Funding Risk	Price Risk
Accounting Risk	Geographic Risk	Principal Risk
Basis Risk	Herstatt Risk	Regulatory Risk
Call Risk	Idiosyncratic Risk	Reinvestment Risk
Clean Risk	Inflation Risk	Relative Risk
Competitive Currency Risk	Insurance Risk	Residual Risk
Compression Risk	Intellectual Risk	Residual Unhedged Risk
Contingent Currency Risk	Integrity Risk	Reverse Equity Risk
Correlation Risk	Interest Rate Risk	Roll-over Risk
Counterparty Risk	Knock-In Risk	Roll Risk
Country Risk	Legal Risk	Security Specific Risk
Credit Risk	Liability Risk	Settlement Risk
Cross-Currency Settlement Risk	Liquidity Risk	Sovereign Risk
Currency Risk	Long-term Rate Risk	Specific Risk
Curve Risk	Marketability Risk	Split Cylinder or Split Risk
Daylight Risk	Market Risk	Spread Risk
Default Risk	Maturity Mismatch Risk	Suitability Risk
Delivery Risk	Maverick Risk	Systematic Risk
Disclosure Risk	Modeling Risk	Systemic Risk
Discontinuity Risk	Moral Risk	Tax Risk
Downgrade Risk	National (Asset) Risk	Transaction Risk
Duration Risk	Non-Systematic Risk	Translation Risk
Economic Risk	Omega Risk	Unsystematic Risk
Equity Risk	Overlay Risk	Unwinding Risk
Event Risk	Overnight Delivery Risk	Volatility Risk
Execution Risk	Pin Risk	Winding-up Risk
Extension Risk	Prepayment Risk	Zero Premium Risk

Source: This (edited) list of financial risk terms was downloaded from the IFCI – International Financial Risk Institute website (http://newrisk.ifci.ch/glossary.htm) on 11/05/2001. The disclaimer to the online glossary states, *The Dictionary of Financial Risk Management* is designed for professional financial analysts and managers. It does not attempt to compete with such general reference works as the *Barron's Dictionary of Finance and Investment Terms* or *The Encyclopedia of Banking and Finance.* The present volume defines and describes many financial terms and concepts that these reference works do not attempt to cover, but it does not list many of the basic terms and concepts a financial analyst learns in introductory courses in finance or in daily experience in financial markets. The principal criterion for inclusion in this volume is that a word or phrase be something that a working finance professional might want to look up

Note:
This glossary is not updated and is provided as is. Some entries could be outdated.

firm-specific, risk-assessment techniques and formal models allows banks and financial firms to further enhance profits by setting aside less capital reserve than would have been required under uniform capital adequacy regulation. Certainly, the state remains an implicit lender-of-last-resort for financial emergencies, however the technology of risk has allowed market institutions to reconfigure the nature of their reliance on the state.

Finally, related to the task of private wealth protection, the technology of risk is also useful in the evasion of undesired regulation and taxation. To the extent that risk-management technology and its diversification strategies may be used to encourage regulatory arbitrage between national jurisdictions, the technology may also function to sustain and enhance value that would be restricted through taxation, legislative acts, or executive orders. In other words, the technology of risk management may be used to defy the sovereign will of the state when laws do not enhance profit. As we will see, the technology of risk assessment and management is consistent with a capitalist norm that implies the interests of creditors should be safeguarded before debtors and a monetarist norm that seeks to limit the intervention of states in market activity.

The next chapter, "Theory of Regulation," extends the current discussion by examining the roles and relationships between market participants and regulatory officials as articulated and activated by the technology of risk. The theory of regulation, which fostered the development of risk technology, is now being transformed by that technology.

4 Theory of regulation

The technology of risk articulates and activates particular roles and relationships between regulatory officials and market participants. In order to understand the complex interrelationships between the state and financial firms it is necessary to examine the social facts, norms, and policies that guide the regulation of financial markets in liberal capitalist societies. The technology of risk emerged within the "factual," normative, and policy constraints of these liberal capitalist societies. This is evident by the ways in which the technology of risk has reinforced the subject status of individual financial firms as the main source of information and the site of technology application. However, the development of risk technology has also contributed to reshaping the regulatory process and the mode of governance by states in response to the *de facto* erosion of the regulatory framework enabled by this technology.

Nevertheless, the state and the firm should not necessarily be seen as rival institutions as they tend to blend, reflect, overlap, and intertwine. As Max Weber noted, there is strong parallel in the organizational structures of state bureaucracies and commercial enterprises. The state is essentially an "enterprise" (*Betrieb*) just like a factory he wrote.[1] In addition, both kinds of enterprise operate through the systematic collection, categorization, manipulation, and analysis of massive amounts of data.[2] Slogans such as "liberalization," "deregulation," and "privatization," mask the extent to which states actively create, negotiate, and manage the social, legal, and institutional framework of international finance.[3] Through legislative acts, court rulings, and executive orders, the "rights" of global capital are accommodated within national territories still under the exclusive control of states.[4]

The relationship between state and market institutions is complicated by the fact that the barrier between state and market institutions is quite porous. States often engage in market operations and market institutions attempt to mimic many central functions of sovereign states.[5] Additionally, an individual person may be labeled a state actor for a particular activity and a market actor for another activity. The career trajectory of individuals often helps to further blur the boundaries, as individuals leave state regulatory agencies to join regulated firms. Through this "revolving door" the financial services industry acquires civil servants with inside knowledge and personal ties to those in control of the regulatory agency.[6] At the same time, the regulatory agency benefits by having persons trained with their broad regulatory outlook involved in advising financial firms.[7] State and market institutions may align along a common "national" identity where drawing boundaries around bodies and spaces functions to privilege individual and collective identities or subjectivities and the space in which these homogenized subjectivities have dominion.[8] Thus, the distinction between state and market institutions is not a boundary between two discreet entities.

In addition, there are varied conglomerations of state and market institutions. Parastatal and extrastatal organizations such as self-regulatory organizations, academic think-tanks, consulting agencies, the financial press, and intergovernmental organizations seek to influence the regulatory environment. These organizations are often composed of leading state officials and market institutions. For example, a former US Federal Reserve Board Chairman, Paul A. Volcker, currently serves as the Chairman of a highly influential private think-tank, the Group of Thirty. The Honorary Chairman for the Group of Thirty is Lord Richardson, a former Governor of the Bank of England. Most of the world's top financial houses are represented on the committees of the G30, including JP Morgan, CSFB, Goldman Sachs, Merrill Lynch, Midland Global Markets, Bankers Trust, Mitsubishi Bank, Morgan Stanley, Barclays Bank, and IBJ. The contemporary financial firm as well as the state elaborates itself in relation to this mass of consultants and experts.

Governance

The governance of international finance requires the coordination of three interrelated policy areas: 1.) *Preventive* (risk and capital reserve policies); 2.) *Regulative* (money and credit policies); and 3.) *Corrective* (debt and debt rescheduling policies). The relative dominance of state and market institutions in these realms is variable. For example, state institutions may focus on the organization of the regulative and corrective spheres and minimize their presence in the preventive sphere.[9] Dominance may also be exercised as apparent self-effacement by masking active involvement with slogans of "liberalization," "deregulation," and "privatization." Hence, the apparent absence of state activity in any particular sphere of international finance should not be mistaken as a sign of the erosion of sovereignty or the irrelevance of the state.

To the extent that the generation, reproduction, and accumulation of wealth sustain the state, states have a structural mandate to cooperate with market participants. To the extent that the state is necessary to establish laws and the relations necessary for contracts, market participants need to cooperate with states.

Social facts

States

States cooperate with market participants because there are particular recognized "social facts" that constrain the ability of states to dictate the substantive value of economic items. The theoretical grounding of the relationship between state and market institutions was advanced by G. F. Knapp's *The State Theory of Money* (1924). Knapp argued that the value of money was conferred by an act of the state. Max Weber later reformulated this thesis in an excursus.[10] Weber's conceptualization deserves elaboration, as it remains a fertile approach for political economists striving to understand how states have historically attempted to govern the market and influence the credibility and value of money.[11] As a historical economist, Weber emphasizes the range of discretionary latitude within the factual rather than arguing that social facts are logically derivative of a small set of axioms.

Weber argued that, "(a) The modern state has universally assumed the monopoly of regulating the monetary system by statute; and (b) almost without exception, the monopoly of creating money, at least coined money."[12] However, as Weber noted, the state loses its ability to regulate the value of money "if it has allowed what was previously an accessory or provisional type of money [for the payment of tax debts] to become free market money (in the case of metallic money) or autonomous paper money (in the case of note money)." This slippage into the market almost always occurs because the provisional money will accumulate in the hands of the government until it commands no other kind and is hence forced to impose this money in its own payments to procure goods and services to operate the government.[13]

The value of money is constrained by other actors once it becomes public, "The public treasury does not make its payments simply by deciding to apply the rules of a monetary system which somehow seems ideal, but its acts are determined by its own financial interests and those of important economic groups."[14] Along this line, Weber notes that the main aim of states (in a gold standard system) is not to regulate the domestic value, but

> . . . to influence the substantive valuation of domestic currency in terms of foreign currency, that is, the market price of the home currency expressed in units of foreign currencies, usually to maintain stability or in some cases to attain the highest possible ratio. Among the interests determining such policy are those of prestige and political power. But on the economic side, the decisive ones are financial interest, with particular reference to future foreign loans, and other very powerful business interests, notably of importers and of industries which have to use raw materials from abroad. Finally, the interests as consumers of those elements in the population which purchase imported goods are involved.[15]

Weber argues that experience has shown "it is possible for the political authority to attain, by such measures as the rationing of consumption, the control of production, and the enforcement of minimum and maximum prices, a high degree of control of this substantive [market determined] validity. . . ."[16] However, it is equally demonstrable from experience, that "there are exceedingly important limits to the effectiveness of this kind of control."[17]

Weber illustrates a complex understanding of the relationship between the state and market in the operation of a monetary economy, and a keen awareness of the political nature of this relationship. The market is not portrayed as an autonomous force akin to nature, rather the market is a reflection of the "power" and "purpose" of the state and other actors.[18] The power and purpose of the state are constrained by the politically organized interests of societal actors, as well as the perceived security of the state as an institution. In comparison to Adam Smith's benignly opaque invisible hand thesis, Weber accords more latitude to the visible hand of the state in its ability to effectively manipulate the economic realm. Nevertheless, Weber also seeks to acknowledge a limit to the state's competence and comprehensive knowledge of the economic sphere. The limit upon the political will and calculative rationality of the state fosters the necessity to cooperate with market participants in the production of substantive value. The limited expertise of state officials coupled with competing interest group pressures also creates the possibility of economic mismanagement and crisis.

Market participants

Theoretically, there is the possibility that market participants may operate in a sphere of economic activity with minimal reliance on the state. For example, Weber wrote in regard to the concept of money,

> It does not, however, seem reasonable to confine the concept [of money] to regulations by the state and not to include cases where acceptance is made compulsory by convention or by some agreement. There seems, furthermore, to be no reason why actual minting by the state or under the control of the political authorities should be a decisive criterion. For long periods this did not exist in China at all and was very much limited in the European Middle Ages. As Knapp would agree, it is only the existence of norms regulating the monetary form which is decisive.[19]

However, Weber believed that legal guarantees enforced by the state are emblematic of modern economic exchange. The political and economic spheres are often fused together, "Economic goods today are normally at the same time *legitimately acquired rights*; they are the very building blocks for the universe of economic order."[20] Thus, state and market participants are linked in a symbiotic relationship. As Weber noted,

> Freedom to contract . . . exists exactly to the extent to which such autonomy is recognized by the legal order. There exists of course, an intimate connection between the expansion of the market and the expanding measure of contractual freedom, or in other words, the scope of arrangements which are guaranteed as valid by the legal order. . . . [21]

Absent the state's ability to enforce private contracts, markets will not function efficiently. Or at the very least, a different group of participants will benefit from the uncertainty of contractual arrangements.

The presence of legal guarantees enhances the degree of certainty in the advanced calculation of economic action, a hallmark of rational capitalism (as opposed to political capitalism for example). It is the complete calculability of the functioning of public administration and the legal order, along with a formal guarantee of all contracts by the political authority that are among the critical components necessary for obtaining a maximum of formal rationality of capital accounting in financial enterprises.[22]

Market institutions' need for calculable public policies also normatively constrains the policy formulation of state actors. The constraint usually occurs when market participants are able to withhold financial investment or relocate assets "offshore" if policies are not calculable. This constraint is contingent on the normative and legal structure of the state.

Legal guarantees coupled with standardized practices are also a mechanism for the advancement of international finance. The fact that the global economy materializes in national territories requires changes in national institutions and legal frameworks to guarantee the "rights" of global capital, i.e., the protection of contracts and property rights. The state remains the ultimate guarantor of the "rights" of global capital.[23] The state is still necessary to produce the legality around new forms of economic activity.[24]

Of course, the state is also necessary, in highly exceptional circumstances, to transgress the legal framework. Laws that significantly hinder the operation of the market can be muted through executive decree. The state's claim to a monopoly on the legitimate and legal use of violence can serve as an essential factor in stabilizing capitalist societies when normative and legal structures become inadequate to ensure social harmony. However, market participants discourage extrajudicial activity where it interferes with the advanced calculation of economic activity. Nevertheless, while violence is not characteristic of activity in the economic sphere, economic activity is also not quite free and voluntary (as liberalism contends) for the majority of individuals driven to labor by the whip of hunger and basic necessities.

Thus, while states reserve significant authority over market actors, the necessity for cooperation in the production of substantive value and the need for calculable public policies in capital accounting generally constrain state actors' ability to regulate market actor activity.

Additionally, the separate institutions of the state's bureaucratic organization may constrain regulatory activity where jurisdictional boundaries are blurred or overlapping. In the United States, for example, there are overlapping and interspersed layers of regulatory agencies.

> A Federally chartered bank can find itself being examined by the regulatory body of the state in which it operates; by the Comptroller of the Currency, an officer of the Treasury whose powers derive from the 1863 National Banking Act; by the Federal Reserve Board, which sets reserve requirements and wields main instruments of monetary policy; by the Federal Deposit Insurance Corporation, which has its own prudential rules to safeguard depositors; and by the Securities and Exchange Commission, which has a special duty to safeguard the interests of stockholders. In addition, banks are deeply affected by the activities of the agencies that regulate their main competitors, such as the Federal Home Bank Board which supervises the savings and loan associations.[25]

Rivalries exist between different agencies over jurisdictional boundaries. Shrewd market participants create financial instruments to exploit jurisdictional ambiguity; they adapt to operate within the spaces between regulatory agencies. As Michael Moran notes, "... there is a premium on circumventing the regulations or on persuading the appropriate regulatory authority or the courts to interpret the law in a new way. A firm that can invent a financial instrument, or a corporate form, allowing it to compete in a new way, or allowing it to enter a previously forbidden market thus gains a significant competitive advantage. ... Regulatory struggles and competitive struggles are thus entwined." Moran cites the chairman of the US Securities and Exchange Commission (SEC), "... competitive advantages increasingly turn on regulatory classifications rather than on the economic merits of financial products and services."[26]

Finally, the system of sovereign states complicates the coordination of international finance. As noted above, market participants maintain a *de facto* exit option if regulatory policies become onerous or unpredictable. Hence, it is often necessary for state actors to coordinate regulatory policies with other major state actors to prevent a deregulatory race to the bottom. However, in the absence of either a supranational organization or unchallenged hegemony, the coordination of regulatory policies between states is very difficult and liable to erosion through market actor manipulation and innovation. National distinctions and "home country" biases persist between markets despite international convergent pressures on regulation.[27] The legal codes of nation states are oriented towards domestic concerns, particularly in regard to financial markets; hence it is difficult to uphold universal regulatory standards without far reaching legal changes.[28]

Norms

In developed countries, two interrelated normative principles build upon the recognized social facts in order to guide the activity of state officials.

First, the monetary order is organized around a *capitalist norm* that implies the claims of investors should be safeguarded by states before the interests of borrowers. The factual force of the normative is such that if wealth is not protected, a capitalist monetary economy will not function. Theoretically, this is due to the fact that advances of money (i.e., investments) determine possible income generation over a period of time. Since resources and labor are generally available in relative excess to investment, employment interests are subordinate to investment interests.[29] A variety of discretionary policy instruments are available to state officials for the protection of wealth (e.g., wage and price controls, capital mobility restrictions, limited liability laws, central bank interest rates, fiscal budget, etc.). Implicit in this norm is the threat of an investment strike, or the massive withdrawal or relocation of investments if the needs of market participants are not accommodated. The effect of the capitalist norm is to privilege the role of financial firms in society.

Since the collapse of the Bretton Woods monetary order in 1971, a more specific normative principle informs the behavior of state officials. The articulation of the second norm is commonly associated with the work of monetarist economists, Ronald McKinnon and Edward Shaw. The *monetarist norm* requires minimal state intervention in the financial sector to achieve economic development. Theoretically, the most efficient allocation of financial resources occurs when credit is allocated on the basis of market determined interest rates. State officials are assumed to lack sufficient information and proper pecuniary motivation to allocate financial resources efficiently relative to market participants in a free-market system. The effect of the monetarist norm is to restrict the regulatory activity of state officials over market participants.

Market participants tend to see these two normative principles as harmonious to the extent that *laissez-faire* policies generally ensure the privileged position of market participants in society. In highly competitive markets however, market participants may seek to use state officials to secure a privileged position *vis-à-vis* rival market participants and developing or emerging country states. Market participants may also call upon state officials to mediate the contradiction between the formal equality of citizens and the substantive inequality between the owners of capital and other groups in society. In essence, the dominant normative principles channel the activity of states in the service of creditor preferences. When the status of creditors is threatened, the capitalist norm takes precedence over the monetarist norm.

These normative principles do not ordinarily conflict with the prospects for popular legitimacy in a democratic state. The realm of international finance continues to remain relatively buffered from popular pressure or debate, especially within developed countries. The buffered status of international finance is probably attributable to its complexity, abstract nature, the impact of money politics and lobbying, and the mediated relationship of international finance (e.g., via collective pension or mutual funds) upon the lives of ordinary individuals. Moreover, within the developed countries these norms did not obstruct the tactical development of the welfare state after World War II. However, these norms effectively act to circumscribe the resources and scope of the welfare state in the post-Bretton Woods/post-Cold War era. Even when financial scandal or bankruptcy does arouse public outcry, the interests of larger financial firms are usually enhanced as regulatory resources are diverted from the regulation of wholesale markets to the scrutiny of retail markets in order to satisfy public outrage.[30]

In the emerging economies, authoritarian states commonly disregard the monetarist norm in order to accelerate economic development. Nevertheless the capitalist norm has been reinforced by conservative ideological formulations and a highly selective appropriation of cultural heritage (e.g., the notion of "Asian values") which restricts the development of an economic order infused with social purpose. Thus, these normative principles are able to create a decisive limit on the possibility and flexibility of democratic governance in many emerging economies. Those emerging economies which permit or accede to a greater voice for popular democracy are faced with irreconcilable claims. In democratic states where the capitalist norm conflicts with popular legitimacy, governments have often had to resort to central bank credits to resolve the deadlock, thereby weakening their monetary economy. Other governments have accepted harsh structural adjustment measures to restore the hierarchy of interests.[31]

Policies

Regulatory policies are broadly derivative of the recognized factual and normative constraints on legitimate governance. Policies confer official recognition upon expertise and disciplinary practices that may originate in localized sites.

The explicit aims of financial regulatory policies in capitalist countries are to maintain the stability and soundness of the financial system, and to protect unsophisticated small consumers from fraudulent practices. The former aim is generally ensured through policies that balance competition amongst financial firms with legal barriers to greater participation. The latter aim, consumer protection, operates upon the assumption of *caveat emptor*. However, there are often attempts to educate consumers and to force firms to make adequate disclosures. An implicit goal of regulatory policy is to ensure the viability and competitiveness of the national financial system in an international context. To the extent that there is a conflict between promoting international competitiveness and maintaining a sound and stable financial system, regulatory officials are charged with balancing these concerns in their policy decisions.

Policy practitioners often divide the regulatory structure by macro-policy and micro-policy categories. The macroscopic is not simply an enlarged projection of the microscopic; the market, the firm, and the individual are not equivalent projections on different scales.[32] The division between the market and the firm allows for homogenizing and individualizing policies; policies may be targeted towards the market as a whole or towards specific firms and individuals. The division of market participants is a useful tactic for the establishment of norms of behavior. The establishment of a norm presupposes the possibility of a homogenizing strategy, in so far as to deviate from the norm is to deviate from the homogenized.[33] Deviations from the norm are measured, quantified, examined, and punished in order to "discipline" subjects (i.e., firms or individuals).

Macro-policy aims to prevent systemic collapse by examining the overall risk and liquidity of the financial system. This task is usually delegated to the central bank and/or treasury. The official aim of the state is to look beyond the interests of individual firms, groups of firms, or economic sectors in order to secure the stability and viability of the entire financial system. Macro-policy decisions apply to all institutions within a particular class of market participants. Micro-policy concerns the regulation of each specific firm, and thereby individual market participants.

The regulatory policy framework can be internally divided amongst three overlapping functional tasks: regulatory policy setting, compliance monitoring, and policy enforcement. It is possible for the monitoring and enforcement of policy to be delegated to market participants such as private stock exchanges or auditing firms with forensic accountants. The statutory power to make regulatory policy is almost always controlled by the state to protect the "general interest" and to prevent conflicts of interest.[34]

Given the normative preferences characteristic of advanced capitalist societies, it is not surprising that private institutions may undertake much of the financial regulatory policy process, often with little or no public supervision.[35] This process of private regulation occurs, at least in part, as

> ... strong market partners often perform the function of providing guidance to other market participants by their own behavior, thus setting "standards" which cannot be ignored without suffering market disadvantages. For example, J.P. Morgan set standards for controlling risk by publishing its "Risk Metrics" but others, including some German institutions, have helped, to a large extent, shape standards by their disclosure practices in the field of derivatives ... [36]

Of course, there are comparative differences across countries in the latitude of private or "self-regulation" depending on the regulatory history, political culture, and legal environment of a particular national market.[37] Furthermore, market participants are not immune from surveillance or criticism by state actors, but they are often entrusted to formulate their own solutions and professional standards. State actors accord to the self-regulatory and professional organizations of private market participants the trappings of a quasi-governmental agency through policy devolution.[38] Nevertheless, while much state regulation depends upon private cooperation for its effectiveness, self-regulation is effective only because it is underwritten by the legal-coercive power of the state.[39]

In general, the art of governance comes to be refracted towards the techniques of self-regulation within the market. Simultaneously, the power to define the actual content of the regulatory framework increasingly comes to be written in the language of market actors.

Regulatory shredding

There is a pattern in the regulation of financial markets. State actors have come to anticipate that market participants will relocate "offshore" to foreign markets if regulatory restrictions become onerous. Serious defection by a large number of financial institutions may threaten the ability of a central bank to implement monetary policy. Hence, in addition to normative constraints, state officials have a practical incentive to avoid increasing the structural complexity of regulation.[40] State officials assume the role of policy critics rather than policy makers. Policy-making authority is delegated to organizations representing private market institutions. State officials influence the policy-making process, but they are no longer the authors.

Market institutions have historically sought to consolidate the authority granted to them by transforming the organizations, markets, norms, discourse, and financial instruments related to risk, money, and debt. Market participants labor to increase the amount of economic activity in accordance with the behavioral principle of self-interest. Market participants also seek to legitimate their status by colonizing the political discourse on freedom, justice, and rights with the language of self-interest. States accept such activity in exchange for either relative economic gains (compared to other states) or absolute economic gains (compared across time).

However, the "efficiency maximization" or factional activities of market participants have often led to the circumvention of the regulatory framework. Market participants accomplish a *de facto* deregulation of markets through financial innovations. Moran states,

> Markets have become arenas where wealthy individuals and corporations practise "tax-efficiency" – in other words, invent instruments to escape tax liabilities. ... The most significant deregulation in financial markets has been accomplished by market operators themselves, who have created regulation-free financial instruments, regulation-free markets and

> regulation-free institutions: banking and insurance have gone 'offshore' to escape national restrictions; actors in securities markets have invented ways of cutting or abolishing regulated commissions on bargains; outsiders have poached business from regulated markets by inventing new organizations capable of slipping through existing regulatory nets. The phenomenon most commonly called deregulation ... has typically been a belated response to deregulation already accomplished in the markets.[41]

Eventually, financial innovations and regulatory evasion may lead to the relative economic decline of the state due to loss of revenue and/or a financial crisis due to regulatory failure. Following periods of economic decline or crisis, states attempt to reassert their legal and traditional authority through the financial markets. In periods of relative economic decline, state actors will work to deregulate domestic market activity in order to lure business back from rival markets. In periods of crisis, state actors attempt to rationalize market activity in order to secure social and economic stability as well as investor confidence.

Security governance

Despite the cunning activities of market institutions, states have not simply retreated towards the "deregulation" of all financial markets. To secure stability, states have come to rely increasingly upon the "elaboration of new rules governing prudence and honesty in the conduct of business."[42] States respond to financial innovation by extending surveillance and supervision beyond national boundaries. For example, the Office of the Comptroller of the Currency, which oversees all national banks in the US, maintains an office in London to supervise the international activity of American banks. State actors also scrutinize the new hybrid institutions and financial instruments existing in the interstices of regulatory categories.[43]

Most importantly, new security enhancing methods of states come to supplement the existing art of sovereign governance. *Sovereign governance* has as its object the extended space of a territory, discipline focused on the individual body, and a legal structure demarcated between the permissible and the forbidden. *Security governance* deals in a series of possible and probable events, it evaluates through calculations of comparative cost, and it specifies an optimal mean within a tolerable bandwidth of variation or compliance.[44]

For example, information gathering, a routine ritual in any bureaucracy, becomes heightened as a mechanical procedure to assure market actor compliance.[45] With advances in computer technology it has become possible for "real-time regulation" whereby the gathering of information on market actor activity is immediately screened for evidence of minor compliance infractions (e.g., securities fraud, or pension misselling).[46] The Federal

Reserve supplements its "on-site" examinations and inspections with "off-site" surveillance and monitoring through programs like "Performance Report Information and Surveillance Monitoring" (PRISM), a personal computer based application that "... supports financial analysis by facilitating access to supervisory and structure data housed in the National Information Center (NIC) and by electronically distributing surveillance and monitoring results."[47]

It is important to note that the extension of surveillance across national boundaries and throughout the membership of international financial institutions, serves to reinforce hierarchies in the international state system. For example on 20 May 1999, the IMF and World Bank announced the creation of two pilot programs known as the Financial Sector Assessment Program (FSAP) and the Financial Assessment Stability Assessment (FASA). These programs to assess and monitor financial systems of member countries were designed to supplement the regular annual ("Article IV") surveillance of member countries' macro-economy carried out by the IMF since the late 1940s. The programs would examine sensitive issues for sovereign states such as compliance with "international" standards, core principles, and good practices (including the Basel Accord). The implicit aim was to discover the sources of risk within emerging market banking and financial systems. Only two developed countries (i.e., Japan and Canada) were amongst the initial pool of thirteen countries requested to "volunteer" for the pilot program.[48] When a developing country member pointedly asked the staffs of the Fund and the Bank whether steps were being taken to achieve a more symmetrical treatment of risk disclosure by countries and private creditors, including hedge funds, the Fund staff replied bluntly in a memorandum:

> The Fund does not set standards in this area. Our role is to encourage acceptance and implementation of standards developed by other bodies. However, in some important areas, notably hedge funds and other highly leveraged institutions, standards, codes, and/or good practices for disclosure have yet to be identified. Fortunately, several international bodies, including the Financial Stability Forum (FSF), and the Committee on [the] Global Financial System, have started work on this topic.[49]

Notably, the FSF does not have any members from the developing world and only two countries are from the emerging markets (i.e., Hong Kong and Singapore).[50] The Committee on the Global Financial System (formerly known as the Euro-Currency Standing Committee) is composed of the central banks of the G10 developed countries.[51]

In essence, the Fund staff deferred the question of symmetric surveillance and decided *de facto* that developing countries required greater surveillance than their creditors and especially speculators. The asymmetric use of surveillance strategies in the developing countries and emerging economies exposed the normative bias toward market participants in the capitalist system and the hierarchical relationship between developed and all other countries in the monetary order.

A few developing countries and emerging economies were concerned that transparency initiatives at the international financial institutions would compromise the confidentiality of the extended surveillance programs. They argued that even the mildest criticism about the health of a developing or emerging country's financial sector could set off a panic amongst investors. The Fund staff reassured these member countries that the utmost level of confidentiality would be maintained. Although several countries eventually agreed to allow the FSAP reports to be made available to the public, others countries have opted to maintain strict confidentiality.

Conclusion

In summary, the governance of international financial markets operates through a dense network of state and market institutions. The categorical boundaries between these entities are porous. Social action within this network occurs in the context of a particular configuration of knowledge, power, and authority. Legitimacy is facilitated through the rationalization of authority within the dictates of power and knowledge. Power and knowledge constrain governance to the recognition of particular social facts, normative principles, and policies. Despite the appearance of technical abstraction, international financial market regulation is an agonistic realm of political struggle. Actions are deflected and modified by the social activity of other participants.

Overall, international financial activity in a capitalist system operates normatively in the service of market participants. Nevertheless, it is excessively reductionist to argue that states have been "captured" by market participants. There is a pattern of regulatory shredding resulting from financial innovation, evasion, and deregulation. States respond to regulatory shredding by articulating a new mode of governance based on security enhancing methods. As surveillance expands beyond the boundaries of developed countries, it may serve to reinforce hierarchies within the international state system, thereby initiating a new process of surveillance and evasion on the international stage.

The next chapter, "Regulating Risk," applies the theoretical discussions in the preceding two chapters through a historical account of the evolution of capital adequacy policies for banks since the collapse of the Bretton Woods system. The chapter analyzes how the technology of risk combined the exploitation of highly profitable but sparsely regulated sites of financial activity with the benefits of a standardized but less profitable financial framework.

5 Regulating risk

The system of regulation inherited from the Bretton Woods regime was riddled with national peculiarities. The earlier system of regulation had emphasized the juridical boundaries of the sovereign state as the "natural space" within which to pursue activities of accumulation, thus cultivating heterogeneous strategies that accorded with, and subordinated financial activity to, the national needs and strategies of post-war reconstruction and development. The growth of "offshore" financial markets (e.g., the Eurodollar and Eurobond markets in London) in the 1960s marked the beginning of an erosion in the system of financial regulation based on the strict partition of regulatory space along national boundaries. Nevertheless, a (limited) array of heterogeneous sites of regulation has persisted long after the collapse of the Bretton Woods system in the early 1970s.

On the one hand, these multiple sites of administration negated one another and multiplied loopholes as transnational financial institutions discovered ways to engage in regulatory arbitrage, triangular and intra-firm trade to move assets outside of any given jurisdiction in order to avoid regulation and taxation. Even today, despite an intensification of the regulatory gaze, pockets of regulatory irregularity (e.g., the Bahamas, the Channel Islands, the Cayman Islands, etc.) have not been deemed as sites of illegality *per se*; nevertheless the sites of heterogeneous regulation have been distinctly marginalized as part of a strategy to strengthen the monetary order.

On the other hand, disparities between sovereign legal frameworks restricted the mobility of financial capital within the circuit of developed countries and the penetration of lucrative emerging markets. Heterogeneous rule structures made it difficult, costly, and legally uncertain to send and retrieve capital from those sites where it could secure the highest rate of profit.

This internal contradiction in the monetary order led to the formation of particular anomalous islands of intense transnational financial activity (e.g., the Eurodollar and Eurobond markets in London) with unclear and ambiguous authority structures. After a few major bank collapses in the 1970s, one sees the emergence of a global strategy to clarify lines of regulatory responsibility. In the 1980s, the persistence of volatility in financial markets, coupled with the failure of this minimalist strategy to prevent serious fraud and hence "systemic risk," led to efforts to standardize regulatory strategies for transnational banks and other transnational financial institutions. While the nominal goals of reformers were to strengthen the quantity and quality of bank capital as a device to shore up the financial system and "level the playing field" (i.e., restrict international competition by limiting heterogeneous strategies of accumulation) the effect of these maneuvers was to increase the homogeneity of the financial terrain as the overwhelming majority of countries adopted the new standards. These tactics served to regularize and rationalize the exercise of power over a smooth, legible, and penetrable financial terrain. Thus, one sees the rise to prominence of sites for the harmonization and standardization of national policies such as the Basel Committee for Banking Supervision (BCBS) hosted by the Bank for International Settlement (BIS).

Within this broader strategy, the emergence and proliferation of the technology of risk assessment and management must be read as a technique that operated to increase the homogenization of the financial terrain. As the majority of states began to approach the regulation of risk in a similar and consistent manner, the heterogeneous spaces of defection were marginalized. However, the application of risk technology also elicited resistance, that is to say the application of the technology created new loopholes and opportunities through which financial institutions recouped the flexibility of the networked heterogeneous system that had emerged at the end of the Bretton Woods era. The application of risk technology led to the current cycle whereby financial instruments are perpetually invented to exploit or insure against newly discovered categories of risk.

The speculative aspects of risk technology necessitated the implementation of an extensive and intensive regulatory supervisory network. Not surprisingly, the endeavor to apply the technology of risk has not diminished the possibility of a systemic collapse; rather these rules have proliferated loopholes, incited the discovery of new risks/speculative opportunities, encouraged mutations in the structure of transnational financial institutions so as to avoid regulation, and mandated the application of risk technology to previously segregated market functions (i.e., securities and insurance markets). Hence, we see the development of a mobile and evolving relationship in the regulation of risk. In summary, the regime of risk is perpetually amended and expanded, as categories of risk are isolated – loopholes emerge, surveillance is made more intensive, and transgression becomes more cunning.

This chapter examines the historical, institutional, and discursive origins of the contemporary international supervisory network on risk management in banking. Through an exploration of the changing principles, policies, and practices endorsed by the Basel Committee on Banking Supervision, the dynamic tactics of state, state/market, and market institutions that constitute an art of global governance is illuminated.

The Basel Committee

One institution has become the symbolic heart of efforts to harmonize and standardize international policies and strategies of regulation, the Basel Committee on Banking Supervision housed at the Bank for International Settlements in Basel, Switzerland. Institutions like the Basel Committee provide a necessary fiction, the fiction of control over both the technology of risk and the general "playing field" in which market participants interact.[1] In reality, the Basel Committee is generally a reactive body that scrutinizes and certifies technological developments and political arrangements that are already in place. Nevertheless, it is at this site that a series of strategic relations between subjects and a generalized art of governance becomes manifest and visible.

The central banks and separate banking supervisory agencies of the G10 countries (Belgium, Canada, France, Germany, Italy, Japan, the Netherlands, Sweden, the United Kingdom, and the United States) plus Luxembourg and Switzerland officially constitute the Committee.[2] Each state has two representatives on the Basel Committee, one from its central bank, the other from its bank supervisory authority.[3] The representatives of the Basel Committee usually meet three to four times per year at the Bank for International Settlements (BIS). The BIS, which was established in 1930 as a public limited company and has been owned and run by central banks ever since, serves as a coordinating body to facilitate cooperation between its shareholders and provides the secretariat for the Basel Committee. The Committee cannot make any binding resolutions, only recommendations, which may be subsequently implemented (with varying degrees of vigor) through national legislation by the respective national banking regulatory agencies. Recommendations require the unanimous support of all the representatives. The inaugural purpose of the Committee was as a forum to discuss, manage, and clarify responsibility and liability for defaults on the international interbank markets. The committee did not originally seek to harmonize or standardize international laws, but to establish broad principles of banking supervision.

It should be noted from the outset that despite appearances, the Basel Committee is not a "state-centric" institution *per se*. The central banks that make up the Committee are quasi-state/quasi-market institutions that work to translate the discourse of financial firms to elected officials and vice versa. Central bankers monitor and regulate the activities of market actors, but central banks also operate within the markets in order to generate revenue, and influence the value of the currency (and hence the viability of fiscal policies). Central bankers occupy an ambiguous middle ground within that porous space that connects state and market institutions. For example, the Bank of England traditionally acted as the Treasury's advisor and agent in financial markets, regulated the conduct of banks and many other financial institutions, and served as the voice of City interests in government.

City bankers had traditionally neglected formally organized pressure groups, preferring to work informally through the Bank of England to influence policy decisions.[4] Even if central banks are treated as a proxy for state institutions, one must keep in mind that there are strong links between market participants and central banks.[5]

Leveling the terrain

Delineating responsibility

In the immediate aftermath of the Bretton Woods system, a minimalist strategy emerged which sought only to delineate clearly the lines of responsibility amongst the major central banks. After the failures of the Franklin National Bank and Banca Privata (American and Italian) and Bankhaus ID Herstatt (German) in 1974, the G10 countries plus Luxembourg and Switzerland formed the Standing Committee on Banking Regulation and Supervisory Practices.[6] Officials at the Bank of England took the lead role in the Standing Committee because the Bank needed to clarify which institution would most likely act as lender of last resort if the London branch of an international bank failed. The failure of a major transnational bank in the London market had the potential to erode confidence in the liquidity or solvency of other banks operating in the same market, thereby potentially setting off a larger financial crisis. The Bank of England also wanted to establish a uniform accounting standard to evaluate the balance sheets of international banks operating in London. By the mid-1970s, London had become a major shelter for bankers fleeing regulatory restrictions in the US financial market. However, the Bank of England could not impose uniform accounting standards without risking a similar defection by the transnational bank branches that sought to operate in those lucrative markets with the least amount of regulation. In essence, the Bank of England needed to insure London's role as a major offshore financial center, and unilateral regulations would have undermined this goal.[7] The heterogeneous regulatory system of the Bretton Woods era that had facilitated the return of London's pre-war status as a major financial center began to impede the Bank's ability to sustain this status; a certain degree of homogeneity or international regulatory cooperation would be necessary to prevent catastrophe or defection.

One year later, in 1975, central bankers reorganized the Standing Committee as the Basel Committee on Banking Supervision (BCBS) at the Bank for International Settlements (BIS) in Basel, Switzerland. In 1975, the "Basel Concordat" was agreed which established the principle of "home country supervision," whereby the host supervisor of a foreign bank agrees to allow the home or parent authority to examine the overall financial soundness and management of an institution and all of its branches. After the 1982 Banco Ambrosiano crisis and the threat of a systemic crisis originating in

Mexico, a revision to the Concordat was finalized in mid-1983.[8] The revision left "parent states" responsible for monitoring the risk exposure and capital adequacy of the home bank and the totality of its operations abroad. The core principles were relatively straightforward: that no banking establishment should escape supervision, and that the supervision should be adequate.[9] However, the Committee also agreed that host authorities had the right to inspect and prevent the creation of banks and subsidiaries on its soil.[10]

These cooperative agreements between states to adjust, extend, and limit the structure of sovereign authority overseas (i.e., the practice of "extra-territoriality") should not surprise us. Since the sixteenth century, an art of governance has emerged in which sovereignty is not exercised so much over a territory and its inhabitants as it is exercised over a complex composed of men and things.[11] Governance involves fostering productive and efficient relations between men and resources, territory, fertility, customs, habits, etc.[12] The aim of government is not the imposition of laws upon men but "... of employing tactics rather than laws, and even of using laws themselves as tactics – to arrange things in such a way that, through a certain number of means, such and such ends may be achieved."[13] The goal of governance is not the preservation of legal or territorial sovereignty *per se.* The goal of governance is in the pursuit of perfection in and the intensification of the processes that it directs. In so far as interstate cooperation permits an intensification in the production of profit, the contemporary art of governance comes into play.[14]

Despite the regulatory extensions and refinements, the principles of the Concordat were "... expressed with a high level of generality, and indeed central bankers continue to disagree about their meaning."[15] The 1975 Concordat and its 1983 successor required no real sacrifices from any of the parties involved.[16] In fact, the $10 billion collapse of the fraud-ridden transnational Bank of Credit and Commerce International (BCCI) in July 1991, dramatically demonstrated the vulnerabilities of the supervisory arrangements for transnational banks. For almost twenty years, the BCCI, a Luxembourg based – Cayman Island registered – bank with branches in more than seventy countries, served as the hub of an international crime network that involved money laundering, drug smuggling, and weapons trafficking. The fraud was detected, not by banking supervisory authorities, but by disgruntled former employees and the bank's auditors who raised the alarm.[17] One year after the BCCI scandal, the Concordat was revised once again with a four-point "minimum standard."[18]

In sum, despite the Basel Concordat, actual responses to crises remained *ad hoc* rather than procedurally formalized.[19] The credibility of these agreements remained dubious since it was unclear who would act to contain a major financial crisis.[20] It is likely that central bankers avoided explicit institutional commitments to act as lender of last resort in order to prevent "moral hazard" problems. In other words, bankers may have used ambiguity to avoid giving market participants the perception of a pre-arranged bailout for the next crisis, thereby avoiding the unwitting provision of incentives towards imprudent behavior.

Creating uniform standards

By the mid-1980s, concerns about "moral hazard" receded as central bankers realized that hazardous conditions already existed throughout the international banking system. The boom in transnational lending, spurred by the need to reinvest the "petrodollars" earned by OPEC countries during the oil crises, had overextended the resources of the transnational banking sector. Bad loans made in good times were coming home to roost. In response to the growing crisis, the Basel Committee in 1986 expanded its role to create uniform standards of capital adequacy to "build confidence" and avert systemic crisis in the banking sector. The objective of regulation shifted from "crisis management" to "crisis prevention" efforts. In reality, periodic consultation to discuss post-crisis management strategies became part of a continuous consultation process on the management of persistent crises.

In the early 1970s, several interrelated events generated increasing concern among US federal financial regulatory authorities and the legislature: oil price increases, the rising incidence of bank failures, the associated increase in Federal Depositors Insurance Corporation (FDIC) expenses, and the continued decline in general capital-to-asset ratios. Expectations of continued inflation had stimulated banks to expand lending to the energy and agriculture sectors in domestic markets, and to non-OPEC countries in international markets. Additionally, banks accepted greater leverage in order to offset competition from Japan and Europe. As a result, among the large commercial banks, the proportion of bank capital to total assets declined from around 10 percent in the early 1950s to 5 percent by the mid-1970s.[21] More than 20 US banks with assets of over $50 million failed during the 1970s.[22] In 1980, the Basel Committee noted that monitoring of foreign exchange business had become a matter of increased interest to supervisory authorities because of the increased instability in exchange rates.[23] By 1981, a major crisis in the domestic banking sector of the US was developing (see Table 5.1).

Despite the warning signs, US banks pursued aggressive lending strategies, as they were not keen to lose market share to the Japanese and Europeans. In particular, Citibank, under the leadership of Walter Wriston, advocated a spurious theory of sovereign debt that claimed that sovereign governments would always honor their debts, because governments owned more than they owed, thus lending to such countries carried little or no risk.[24] Citibank argued in a public forum that its dollar-denominated exposures in Mexico were safe because with 7,000 borrowers, its assets were adequately diversified. Citibank would only realize too late that all of these borrowers had only one source of dollars, the Mexican central bank.[25] International bankers had bought their own rhetoric and convinced themselves of the possibility of risk-free lending.

The announcement in 1982 by the Mexican government that it would default on its international loan payments focused intense attention on the ability of the international financial system, and US banks in particular, to withstand such a major default and the general strength of internationally active banks. By recycling petrodollars after the oil shocks, some banks had acquired significant exposure to Argentina, Brazil, Mexico, Poland, Venezuela, and Yugoslavia, which experienced debt-servicing difficulties. For example, the nine largest US banks had lent over 140 percent of their capital, which amounted to $30 billion, to Mexico, Argentina, and Brazil.[26] Eventually, these countries entered into negotiations to reschedule their debt, linked to the provision of new finance and economic adjustment programs. The US government encouraged American banks to roll over loans to nearly insolvent countries by permitting its banks to increase interest charges and pocket gigantic "rescheduling fees" on non-performing sovereign loans. The extra interest and fees were simply added onto the borrowers' indebtedness with the consent of the US government and private auditors.[27] By lobbying the US government, American banks actually profited from their reckless international lending, rather than having to strike bargains with debtor countries and sharing in the cost of the bailout. The cost of bailing out bad loans was resolved through an $8.4 billion contribution from US taxpayers to the IMF and the acceptance of austerity measures by citizens in afflicted developing countries.

However, the 1982 debt crisis highlighted a liquidity problem for regulators whereby, "the overseas branches of banks from countries experiencing external debt problems have, in some cases faced liquidity difficulties particularly where, in nervous market conditions, their funding has depended in substantial measure on borrowing at short term in the interbank market."[28] Liquidity, and hence the possibility of a broader crisis, had been contained mainly by pressure and side payments from central banks to lending banks not to withdraw deposits precipitately from banks in the debtor countries.[29] A long-term solution would need to be devised to prevent future crises.

Of course, different countries adopted different approaches to strengthening their financial system in the wake of the debt crisis. Japan changed its tax codes to allow its banks to write off bad debts. European regulatory adjustments reflected not only the debt crisis but also efforts to harmonize and facilitate European integration.[30] The US regulators focused on capital adequacy, balance sheet transparency, and new accounting rules.

Despite these initial reform attempts, by May 1984, the eighth largest bank in the US, Continental Illinois, collapsed notwithstanding a $6 billion infusion from the Federal Reserve to meet its immediate financial obligations.[31] By 1986, the number of bank collapses in the US had jumped into the triple digits. Whereas in 1965 there were 5 bank collapses with a total of $58 million in assets, by 1986 there were 138 collapses with assets totaling $7 billion (see Table 5.1). These bank collapses within the US and the specter of the international debt crisis set in motion and reinforced a process that would lead first to a proposal for a uniform domestic capital standard and then to a joint proposal by the US and UK to create a uniform capital standard for all of the members of the Basel Committee.

In 1981, the newly commissioned Federal Financial Institution Examination Council (FFIEC) proposed a uniform definition of capital to promote uniformity in supervisory policies among the federal banking agencies, i.e., the US Federal Reserve Bank, the Federal Depositors Insurance Corporation (FDIC), and the Office of the Comptroller of the Currency (OCC). The proposals stated that an objective was to redress the long-term decline in capital ratios.[32] The agencies set a minimum acceptable level for primary capital and established three zones for classifying institutions according to

Table 5.1 Number and assets of bank-insurance-fund insured banks closed because of financial difficulties in the US, 1965–1990

Year	*Number of closed banks*	*Assets ($ in thousands)*
1990	168	15,660,800
1989	206	29,168,596
1988	200	35,697,789
1987	184	6,850,700
1986	138	6,991,600
1985	120	8,741,268
1984	79	3,276,411
1983	48	7,026,923
1982	42	11,632,415
1981	10	4,859,060
1980	10	236,164
1979	10	132,988
1978	7	994,035
1977	6	232,612
1976	16	1,039,675
1975	13	419,950
1974	4	3,822,596
1973	6	1,309,675
1972	1	22,054
1971	6	196,520
1970	7	62,147
1969	9	43,572
1968	3	25,154
1967	4	11,993
1966	7	120,647
1965	5	58,750

Source: Adapted from Federal Deposit Insurance Corporation (2000) FDIC Annual Report 1999, Washington, D.C.: FDIC), p. 86.

the adequacy of their total capital. The FDIC actually adopted a more stringent definition of reserve capital, which included only equity capital, than the Federal Reserve or the OCC. The FDIC's stance reflected the fact that it served as the main depository insurer. The FDIC argued that secondary capital instruments lacked permanence and would not be available to absorb losses in an emergency. Eventually, all three regulatory agencies came to agree that only equity capital could count as the prime factor in a definition of capital.[33]

Congress also passed the International Lending Supervisory Act (ILSA) in 1983. Section 908 of the ILSA directed the three federal regulatory agencies to ensure that all banking institutions would achieve and maintain adequate capital levels. The ILSA provided the regulatory agencies with the statutory authority to enforce capital adequacy standards. The ILSA also directed US bank regulators to seek an international agreement on the harmonization of capital adequacy standards.[34] Specifically, the ILSA directed the Chairman of the Board of Governors of the Federal Reserve System and the Secretary of the Treasury to "encourage governments, central banks, and regulatory authorities of other major banking countries to work toward maintaining, and where appropriate strengthening, the capital bases of banking institutions involved in international lending."[35] Congress asked the regulators to seek an international agreement on capital adequacy standards within the framework of the Basel Committee, and to report back to the Congress within a year on the progress towards such an agreement.[36] Wolfgang Reinicke states,

> The pressure that ILSA exerted upon US regulators was thus not only reflected at the domestic level, culminating in the harmonization of capital adequacy rules for all U.S. banks. U.S. regulators were also increasingly pressing the other members of the Basel Committee to continue to search for ways to arrive at an international agreement to resolve the same issues at the global level.[37]

By the mid-1980s, growing bank collapses, the practice of regulatory arbitrage, whereby banks moved to alternate jurisdictions to avoid regulations, as well as the concern of American bankers to limit increasing competition from Japanese banks (that appeared undercapitalized by American standards) motivated regulatory officials to work for regulatory harmonization at the Basel Committee. As Reinicke argues,

> By the end of 1986, it was generally accepted by policymakers that global regulatory harmonization was required to stem the increasing tendency of private actors to engage in regulatory arbitrage. . . .
>
> There existed a broad agreement in the Basel Committee on the necessity to strengthen as well as harmonize capital ratios across the G10

> countries. In fact through its efforts the committee had, by the end of 1986, succeeded in the formulation of a complex definition of capital that all countries agreed on. The definition contained a variety of characteristics that were used in some, though not all, countries' regulatory systems, reflecting the increasing willingness of members to contemplate changes in their own system in the interest of greater convergence among the countries represented on the committee.[38]

The product of the Committee's extensive negotiations was the 1988 Capital Adequacy Accord.

Constructing the regime

Political economists consider the 1988 Capital Adequacy Accord or "Basel Accord" a landmark event in international finance and international cooperation in general. The Accord established uniform rules for internationally active banks in several countries and set a minimum capital reserve ratio based on the "risk-weighted" value of assets.[39] In other words, the amount of capital that a bank would need to set aside in case of a liquidity crisis would be a function of the "riskiness" of the assets in its portfolio. Most importantly, the Accord claimed to include all assets both on- and off-balance-sheet.

The appearance of uniformity masked the compromises embedded in the final agreement. For example, Charles Calomiris and Robert Litan note, "... Germany was influential in gaining a discounted risk weight for mortgage loans (which survives to this day) and also held up the most recent proposal to ensure favorable treatment for its banks' mortgages."[40]

Although designed to set standards for the banks of the twelve most developed countries, by 1999 the Accord had been implemented in approximately 100 countries.[41] While a large number of countries "voluntarily" adopted the Accord as a means to attract foreign investment, it should be noted that the Accord was created for an abstract developed economy. Hence, the design of the Accord may not be suited to the banking needs of developing countries and emerging markets. For example, the Accord was not designed for a developing country that is dependent on the agricultural sector.[42] In other words, the Accord may be ill suited to an economy characterized by seasonal fluctuations in lending practices. Similarly, the Accord may not be ideal for a primary product exporting economy that is highly vulnerable to small shifts in commodity prices. In emerging economies, which generally have a larger industrial base and greater export diversity than developing countries, the weak adaptation of accounting standards set in the developed countries and the widespread practice of politicized lending may make the application of the Accord an insufficient standard to strengthen their financial systems.[43] The Accord may also lead to a misallocation of the capital needed to sustain strong economic growth in the emerging markets. For example in India, although the implementation of the Accord in 1999 led to a significant drop in non-performing assets from 8.1 percent in 1999–2000 to 2.9 percent of net bank credit by 2003–4; the diversion of bank assets to government securities to meet the Basel standards led to a major decline in bank credit to small-scale industries from 17.3 percent to 7.0 percent in the same time period. Small-scale industries in India, which are profitable, collateralized, and do not constitute a greater portion of non-performing assets than other sectors, are being starved of working capital. In India, small and medium enterprises (e. g., small-scale industries) constitute the major component of the unorganized sector which generates 86 percent of employment in manufacturing, contributes to 40 percent of industrial production, and generates over 34 percent of national exports.[44]

Finally, the Accord did not address the practice of dollar-denominated borrowing by banks in emerging market economies, a major source of vulnerability during a speculative currency assault. The reason for the silence is attributable to the fact that the developed countries already have generally stable and credible currency regimes.

The 1988 Accord dealt with differing regulatory practices and economic contexts by simply dividing the world into two camps – OECD and non-OECD – with a preferential reserve requirement for the former set of developed countries and for short-term loans to the latter. This simplistic framework was strongly criticized after the Asian financial crisis. The framework fueled volatile short-term lending in the non-OECD emerging economies (discussed in Chapter VI) while giving a categorical stamp of approval for short- and long-term lending (without sufficient scrutiny into financial regulatory practices) to the newest member of the OECD, South Korea. The binary division may have reflected an implicit bias about the financial regulatory standards of democratic, capitalist, developed countries of Europe, Japan, and North America. The attempt to couch this bias in a formal organizational classification, whose membership included a select number of emerging economies, exposed untested assumptions. The near default of the South Korean financial system during the Asian financial crisis while Singapore, a non-OECD member, maintained a high credit standing poignantly illustrated a need to reassess aspects of the Accord's risk-weighting system. Moreover, the establishment of segregated regulatory spaces belied the Basel Committee's stated objective of wanting to promote a "level playing field."

Discursive origins

It would be incorrect to argue that the modern discourse on risk arose because of the need to homogenize spaces of financial activity among the developed countries. The concept of "risk-based" capital predates its actual implementation. The need for a "risk-based" capital appears to have first been formulated in the US shortly after World War II. Federal regulators had indicated that they favored adopting a capital-to-assets ratio that included a "risk-weighting" provision.[45] However, this notion would not be implemented in the US until the late 1980s. The strict partitioning of financial space and fixed exchange rate arrangement in the Bretton Woods system muted the need to foster a risk-based approach. Thus, throughout the Bretton Woods era, regulators in the US focused upon calibrating the appropriate capital-to-assets ratio, which represented a broader approach than the pre-war capital-to-deposit formula.

The risk-weighted capital standard was first applied by the Bank of England in the wake of the "fringe" banking crisis that threatened Britain's domestic financial system in the mid-1970s. As Kapstein writes, "Traditionally, capital had not been a focal point of British regulation, but with the collapse of a number of poorly capitalized institutions that had over-extended themselves in real estate (akin to the savings and loan crisis that would later ravage the United States), the bank began to develop new standards."[46] Several G10 countries had already adopted the risk-weighted system at the time that the US began looking to create a uniform international standard for capital adequacy.[47] In essence, the US borrowed and refined a concept that was already in use when it promoted the idea of risk-based capital adequacy standards at the Basel Committee.

Even though the contemporary discourse on risk predates the current monetary order, it is important to note that the contemporary discourse on risk assessment and management stands in contrast to earlier monetary orders where the conception of "risk" was quite vague and financial stability was ensured through traditional social structures and blanket approaches to prudential behavior. In late nineteenth century London, for example, a "gentlemanly order" based on highly visible class, gender, and ethnic divisions structured the boundaries of the creditworthy community.[48] The performance of these signs allowed market participants to recognize the outsider from the insider, and therefore the trustworthy from the non-trustworthy. The members of this class stratum were also interlinked through a constructed common background, i.e., the public school and the Oxbridge university experience. Similarly in the United States in the late eighteen hundreds, creditworthiness was conferred through membership in religious sects. Max Weber writes,

> A person who wants to open a bank joins the Baptists or Methodists, for everybody knows that baptism, respectively admission, is preceded by an *examen rigorosum* which inquires about blemishes in his past conduct: frequenting an inn, sexual life, card-playing, making debts, other levities, insincerity, etc.; if the result of the inquiry is positive, creditworthiness is guaranteed, and in countries like the United States personal credit is almost unthinkable on any other basis.[49]

The emphasis centered upon producing and recognizing the signs that indicated trustworthiness whereas approaches toward risk were vague and undifferentiated. For example, after the Bank of England rescued Barings Bank from bankruptcy in 1890, John Baring coined what became an unwritten motto of the institution for almost one hundred years, "I am going to take no risks."[50]

The performance of the signs of trustworthiness remains an important component of the contemporary monetary order, even though the homosocial environment of the nineteenth century has certainly changed. Nevertheless, the conception of risk has become an autonomous realm of discourse that generates its own signs of trustworthiness.

Refining the regime

The 1988 Basel Accord formally inaugurated the "risk-related" approach to capital adequacy for internationally active banks. Since 1988 the Accord has been continuously formalized, refined, and expanded to incorporate new categories of risk and to certify new techniques and domains of risk management. At the same time, a pattern of regulatory transgression has emerged whereby the technology of risk opens spaces of financial activity beyond the gaze of regulatory officials. Each pattern calls forth its other; each advance in precision is matched by transgression.

Precision

The Accord has been amended several times in order to make the measurement of risk more precise and the capital reserve ratio "proportionate" to the risk. Specifically, the 1988 Accord was amended in November 1991 to give greater precision to the definition of those general provisions or general loan-loss reserves, which could be included in capital for purposes of calculating capital adequacy.[51] In April 1995, the Committee amended the Accord to recognize the effects of "bilateral netting" of banks' credit exposures in derivative products.[52] In April 1996, Committee members accepted the effects of "multilateral netting" arrangements. In January 1996, the Committee amended the Capital Accord to incorporate the market risks arising from banks' open positions in foreign exchange, traded debt securities, equities, commodities and options.[53] Finally, in 2001 a revised accord ("The New Accord") was proposed based on three "complementary" pillars: 1) minimum capital requirements; 2) supervisory review process; and 3) market discipline.[54] The New Accord or Basel II will be implemented in 2008. Under the rubric of "efficiency," the Accord has been consistently modified to enhance the profit of financial institutions while intensifying the techniques of supervision.

This movement toward "precision" must not be cast simply as a struggle between state and market institutions. The contemporary art of governance involves establishing an "economy" or a field of efficient and productive relations between state and financial institutions while monitoring the behavior of each and all with an attentive form of surveillance that facilitates strategies designed to produce compliance to rules and norms. The process that moves the monetary order toward greater precision in the assessment and management of risk interpellates state and market participants as well as a host of state/market conglomerates. The stated aim of numerous working papers and pamphlets released by organizations like the Basel Committee is to establish a complementary relationship between "external" and "internal" surveillance mechanisms through the production of a constant stream of knowledge about the financial institution. A Basel Committee publication states:

> Strong internal control, including an internal audit function, and an independent external audit are part of sound corporate governance which in turn can contribute to an efficient and collaborative working relationship between bank management and bank supervisors. An effective internal audit function is a valuable source of information for bank management, as well as bank supervisors, about the quality of the internal control system.[55]

The subjects of power are determined to speak about risk, to hear it spoken about through explicit articulation and endless detail.[56] As the Basel Committee recommended, "An effective internal control system requires that the material risks that could adversely affect the achievement of the bank's goals are being recognised and continually assessed. . . . Control activities should be an integral part of the daily activities of a bank. An effective internal control system requires that an appropriate control structure is set up, with control activities defined at every business level."[57] While reports to senior level management are usually generated on a monthly basis within a firm, risk oversight managers usually receive daily reports, particularly on any deviations from standard credit arrangements or exceptions to set spending limits. These daily reports feed into the risk committee structure of the firm.[58]

Many financial institutions have implemented additional surveillance procedures to supplement the internal control system and the internal audit department. One supplementary process is known as self-assessments, or ". . . a formal and documented process whereby management and/or a staff team analyse their activity or function and evaluate the efficiency and effectiveness of the related internal control procedures."[59] Another self-surveillance mechanism involves the board of directors of the financial institution who are charged with verifying that the senior management has put in place a well-ordered system of internal surveillance. The board of directors is considered legally responsible for the overall risk-assessment and management system within their financial institution.

The internal audit system is usually supplemented by a "private" external audit as well as the "public" audit performed by the supervisory authorities. This multi-layer approach to regulation is not only necessary to deal with the volume of documents produced by a financial institution, but also it is necessary because "judgment permeates the auditor's work."[60] Auditors must determine whether or not inconsistencies in the records of the financial institution are merely errors or material evidence of fraud. The point of these multiple internal and external sites of investigation must be viewed as an attempt not only to detect risks that may be overlooked by a single set of eyes, but also to balance or reinforce the judgment of various professionals. As many of the major private auditing firms and credit rating agencies are headquartered in the US, one must also assume that the reliance on such "independent" agencies is a device to standardize the judgment of financial professionals along a narrow set of ethnocentric norms (while also providing a wealth of business to US auditing firms). Furthermore, it should be noted that external auditing firms usually apply an upper ceiling on the credit rating assigned to a financial or corporate institution based in a developing country or emerging economy, regardless of that institution's individual creditworthiness and past debt-service record.[61] In essence, the reliance on external auditing allows for a built-in bias against the financial institutions of the developing economies.

The concern with auditing has involved the Basel Committee in ensuring the ethics of the private external auditors, thereby implicitly acknowledging that the regulation of the financial system rests upon norms of trust at least as much as institutional design. The Basel Committee has sought to influence the ethical standards of professional organizations such as the International Federation of Accountants to ensure the "independence" of bank auditors. The Committee has acknowledged that the "independence" of auditors is ultimately a state of mind, nevertheless it argues that "... precise rules that support that state of mind will enhance the independence in appearance."[62] The ultimate aims of the Committee are to ensure that "... the public interest be internalised in the culture of international audit standard setting."[63]

The process of internalization is supplemented with perpetual surveillance. Basel Committee pamphlets encourage bank supervisors to conduct surprise on-site inspections in order to ensure that limits on foreign exchange exposures are adhered to on a "permanent basis."[64] In fact, the Committee believes that "[t]he development of sophisticated real-time computerised information systems has greatly improved the potential for control."[65] Not surprisingly given the discourse on risk, the Committee adds that real-time surveillance, "... has brought with it additional risks arising from the possibility of computer failure or fraud."[66]

Self-regulation

The contemporary desire for rigor has often been initiated by the financial institutions themselves, as an increase in the precise measurement of risk often results in a decrease in capital charges for the financial institution. The vocabulary of risk is equally accessible to state and market participants.

For example, even before the implementation date of the Basel Capital Accord, market participants began working to amend the rules to incorporate more precise risk-assessment strategies. Bankers aimed their major criticisms of the 1988 Accord toward the failure to incorporate market risk, or the risk of financial loss during the minimum period required to liquidate transactions in the market. Bankers argued that their technical ability to assess market risk was superior to the resources available to their regulators; therefore, bankers sought an expanded scope for self-regulation. Specifically, bankers argued that the Basel approach did not reward "risk-reducing diversification strategies" with lower capital requirements; riskier activities were incoherently accorded lower capital requirements; and the "traditional" or Basel approach was not designed to cover non-linear risk, as incorporated in derivatives instruments.[67]

The Basel Committee attempted to directly address the issue of market risk in a paper titled, "The Supervisory Treatment of Market Risk."[68] The Committee drew a distinction between the long-term investments of a bank and its trading book. The purpose was to apply the existing accord to the long-term investments and the new proposals on market risk to the trading book. However, bankers and economists mocked the proposed standardized formulas for determining risk as too clumsy and outdated relative to the methods already in use by the banking community.[69]

Partly in response to the Basel Committee paper in April 1993, JP Morgan placed in the public domain its RiskMetrics data set and Value-at-Risk (VaR) model for market risk.[70] JP Morgan's objective was to gain the official endorsement of regulators for the use of such in-house models by displaying its advantages over traditional risk-management approaches. At the same time, the Institute for International Finance (IIF), a private think-tank supported by 280 major commercial banks, severely criticized the Basel Committee. It chastised the Basel Committee for failing to encourage the use of more sophisticated hedging instruments that would reduce risk beyond the regulatory minimum. The IIF also suggested that banks with superior internal risk-measurement and control procedures should qualify for preferential capital treatment.[71]

In July, the Group of Thirty (G30) released a survey of market actor practices titled, *Derivatives: Practices and Principles.* Most of the world's top derivative houses were represented on the working committee (including JP Morgan, CSFB, Goldman Sachs, Merrill Lynch, Midland Global Markets, Bankers Trust, Mitsubishi Bank, Morgan Stanley, Barclays Bank, and IBJ), which formulated the report. The report championed the use of derivatives instruments and, more broadly, internal Value-at-Risk (VaR) models to assess risk.[72] The G30 report served to provide an alternative to the proposals of state regulators. Additionally, the G30 report had the appearance of illuminating a method, which if properly managed, promised scientific precision in teasing out and efficiently minimizing different types of risk. The general thrust of the report was that derivatives instruments did not introduce new or greater risks and therefore did not pose a threat to systemic stability. The G30 authors believed that the "amount of capital needed to support derivatives exposure is a matter of judgment for individual institutions, depending upon their appetite for risk and their ability to measure and manage it." The report argued that their approach was "not necessarily inconsistent with the view of regulators, who see the problem from a systemic perspective and conclude that certain minimum capital standards are appropriate as well."[73]

While most of the G30's recommendations were oriented towards market actors, the report urged legislators, regulators, and supervisors to: 1) recognize close-out netting arrangements and amend the Basel Accord to reflect their benefits in bank capital regulations (i.e., reduce capital reserve requirements where bankruptcy arrangements were pre-specified by the contracting parties); 2) work with market participants to remove legal and regulatory uncertainties regarding derivatives; 3) amend tax regulations that disadvantage the economic use of derivatives; and 4) provide comprehensive and consistent guidance on accounting and reporting of derivatives and other financial instruments.[74] Not surprisingly, market participants recognized the necessity for state actors to agree to the legal enforcement of the new financial instruments.

In April 1995, the Basel Committee acquiesced and they released a new proposal that indicated banks would be allowed to use either a standardized approach or their own VaR models to assess and monitor market risks. This revision by the Basel Committee was seen as a response to the pressure from the banking community for increased self-regulation. Nevertheless, the new proposal included "stringent qualitative" criteria on risk management models before they could be permitted.[75] Essentially, the Committee recommended using the VaR models and (arbitrarily) multiplying the recommended capital reserve by three. The Committee argued that the banks' VaR models contained unrealistic assumptions about the way markets move. Because the triple multiplication of the VaR calculations could result in higher requirements than the standardized approach, bankers immediately balked at the notion of setting aside more capital than the original proposal, thus initiating a new wave of debate between state, market, and state/market institutions.[76]

Transgression

Coupled with the expanding precision of the Accord is a process of regulatory transgression. As the process of regulation remains reactive to crises, the transgression of existing regulations is usually followed by calls to increase the state's surveillance to cover the new space occupied by market participants and/or to increase the precision in risk measurement in order to neutralize the danger posed by the new mode of activity. The reactive regulatory process effectively legitimates the act of transgression *ex post facto* and paves the way for new transgressions.

As the Basel Committee noted with obvious frustration, over time banks have "... learnt how to exploit the broad-brush nature of the requirements – in particular the limited relationship between actual risk and the regulatory capital charge. For some banks, this has probably started to undermine the meaningfulness of the requirements."[77] These complaints are similar to the Committee's frustrations with bankers in the mid-1980s prior to the approval of the Accord. In 1986, the BCBS had issued a report that argued:

> A prime motivation for some innovations has undoubtedly been the avoidance of prudential capital requirements, and these are, naturally enough, of particular concern to supervisors. There is also a more general concern that a number of the instruments ... may have the effect of concentrating risks within the banking system as whole which were previously more widely dispersed. This applies particularly to foreign exchange and interest rate risk. At the same time, it is recognised that while some banks will have increased their risk profiles, other banks, as well as bank customers, now have considerably greater opportunities to limit and control their overall risk exposures and to reduce their cost of borrowing. Some banks – the consumers as opposed to the market makers in these instruments – may thus have managed to reduce their total risk exposure.[78]

In essence, despite a decade of regulation, transnational banks continue to "discover" sophisticated techniques to manipulate regulations or create technical and institutional innovations to avoid existing regulations altogether.

Of course, there are also much simpler ways to avoid regulatory scrutiny such as non-compliance or minimal compliance with information gathering requests. For example, as the measurement of risk seemed to become more sophisticated in the 1980s, central banks in Europe began to show concern that their existing risk-to-asset ratio for determining capital reserves had not factored in the risks arising from growing off-balance-sheet exposures such as stand-by letters of credit.[79] In the US, federal regulators began requesting regular reports from banks regarding their off-balance-sheet items in 1983. However, American regulators feared that, as they began to press banks to increase capital reserves in proportion to their loans, banks might try to shift some direct loans into categories that did not show up on their balance sheets, thereby circumventing the demands for increased capital.[80] The Federal Reserve had good reason to anticipate resistance. Salomon Brothers estimated in 1984 that if the US government required banks to maintain capital against standby letters of credit alone, the 35 banks it advised could be forced to raise \$2.7 billion to \$5.3 billion in new capital.[81] Of course, all parties knew that a comprehensive understanding of the risks could only come from experience accumulated over a variety of cyclical conditions.[82]

Information collection requests may have fueled financial innovation. Efforts of state regulators to monitor new financial activities by banks in the securities markets were continuously frustrated by the nature and pace of innovation. The Bank of England noted that their supervisory response to new financial instruments affected the development of those instruments. The Bank of England indicated that their attempt in April 1985 to incorporate banks' underwriting commitments under the "Note Issuance Facilities" category in the risk asset ratio, probably accelerated the trend towards non-underwritten Eurocommercial paper programs.[83] The frustration experienced by central bankers in attempting to regulate new financial instruments was a factor that heightened prudential concerns.

States have adopted some general responses to noncompliance and innovation. They have worked to establish a homogenous regulatory terrain through common minimum standards across the spectrum from developed to developing countries, and regulators have consistently expanded their gaze toward the marginal sites of heterogeneous regulation through cooperative agreements with regulatory officials in emerging economies and developing countries. In July 1992, for example, after several major bank collapses, certain of the principles of the Concordat were reformulated as "Minimum Standards."[84] The Basel Committee has also increased cooperation with "offshore" money centers to remove obstacles to consolidated cooperation. In 1996, 140 countries attending the International Conference on Banking Supervision (ICBS) endorsed a report with proposals to overcome barriers to the supervision of the cross-border activities of international banks. Nevertheless, official policy guidelines remain reactive to crises and innovations.

Institutional adaptation

Despite the cooperative transnational efforts of regulatory officials, institutions have continuously adapted to maneuver within the silent spaces between regulations. As the Basel Committee noted in a discussion on the techniques for regulating holding companies, "... gaps in supervision can arise out of structural features of international banking groups."[85] In less diplomatic terms, the Committee stated that the structural features of banking groups may have the effect or be designed so as to evade regulatory scrutiny. Enhanced supervision will only have the perverse effect of eliciting even more convoluted financial institutions. However, it is not even necessary for banks to modify their structure; banks may create selective linkages with unregulated institutions in order to achieve high rates of profits from extremely speculative strategies. One such example of this type of selective linkage is between banks and hedge funds.

Hedge funds or "Highly Leveraged Institutions" (HLI) are essentially mutual funds that use derivative instruments, high leverage strategies, and computer models to shift positions rapidly in one or more markets so as to maximize profits. It is estimated that there are close to 5,000 hedge funds – with approximately 3,000 operating in the US. The vast majority of hedge funds are quite small – with the average fund having less than $100 million in capital – although some have over $100 billion in assets.[86] The most famous hedge fund, George Soros' $10 billion Quantum Fund, based in the US but registered in Curaçao in the Netherlands Antilles, is credited with knocking Britain off the Exchange Rate Mechanism in 1992.[87]

These institutions were specifically designed to operate beyond the gaze of regulatory authorities.[88] Hedge funds are usually registered in offshore tax and regulatory havens in order to minimize taxation and oversight, even though the funds generally operate within the G10 countries.[89] In the US, hedge funds are structured as limited partnerships that are exempt from federal securities law and regulation.[90] Hedge funds operating in the US are subject to the Federal Reserve Bank's weekly and monthly reporting system if they have foreign currency positions equivalent to $50 billion (US) in any of five currencies (British pound, Canadian dollar, German mark, Swiss franc, Japanese yen). Quarterly reports are required of funds that have more than $1 billion outstanding at the end of any quarter during the previous year. Hedge funds intentionally limit the sales of securities to fewer than 100 partners, all of whom would meet the definition of qualified purchasers – "sophisticated" institutions or individuals – meaning institutions with total investments exceeding $25 million and individuals with investment portfolios of at least $5 million.[91] Hedge fund advisors are not required to be registered or subject to the Investment Advisors Act. Hedge fund managers can avoid the definition of investment advisor by limiting their client base to fewer than 15 hedge fund "clients." Thus, the limited partners (investors) in such funds are a small number of wealthy, financially sophisticated parties, who must perform their own due diligence of the hedge fund, since the fund is not subject to standardized disclosure requirements.[92] All of these features combine to provide the hedge fund with a high degree of privacy, flexibility, and secrecy in its operations.

In the case of the Connecticut based – Cayman Island registered – Long Term Capital Management (LTCM) hedge fund that collapsed in 1998, the minimum investment was $11 million per investor. The central bank of Italy, a client of LTCM, invested $250 million from its currency reserves.[93] LTCM had over $125 billion in assets and used leverage in excess of a 30 to 1 ratio in their market transaction. In other words, they were able to borrow in excess of $30 billion for every $1 billion in collateral in order to engage in derivatives trading. In fact, some banks may even have waived the collateral requirement for LTCM.[94] The structure of this HLI was designed to dovetail with the lending institutions that fueled its trading strategies. US national banks are legally permitted to invest directly in a hedge fund provided that the portfolio of the fund consists exclusively of assets that a national bank may purchase and sell for the bank's own account, and the fund otherwise meets all applicable requirements for ownership by a national bank.[95] The notional value of the contracts traded by LTCM was approximately $1.25 trillion (a sum that was greater than the total GDP of almost all of the emerging market economies). Nevertheless, due to the secretive nature of the hedge fund, lending institutions had little or no idea about the fund's degree of leverage and counterparty obligations; and the banks had little incentive to ask too many questions as long as they were making large returns on their investments.[96] HLIs occupy a structural position within the social division of labor that permits banks to engage indirectly in extremely leveraged activities despite norms and regulations prohibiting banks from direct involvement in such transactions.

As the trading strategies of LTCM encountered adverse conditions in the wake of the Asian financial crisis and the Russian debt default (discussed in Chapter VI), the hedge fund became incapable of repaying collateral calls from lenders. A cash infusion $3.65 billion from a handful of securities firms and banking institutions coordinated by the US Federal Reserve Bank of New York averted a systemic crisis.[97]

The LTCM debacle served as part of the public justification for the formation of several new committees and the announcement of new commitments to investigate the role of hedge funds in international financial markets. The Basel Committee created a new working group and announced a revision of the 1988 Basel Accord. William McDonough, Chairman of the Basel Committee, said that, "We have been reminded dramatically of the importance of banks in the last few years (these rules are) meant to strengthen the world's banking systems and banking supervision."[98] The threat posed by hedge funds was not new. As an IMF report reveals, hedge funds had been implicated in a series of crises since 1992:

> Each bout of turbulence in international financial markets heighten the attention of government officials and others to the role played by institutional investors, and hedge funds in particular. This was the case in 1992, following the ERM crisis. It was the case in 1994, a period of turbulence in international bond markets. It was again the case in 1997 in the wake of the financial upheavals in Asia. In each case, it has been suggested, hedge funds precipitated major movements in asset prices, either through the sheer volume of their own transactions or through the tendency of other market participants to follow their lead.[99]

Nevertheless, as the *Financial Times* shrewdly observed, the fervor for increased regulation died down as markets returned to normalcy:

> The working group was set up as part of a flurry of official initiatives when financial markets froze and banks took heavy losses in the aftermath of the LTCM collapse in autumn 1998.
>
> Since then many observers have noted that the relative calmness of financial markets has reduced the sense of urgency around regulatory reform.[100]

It is likely that hedge funds will eventually fall under the regulation of states; however by that time newer institutions will have emerged to exploit regulatory loopholes.

Lateral expansion

The relentless expansion of the technology of risk has resulted in the opening of sectors of financial activity that had been closed to international bankers in the Bretton Woods era. In an effort to diversify risks, financial institutions have justified moving into securities markets.

Of course, banks had sought to move into the securities sector even before the 1970s, but they had been lured toward syndicated lending activities after the petrodollar surplus emerged in the mid-1970s. Five years after the 1982 debt crisis, however, provisioning against problem country debt resulted in a sharp fall in pre-tax profits in many large banks.[101] The decline in retained earnings meant that banks had to resort to other sources of capital to support balance sheet growth.[102] Additionally, bankers faced pressure as highly rated corporate borrowers turned to the direct credit markets (e.g., stocks and bonds) for finance. International banks began to lose their comparative advantage to international securities firms as a channel for credit intermediation for the largest, high-grade borrowers. As a response to the competition as well as the need for capital, banks moved into certain capital markets and left development lending behind.[103] The movement away from lending to developing countries should not be viewed as a retrenchment of international capital. To the contrary, the invention of new financial instruments had the effect of transforming more and more components of finance or financial assets into marketable instruments. There was an enormous increase in liquidity and in the circulation of financial capital through the marketing of financial instruments rather than lending.[104]

Banks vigorously pursued large corporate businesses by acting as managers and underwriters of capital market activity. Banks also raised new capital by issuing and purchasing shares. Increasingly, this new role placed banks in direct competition with domestic and international securities firms. In order to become more efficient, banks restructured their internal organization, cut costs, and acquired securities firms. This functional integration of banking and securities activity continued throughout the 1980s.

The securities market also offered an opportunity for bankers to market the debt on their ledger books in order to liquidate holdings in times of uncertainty.[105] Existing loans could now be sold as bonds on the international market, freeing banks' balance sheets of the need to wait for the loan to reach maturity. For example, the risk of default from a loan to a sovereign developing country could be sold off as bonds, thereby resolving the problem that imperiled banks in the 1982 debt crisis. Of course, banks could also purchase securities, thereby increasing their profits (and risks) in times of certainty. As many countries did not initially require banks to report securities holdings as claims for statistical purposes, banks that purchased securities were essentially able to move more assets off the balance sheet. This meant that lending to countries that issued securities (e.g., Thailand) would be under-reported in banking statistics.[106] Central banks would eventually realize that while some institutions were diversifying risks through the securitization of debt, other banks were adding risks to their assets by purchasing securities without the provision of extra reserve capital.

Nevertheless, pressure mounted on regulatory authorities to permit banks to deal in securities. In October 1986, the UK initiated its "Big Bang" to officially eliminate barriers between the banking and securities sectors. But the "Big Bang" only served to recognize a *fait accompli*. Even before the "Big Bang," four large British banks had acquired seven former London Stock Exchange brokerages and jobbers; and ten of the solo-authorized banks (i.e., the Accepting Houses Committee members) had acquired twenty London Stock Exchange member firms. In fact, in 1984 there was a 67 percent increase in Eurobond issuances from the previous year reaching a staggering $80 billion.[107] A dramatic shift had begun in 1980s whereby international lending, particularly to sovereign countries, was being replaced by international bond issuances. In 1982, bank loans were worth nearly $100 billion, while bonds were $70 billion; one year later bonds were worth over $100 billion while bank loans were worth only $60 billion.[108]

Gradually, as this lucrative market skyrocketed in value, transnational banks in other developed countries were able to pressure their states to officially sanction the expansion into the securities market in order to preserve competition and prevent defection to rival jurisdictions. In 1990, the US Federal Reserve Board approved the applications of five major American banks to underwrite corporate debt, provided that a separately capitalized subsidiary unit conducted the underwriting. State-chartered member banks were also authorized to own shares in certain investment companies and money-market mutual funds. In the same year France's Finance Ministry proposed changes in the mutual fund law permitting the securitization of bank credits. Similarly, in Japan the Ministry of Finance allowed mutual banks to be converted into commercial banks, and eased banks' branching restrictions. Furthermore, in exchange for allowing securities houses to deal in currency futures, the Ministry of Finance permitted banks to broker government bond futures.

While central bankers agreed that participation in securities activities could counter risk through portfolio diversification, it was equally becoming clear that "trading losses incurred in investment banking and securities operations can significantly damage the earnings of even the largest institutions. ..."[109] Securitization increased the banks' risk relative to minimum capital levels. Empirical evidence indicated that this practice of arbitrage (or "securitization") was substantial at around 25 percent of these banks' risk-weighted loans. In fact, European banks had been using the US markets for securitizations and securitization outside the US markets had been growing exponentially.[110] The possibility that a collapse in the securities sector could spread to the banking sector emerged.

Beginning in July 1989, the Basel Committee started working with the International Organization of Securities Commissions (IOSCO) on the issue of securities trading by banks. The Committee adopted a strategy to homogenize the financial terrain by incorporating securities firms within the existing capital adequacy framework for banks. Discussions took place at the same time that IOSCO was working on setting capital requirements for securities firms in September 1989. The Technical Committee of IOSCO issued a tentative agreement that there was a need for a common conceptual framework regarding the capital requirements of securities firms.

The IOSCO framework would include a risk-based measure of capital adequacy similar to the Basel Accord that would cover all risks to a firm, including the risk arising from both on-balance-sheet and off-balance-sheet activities. Allowances were provided for the use of risk reduction strategies such as diversification. The framework was supposed to correspond to those already in use in the US and UK. However, the proposals would be less rapidly applied in countries such as Germany with universal banking systems, in which a minimum capital base is required of a bank as a basis for all its operations, irrespective of scale.[111] The definition of capital was to be expanded beyond what had been previously agreed at Basel in 1988. As countries maintained highly divergent regulation between banks and securities firms with respect to subordinated debt, a compromise was proposed that the capital requirements resulting from the new market risk regulations may be met by an additional "own funds" category.[112]

Concurrent to the discussions between the Basel Committee and IOSCO, a set of EC regulations that would apply to all financial institutions rather than only to banks was being contemplated. The legislative foundation for the establishment of a "single unified financial area for Europe" was set in 1977 by the *First Banking Coordination Directive*, which required that all member countries adhere to certain minimal capital and management standards for authorizing the establishment of banks and other credit institutions. The Directive also required that branches of EC country banks be subjected to the same regulations as national banks in the host country. The *Second Banking Coordination Directive* was adopted in December 1989. This directive replaced the First Directive's principle of national treatment with the principle of "mutual recognition of rules." The Second Directive gave EC banks a "passport" to do business in any other member country subject only to the rules in force in its home country. Exceptions to the Second Directive were provided for codes of conduct and for consumer or investor protection. The Second Directive also provided for reciprocity of treatment to non-EC banks. EC banks were to be granted equal "national treatment" in the non-EC country, otherwise banks from the host country could be suspended from practice within the EC.[113]

Initial talks between the Basel Committee, IOSCO, and EC broke down in 1992 over the attempts to set a common minimum capital reserve standard. However, a solution was proposed in 1995 whereby the internal risk calculation (or VaR) models of financial institutions could be used to determine the appropriate level of capital. In other words, the capital adequacy criteria would be designed by the market participants themselves. As one newspaper commented,

> ... there has been considerable progress since the worst days of bickering over how much capital institutions should be set[ting] aside to cover trading risks. The recent shift towards allowing institutions to use their own computer models to calculate risk should allow more efficient use of capital – though it will take some policing. A level playing field, regulators now agree, does not necessarily mean identical capital requirements for all.[114]

In essence, the "internal" risk-management procedures of each individual financial institution would become the basis for "external" regulators to evaluate risk in both banking and securities sectors. Inevitably, this will mean that external regulatory agencies will become involved in the intensification of the disciplinary processes within the financial institution. If banks are to regulate themselves, regulators will need to be certain of the ethics and trustworthiness of the members of the firm.

Conclusion

It would be inaccurate to assert that the processes of precision and transgression result in an "equilibrium" for the monetary order. In fact, the perpetual discovery of risk and expansion of financial activity leads to periods of intense volatility, which can have severe economic, political, and social consequences around the world. The ever-evolving technology of risk means that volatility will continue throughout the life of the monetary order. However, it seems likely that the sources of volatility will generally come from new species of financial institutions, or newly discovered categories of risk, and/or newly incorporated sectors of the market, etc. The state's regulatory gaze is reactive; states focus upon and seek to repair breeches in the monetary order, but only after these breeches have been exposed through crises. Market institutions are proactive; the need for economic survival impels them to exploit opportunities revealed by risk technology.

The next chapter, "Political Arena," examines the forum in which the technology of risk evolves. The fallout from the Asian financial crisis demonstrates that the spirals of speculation and insurance initiated by the operation of risk technology have had devastating, long-term, and asymmetric consequences for those at the margins of the financial system. The normative framework within which risk technology has developed has meant that the solutions developed to counter the effects of crises (e.g., political risk insurance) has served the interests of the owners of capital in the developed countries before the interests of all others in the international political economy.

6 The political arena

The drama of financial risk is performed in a political arena. The technology of risk affects its audience and is reactive to its context; it is not an abstract discourse. The technology of risk management responds to and generates social and political phenomena. War, civil unrest, oil embargoes, expropriation/nationalization, terrorist attacks, speculative assaults, labor unrest, mass layoffs, race riots are all influential upon the evolution and operation of the technology of risk management. Social and political phenomena that potentially affect the production and distribution of commodities and services are incorporated quickly into financial market calculations. At the same time, volatility in financial markets generates social and political phenomena and affects the lives of subjects even at the margins of the international financial system.

This chapter is divided into two sections. The first section links the technology of risk to the Asian financial crisis. It seeks to elaborate some of the ways in which elements of risk technology facilitated and fueled the regional and ultimately global financial crisis. The lasting economic and social effects generated by the crisis are sketched out to illustrate the long-term and asymmetric consequences of a speculative assault. The second section discusses the development of the technology of political risk insurance which claims to transcend social and political instability in order to promote economic development. What the technology of political risk insurance actually demonstrates is the ways in which the discourse on risk facilitates a reconfiguration of public and private spheres as well as the actuarial and political realms to serve particular interests.

Risk and crisis

The technology of risk has played an important role in several major financial crises. This section examines the relationship between the technology of risk and the Asian financial crisis, which was arguably one of the most severe global economic crises in the post-Bretton Woods monetary order. What began as a speculative assault on a pegged exchange rate by large financial houses and hedge funds using sophisticated derivatives in offshore markets resulted in a region-wide economic contraction. The East Asian region went from a $93 billion investment inflow prior to the crisis to a $105 billion outflow. The affected countries witnessed a massive 11 percent drop in their cumulative GDP. It is clear that while long-term foreign direct investment in tangible assets across the region remained relatively constant at $7 billion, there was a significant shift in liquid capital flows with a $77 billion drop in commercial bank lending, a $24 billion decline in portfolio equity, and a $5 billion cut in nonbank lending.[1] Notably, the East Asian crisis countries did not have particularly risky policies before the crisis set in; the East Asian crisis countries were characterized by macroeconomic stability, low public debt, increasing output, moderate to low inflation, and balanced or surplus fiscal positions throughout the preceding decade.[2] Nevertheless, the technology of risk set the stage, provided the weapons, and heightened the drama.

First, the rapidly evolving technology of risk promoted the type of infrastructure that facilitated the financial crisis. The technology resulted in the development of investment instruments, institutions, markets, and rules that were specifically designed to move capital rapidly between financial markets in order to exploit arbitrage and short-term profit opportunities.[3] The most important infrastructural elements, the establishment of offshore markets and the liberalization of capital controls, were put in place in the early 1990s.[4] This infrastructure was strongly recommended by policy makers from the major financial centers as well as the intergovernmental financial institutions. However there was less emphasis on fostering the associated norms and institutions to support the new financial environment.

Thailand, which would become ground zero for the Asian financial crisis, began its financial liberalization in 1990 when it agreed to lift foreign-exchange controls on current account transactions in accordance with Article VIII of the IMF. The next year Thailand abandoned restrictions on capital account transactions.[5] In 1993, Thailand created an offshore market called the Bangkok International Banking Facility (BIBF). The BIBF was intended to serve as a regional hub and as a first step in granting foreign banks full access to the domestic market. In order to make the center competitive with Malaysia's offshore market on Labuan Island[6] (set up only three years earlier) as well as the established regional financial markets in Singapore and Hong Kong, certain transactions were granted tax privileges and breaks. These concessions along with the lucrative potential of the market encouraged large net capital inflows. The BIBF lent $32 billion to companies in Thailand in the years prior to the crisis.[7] A significant portion of the funds raised from the BIBF helped to pump up the value of stocks and real estate in Thailand. Professor Eisuke Sakakibara, Japan's former Vice Minister of Finance for International Affairs, argues,

> ... the total value of stocks, against a 1975 index base of 100, rose almost 15-fold to 1,494 by January 1994, while the foreign debt of

> financial institutions in Thailand surged to a level equivalent to 28 percent of the country's 1995 gross domestic product. This is a clear indication that a bubble economy had been created by an influx of foreign capital that inflated the value of stocks and real estate.
>
> After peaking in 1994, the Thai bubble economy began showing signs of collapse. The influx of foreign capital was due mainly to the exchange rate of the baht, which was pegged to the dollar. ... [8]

The hard currency funds borrowed from foreign banks in the offshore market tended to be short term in maturity because of the provisioning requirements of the Basel Capital Accord. As noted earlier (see Chapter V), a loan to a non-OECD country with a maturity date beyond one year required a 100 percent risk weighting for assets. Short-term loans to non-OECD countries carried a lower risk-weighting charge. Hence banks preferred to lend only on a short-term basis.[9]

Of course, the over-inflated Thai economy was only part of a broader regional trend. Throughout the 1990s, short-term capital investments poured into the financially liberalizing emerging markets of East Asia in accordance with portfolio diversification and earnings maximization strategies. In fact, all three of the countries that would eventually have to turn to the IMF for loan packages (Thailand, South Korea, and Indonesia) had short-term foreign debts relative to official reserves in excess of 100 percent in 1996.[10]

Capital flowed to Asian countries despite common knowledge of crony capitalism and weak financial regulatory institutions in the host countries. Investors were particularly attracted to real estate and equity markets which were characterized by high profits with short time horizons. For borrowers within the emerging market economies, access to foreign capital ensured by a stable exchange rate encouraged the adoption of highly leveraged growth strategies and speculative activity. (After the crisis, it would be commonly argued that Asian borrowers had failed to hedge against the risk of currency devaluation – despite the officially pegged exchange rate – and hence failed to apply properly the technology of risk management.) Easy access to dollar-denominated loans from offshore international banking facilities coupled with crony capitalist practices resulted in domestic banks funding low-quality projects and speculative investments. The end of the real estate bubble as well as a slowdown in export growth led to a deterioration of banks' loan portfolios and corporations' balance sheets; hindering their ability to repay their dollar-denominated debt, eroding confidence in the domestic economy, and placing pressure for currency devaluation.[11]

Second, the technology of risk supplied the derivative instruments that were pivotal in the assault and defense of the exchange rate that set off the crisis.[12] The speculative attack on the Thai baht, which was pegged primarily to the dollar, began in May 1997. Although the end of the property bubble and decline of export growth were the main reasons for pressure against the Thai currency, many commodity and currency futures traders had an interest in speculatively selling baht to bring down its value and thereby dramatically increase their profits on the delivery date of their futures contract.[13]

In response to the speculative assault, the Thai central bank in coordination with monetary authorities in Hong Kong, Malaysia, and Singapore committed billions of dollars in foreign exchange reserves to support the value of the baht over several weeks. The government was able to mount its heroic defense using sophisticated derivatives contracts known as "repos" or repurchase agreements. Repos are essentially agreements (between central banks in this case) to extend cash (US dollars) in exchange for (US government) securities. In this manner liquid assets can be used to defend the currency from a speculative attack on the open market, but the central bank is obligated to repurchase its securities at the same or similar price on a set date. In essence, these derivatives permit a massive accumulation of liquidity but these resources must be repaid in the future, thereby limiting resources available for future crises. The Thai central bank gambled on a long shot that a vigorous defense would drive the speculators away for the foreseeable future.

The defensive measures were of limited success as the baht fell to a ten-year low on offshore markets. Nevertheless, false rumors that the Japanese central bank was helping to support the baht kept speculators at bay. Moreover, the Thai government inflicted some pain on speculators by cutting off their access to the local currency and by raising interest rates in the offshore market to over 1,000 percent. After a brief respite, pressure on the baht mounted again as domestic borrowers began selling baht for dollars to repay their dollar-denominated loans. In a bid to stop the hemorrhaging, the Thai government decided to abandon the fixed exchange rate and float the baht in July 1997. Hedge funds and financial houses gambled that the Thai government's decision to float its currency; the central bank's reliance on dramatic interest rate hikes to support the currency; and the introduction of new rules limiting nonresidents from access to the currency indicated dwindling foreign exchange reserves and the possibility of further devaluation with sufficient market pressure.

The speculators were correct. After commitments to repurchase securities were deducted, Thailand was left with only $2.8 billion in foreign exchange reserves by June 1997, barely enough to cover three months of imports much less the $48.5 billion in short-term debts which were coming due. Thailand could not rely on a bailout from the Japanese central bank because the Thai central bank was unwilling to reveal the limit of its dwindled foreign exchange reserves to any foreigners. In essence, the first speculative assault left blood in the water and a weakened, isolated victim, which brought the sharks back; a feeding frenzy became inevitable.

In the weeks that followed the initial float, the baht lost nearly a fifth of its value. Eventually, the government of Thailand would have to turn to the IMF for a $17 billion assistance package in exchange for the implementation of fiscal austerity and the closure of 58 finance companies. The level of austerity negotiated by the IMF was highly intrusive:

> ... the IMF was insisting on an increase in bus fares, because of the costly government subsidy that kept fares low. The two sides finally agreed that only fares on air-conditioned buses would rise; fares on buses without air conditioning would remain subsidized, since the non-air-conditioned buses tended to serve the poorest riders. But the Fund held its ground on the basic issue and won agreement on a major tightening of fiscal policy. ... [14]

The imposition of austerity led to a severe recession; the economy contracted by 10 percent in 1998. The currency continued to depreciate significantly even after the IMF bailout; the exchange rate fell from 25.8 at the end of June 1997 to 53.8 in January 1998. The currency depreciation drove domestic borrowers with dollar denominated debt into bankruptcy. It would take five years for Thailand just to regain the output level it lost in the crisis.

Notably, the IMF package served to reaffirm the rights of financial capital as restrictions on capital flows were not permitted; state owned enterprises were privatized; and full guarantees were extended to (mostly foreign) creditors of financial institutions.[15]

Billions upon billions of dollars were spent in the speculative assaults and counter-thrusts of the "battle of the baht." A measure of the stakes wagered by the financial houses can be inferred from the build-up of Chase Manhattan Corporation's trading account (i.e., the value of all the securities and derivatives it trades) from $47 billion in 1994 to $72 billion by September 1997, with an increase in the share of its emerging market instruments rising from 7.5 percent to 17.4 percent of its trading account. Similarly, JP Morgan increased its trading account from $57 billion to $115 billion in the same time period.[16]

Despite the combined power of the financial speculators, they were occasionally caught off guard by the coordinated actions of central banks. Losses from derivatives trading during the crisis are evident by the decision of Citicorp to place $59 million worth of derivatives contracts on a "non-accrual" basis and JP Morgan's decision to designate an astounding $587 million worth of financial contracts, mainly swap arrangements, in Asia as "non-performing."[17] Final quarter earnings in 1997 for JP Morgan were down 35 percent from the previous year, "primarily because of derivatives trading."[18] Chase Manhattan Corporation which lost $126 million in the heat of the crisis ended the quarter with $78 million in pre-tax trading losses; and Deutsche Bank may have lost as much at $100 million on derivatives trading during the crisis.[19]

In addition to the large financial houses, it is understood that hedge funds played a critical part – although the precise roles are still hazy. As hedge funds rely upon leveraging strategies to maximize profits, their gross balance sheets may have been worth several trillion dollars. Profits and losses by these institutions during the crisis were more difficult to gauge as they are not required to make disclosures to the public, however market watchers stated that one hedge fund lost $450 to $500 million in the initial assault on the Thai baht.[20]

The defeat of the Thai central bank tempted speculators to test the other emerging markets in the region. As the crisis spread from Thailand to Malaysia, Indonesia, the Philippines, Hong Kong, South Korea, Russia, and Brazil volatility increased, resulting in a general crisis of confidence in emerging markets.

Of course, the financial houses and hedge funds place the blame for the crisis on the East Asian governments which failed to regulate their financial sector and East Asian central banks which initially raised interest rates unrealistically to defend the exchange rate and extended credit to prop up ailing domestic financial institutions instead of accepting dramatic currency devaluation and bank closures. While there is merit to the currency traders' argument, it is clear that the regionally clustered pattern of speculative assaults as well as varying economic conditions in crisis-afflicted countries indicates an element of irrationality and opportunism which resulted in an over-correction of asset prices and economic output.

Third, the deployment of common strategies of risk management exacerbated the crisis. Volatility increased as large American and European pension funds pulled out of their investments in the region. Institutional investors are generally prohibited from investing in speculative grade bonds and hence must sell off their holdings if the credit rating declines. However, when large funds begin to liquidate their positions simultaneously in response to market volatility, asset prices will plunge.

A report by the IMF confirms that fluctuations in asset prices, which may increase the credit exposures of large firms, are linked with volatility across the financial system.

> When asset prices adjust rapidly, the size and configuration of counterparty exposures can become unsustainably large and provoke a rapid unwinding of positions. Recent experience strongly suggests that the ebb and flow of credit exposures among the large internationally active financial institutions can be severely affected by some events, which cannot be easily predicted and which can lead to potentially disruptive systemic consequences.[21]

In other words, as major financial firms seek to shed undesired risk exposures simultaneously, volatility in the global derivatives markets may increase. The dynamic of simultaneous risk shedding creates a liquidity crisis in a manner similar to a classic run on the banking system where depositors rush to empty their accounts thereby ensuring the bank's collapse. These liquidity crises are not anomalous events. It is apparent that there has been a dramatic increase in the volatility of derivatives markets in the 1990s. The IMF report continues,

> … in the 1990s, OTC derivatives activities have sometimes exhibited an unusual volatility and have added to the historical experience of what volatility can mean. For example, in the 1990s, there were repeated periods of volatility and stress in different asset markets (ERM crises, bond market turbulence in 1994 and 1996; Mexican, Asian, and Russian crises; LTCM; Brazil) as market participants searched for higher rates of return in the world's major bond, equity, foreign exchange, and derivatives markets. Some of these episodes suggest that the structure of market dynamics has been adversely affected by financial innovations and become more unpredictable if not volatile.[22]

In fact, derivatives instruments served to facilitate the preferences of investors seeking to rapidly liquidate their positions in the midst of the crisis. For example, during the financial crisis, foreign creditors forced a bank linked to the Thai government to repay a $500 million bond several years before maturity by exercising a credit derivative (i.e., a "put option" linked to the bank's credit rating). The Thai bank borrowed money from the Thai Finance Ministry, the World Bank, the Asian Development Bank (ADB), and the Import-Export Bank of Japan to repay its obligations.[23] If the bank had not been able to secure funds from these (quasi-political) institutions, the crisis would have widened.

Even in highly liquid markets, some cost-effective hedging instruments seem to have contributed to, as opposed to dampened, significant volatility. For example, the use of "knockout options" in the yen-dollar foreign exchange market has been linked to extreme market volatility in 1995 and 1998.

> In both cases the yen-dollar exchange rate exhibited what might be characterized as extreme price dynamics – beyond what changes in fundamentals would suggest was appropriate – in what was, and is, one of the deepest and most liquid markets. The extreme nature of the price dynamics resulted in part from hedging positions involving the use of OTC derivatives contracts called knockout options. … These OTC options are designed to insure against relatively small changes in an underlying asset price. Yet once a certain threshold level of the yen-dollar rate was reached, the bunching of these OTC options drove the yen-dollar rate to extraordinary levels in a very short period of time – an event that the OTC options were not designed to insure against.[24]

Japanese exporters who had bought the "knockout options" to protect against a moderate depreciation of the dollar dumped their dollars to prevent further losses when the knockout options were cancelled. At the same time, the sellers of the knockout options also dumped their dollar holdings to re-hedge their positions.[25] Hence, the financial instruments that were designed to absorb market volatility generated heightened levels of volatility.

It is also worth noting that some of the sophisticated derivative instruments and risk management techniques used to limit the effects of the Asian financial crisis did not always perform very well even after the crisis was well underway. For example, Chase Manhattan Bank arranged a hedge for a decline in Brazilian and other foreign government bonds that were tied to the US bond market. The logic was that if Brazilian bonds declined, there would be a flight to US bonds. Instead, the US bonds fell as the crisis spread to Brazil thereby exacerbating Chase's losses. Chase executives decided that they had relied too heavily on computer models that predict future risk based on past market volatility.[26]

Socializing risk, transferring wealth

Regardless of the sophistication of private risk-management strategies and instruments, once a serious financial crisis is underway, private risk is generally socialized. Meredith Woo-Cummings writes:

> The state can achieve its goal by manipulating the financial structure, but once it does so, it has to socialize risk, either through inflationary refinancing (monetary means) of the nonperforming loans to bail the firms out, or through expansion of the state equity share of the banks (essentially fiscal means) so as to write off the bad loans. The former is indirect taxation on the populace, and the latter, direct.[27]

In essence, wealth is transferred either directly or indirectly from the general population to compensate private market actors.

In this regard, the massive bailouts by states and intergovernmental financial institutions can also be viewed as wealth transfers from the taxpayers of member states (who supply, replenish, and expand the endowment of their states and the intergovernmental financial institutions) to debtor governments and ultimately to the (mainly Western) private financial institutions which demand repayment. For example, in the month of December 1997, almost all of the $9 billion first disbursed by the IMF to assist South Korea had gone to pay off foreign banks that were calling in their loans to Korean borrowers. Nevertheless, as the Korean won fell forty percent over the course of the month, the bailout failed to rescue Korea from the brink of default.[28]

Despite the initial losses to US-based financial houses and hedge funds, and official "assistance" to crisis afflicted countries, the Asian financial crisis may have resulted in an aggregate transfer of wealth from Asian countries to the United States. A paper by the Bank for International Settlements states,

> It is not difficult to document the "beginning" and the "end" of the money trail insofar as it involves the Asian countries and the United

> States. Capital outflows from the Asia-5 from the start of the crisis (1997Q2) to the end of 1998 amounted to about $80 billion. The United States ran a current account deficit in 1998 of $221 billion, an increase of $77 billion over the 1997 current account deficit. The increased deficit was obviously financed by increased capital inflows.
>
> It is more difficult, however, to document the precise trail of money from these Asian countries to the United States. Using Bank for International Settlements (BIS) data, and data drawn from the US Treasury Department's Treasury International Capital (TIC) system, we are able to follow the trail to a certain extent. We find that banking flows were the major source of the outflows, and that these outflows were dispersed all over the world, including Japan, Europe, the United States and offshore banking centers. The majority of the flows went to the offshore centers. Our findings also suggest that most of the offshore centers funneled their money to European banks. From there the trail runs cold, but we do conclude that banks clearly played an important role at the beginning of the reallocation process, and the money clearly came to the United States in a roundabout fashion.[29]

The controversial paper goes on to argue that the US economy received a +0.2 percentage point growth in GDP as a result of the redistribution of wealth.

Regardless of the aggregate benefits and losses, it is clear that the Asian crisis nearly culminated in a systemic collapse of the international financial system after the hedge fund Long-Term Capital Management (LTCM) folded in the wake of the crisis. The IMF reported that

> ... the turbulence surrounding the near-collapse of LTCM in the autumn of 1998 posed the risk of systemic consequences for the international financial system, and seemed to have created consequences for real economic activity. ... This risk was real enough that major central banks reduced interest rates to restore risk taking to a level supportive of more normal levels of financial intermediation and continued economic growth.[30]

The fifteen partners and 150 employees of LTCM managed over $125 billion in assets which belonged primarily to financial institutions. Using highly leveraged strategies common to all hedge funds, LTCM traded mainly in swaps and the spread between fixed interest rate swaps and government bond yields with similar maturity periods and currency denomination. Reportedly, LTCM earned over 25 percent return on investment per year for over three years, with returns as high as 46 percent in 1995 and 41 percent in 1996.[31] The total notional value of their trading book at the height of their crisis was approximately $1.25 trillion covering 10,000 swaps agreements.

Despite its highly leveraged strategy, the firm was generally considered to be conservative in its investment approach. LTCM used the latest technology of risk, i.e. the VaR approach, as well as geographic diversification to hedge their positions carefully and ensure some level of profit regardless of market conditions. LTCM had only limited exposure to emerging markets and junk bonds, where the risk of default was great. The firm also added additional conservative weights to their models and stress tested their strategies against hypothetical catastrophic scenarios. The Achilles heel of the firm was that it was not able to disguise its trading positions from other arbitrage firms despite using different counterparties because of the social character of the derivatives market and the requirement to reveal trading strategies to potential investors.[32]

Ordinarily imitators would not have posed a problem for LTCM's arbitrage strategy which relied on a convergence between spreads. In fact, imitators would help reduce the spreads more quickly by piling on to an arbitrage opportunity. However, as the Asian financial crisis moved to Russia, spreads widened considerably after Russia defaulted on its domestic debt. (Critics would later argue that LTCM failed to account for the largely unquantifiable "event risk").[33] Arbitrageurs who incurred losses began to reduce their positions. As more and more arbitrage firms liquidated their positions to stop losses, they exacerbated price pressures and widened spreads. In his illuminating study of the LTCM debacle, Donald MacKenzie notes the perverse impact of the VaR approach used by the firm during the crisis,

> Another factor may paradoxically have been modern risk management practices, particularly the "value-at-risk" method of measuring and managing the exposure of a portfolio of assets to losses. This statistical technique allows senior management to control the risks incurred by trading desks by allocating them a risk limit, while avoiding detailed supervision of their trading. When a desk reaches its value-at-risk limit, it must start to liquidate its positions. Says one trader: "a proportion of the investment bank[s] out there are managed by accountants, not smart people, and the accountants have said, 'well, you've hit your risk limit. Close the position'" (Wenman Interview). An international change in banking supervision practices increased the significance of value-at-risk. Banks are required to set aside capital to meet the various risks they face, and in 1996 they began to be allowed to use value-at-risk models to calculate the set-aside required in respect to fluctuations in the market value of their portfolios (Basel Committee on Banking Supervision 1996). The change was attractive to banks because it reduced capital requirements, but it had the consequence that as market prices move against a bank and become more volatile, it has either to raise more capital to preserve its trading positions, a slow and often unwelcome process, or to try to liquidate those positions.[34]

When the crisis peaked, correlations between fundamentally unrelated components within LTCM's portfolio rose. In other words, despite maintaining a diversified portfolio the firm began to incur losses across the board. As losses mounted and LTCM published its monthly report, rumors spread of the firm's imminent collapse resulting in a fire sale of assets which LTCM was alleged to have in large quantities.[35] By late September 1998, the firm had lost almost 90 percent of its capital.

The international financial system narrowly escaped collapse because of a central bank coordinated private-sector bailout to the tune of a $3.6 billion. The bailout required the Federal Reserve Chairman to twist the arms of the New York banking community whose sixteen top executives were reportedly summoned to the NY Federal Reserve at 1 pm and kept in a conference room until 3 am when the terms of the private bailout were agreed.[36] In the wake of the collapse and bailout, the exposure of financial institutions to LTCM was divulged: amongst the most exposed to LTCM were Chase Manhattan with $3.2 billion, Merrill Lynch with $1.4 billion, and JP Morgan with $1.1 billion. It was estimated that without the capital injection, LTCM's losses could have mounted to $14 billion. Notably, many banks had not demanded any margin (i.e. funds to be set aside) when they traded with LTCM. Moreover, the Basel Accord did not require banks to set aside capital against hedge fund exposures.[37]

Although a systemic collapse was averted, the cost of the entire Asian financial crisis was remarkably high. In economic terms, billions of dollars were disbursed trying to bailout the afflicted countries, including $14.3 billion for Thailand, $21.9 billion for Indonesia, and $30.4 billion for South Korea. In aggregate, the bailouts were the costliest in history. In social terms the crisis negatively impacted the lives of millions of people living at the margins of the international financial system.

Social Effects

Financial crises are usually short-lived in duration; however losses in actual output may be large and persistent, particularly in less developed economies and/or in situations where a banking crisis is combined with a currency crisis.[38] The economics literature and financial press tend to focus on the restoration of trend growth rates after a crisis rather than the trend level of output prior to the crisis. As Boyd, Kwak and Smith argue:

> Proceeding in this way is problematic in several respects. First, the level of output is typically still well below what would be predicted on the basis of pre-crisis trends, even at the point where the rate of growth has recovered to its pre-crisis value. Second, by focusing on growth rates rather than levels, the effects of a crisis are not allowed to compound over time, something that they clearly do in practice. Third, this method of estimating output losses does not discount future output losses, and

> thus aggregates magnitudes that are not inter-temporally comparable. . . . Additionally, they assume that all output losses associated with a crisis have been incurred by the time the crisis is over. As we will see, this is not usually the case.[39]

Losses in output and related losses in government revenue may imply lasting and asymmetrical social impacts on the relatively most vulnerable segments of society in developing countries and emerging economies. For example, after the Mexican debt crisis of 1982, the fiscal adjustment programs adopted by Latin American countries reduced spending on education in real terms as well as a portion of total government expenditures. Lower levels of education suffered deeper fiscal reductions than higher education.[40] Although very little evidence on the quality of education was gathered, one can reasonably infer that a reduction in educational funding has an impact on the quality of education in developing countries. In other words, a short-lived financial crisis may quietly cripple an entire generation of a society through little noted changes in government spending.

Similarly, the Asian financial crisis resulted in significant output losses and had a disproportionate impact on some of the most vulnerable sectors of society. In 1998, output losses from the crisis were estimated at 15 percent in Indonesia, 7 percent in South Korea, 5 percent in Malaysia, and 7 percent in Thailand.[41] As a report by the ADB noted (in a language that was intended for market participants): "The poor, unskilled, and uneducated are least able to protect themselves by hedging their incomes and diversifying their investments; it is not surprising that they should suffer disproportionately from volatility."[42]

The Asian financial crisis began in a region of the developing world that had become a living testament for the notion that financial market liberalization and export led growth helps economic development and poverty reduction. Before the financial crisis, a litany of statistics showed that the East Asian countries were at the forefront of development efforts to lift their populations out of poverty. Between 1975 and 1995, absolute poverty in East Asia dropped by two-thirds according to the region's headcount index with respect to the constant US$1-a-day poverty line (in 1985 purchasing power parity terms), and the pace of poverty reduction was faster than in any other developing region.[43] In 1975, six out of ten East Asians lived in absolute poverty according to this standard; by 1995 the ratio had dropped to two out of ten. This means that the number of poor people in the region was more than halved, from 720 million to 345 million.[44] From 1975 to 1995, Thailand had the largest proportional reduction as the 8 percent of the population living in poverty was reduced to less than 1 percent living in poverty.[45] Similarly, the number of poor persons declined by almost three-quarters over the same period in Indonesia. While the discourse of poverty always defines its subjects in debatable terms, it is certain that aggregate economic conditions in East Asia were generally improving before the financial crisis.

The financial crisis imperiled these significant achievements across the region and particularly in South Korea, Thailand, and Indonesia. The number of people living below the poverty line increased dramatically and the economic growth rate fell to its lowest point since World War II. For example, South Korea witnessed a jump in the portion of urban poor persons from 9.6 percent just before the crisis to 19 percent in 1998 (see Table 6.1).[46] Similarly in Thailand, because of the crisis, more than one million Thai citizens were without a job four years later. Poverty incidence increased sharply from 11 percent in 1996 and 13 percent in 1998 to 16 percent of the population in 1999. In other words, 9.8 million Thai citizens were living on less than the purchasing power equivalent of $1.50 per day.[47] A significant portion of the steady poverty reduction achieved by Thailand since 1981 was wiped out by the financial crisis.[48] In Indonesia, it was estimated that 17 million more Indonesians would fall below the $1 a day (extreme) poverty line in 1998. An additional 5 million Indonesians would fall below the poverty line if it were set just a bit higher at $1.25 per day.[49]

Many workers who were not laid off were forced to accept large wage reductions resulting in significant decreases in real earnings. For example, in South Korea many companies cut wages by as much as 30 percent and even unionized workers accepted wage cuts averaging 3 percent.[50] By May 1998, nearly 80 percent of South Koreans suffered a significant reduction in income.[51] Women were disproportionately laid off or forced to accept "voluntary" leaves under the patriarchal assumption that women were not breadwinners.[52] The female labor force declined by 3.8 percent during the crisis, while the male labor force actually increased by 1.0 percent.[53] In Indonesia, one in five jobs in the formal sector was lost. Out of a workforce of 100 million persons in the formal and informal sectors, almost 14 million people were unemployed – mainly in the informal sector. In fact, 5.4 million people shifted to the agricultural workforce from 1997 to 1998.[54]

Income inequality increased in most of the countries afflicted by the crisis: Thailand (20.5 to 22.5 percent), South Korea (22 to 24.5 percent), and the Philippines (39.3 to 42.9 percent). However, Indonesia reported an improvement in income equality. Within countries, the regional distribution of income also shifted. In Thailand, Bangkok and the central region gained while other regions worsened. In Indonesia, the island of Java, where two-thirds of the population lives, suffered the worst impact of the crisis.[55]

The countries afflicted by the financial crisis historically had low levels of government commitment to social insurance, even in comparison to countries with similar levels of economic development.[56] In fact, it was the low commitment to social spending and hence the semblance of "fiscal discipline" which had attracted foreign investors prior to the crisis. Thus, the governments impacted by the crisis had limited economic stabilizers in place and inadequate mechanisms for targeting aid to the most vulnerable segments of society.[57] Moreover, the traditional reliance on extended family networks and rural-urban linkages were of limited utility in a regional economic downturn. Ironically, the waves of reverse migration of urban and regional migrant laborers to rural areas expanded the scope of the crisis and threatened local economies which were just emerging from the grip of entrenched poverty.

The rapid increase in unemployment and the deterioration in the standard of living threatened the social stability of several countries in the region.[58] For example, with inflation spiking to 80 percent and a severe drop in real income, riots broke out in several towns across Indonesia as townspeople looted shops owned by ethnic Chinese whom they accused of charging excessive prices for staple foods.[59] Hundreds perished in the months of riots and thousands of buildings were burned. After a 70 percent increase in petroleum prices, violent riots spread to the capital, leaving over two hundred people dead and ultimately toppling the government.[60]

Less noted than violent protests were the quiet tragedies caused by the crisis. For example, in Korea an average of 28 people per day took their own lives in the first quarter of 1998 – up 36 percent from a year earlier.[61] In Thailand, 150,000 out of 1 million students dropped out of school in 1998 and NGOs reported increases in child prostitution, child labor, and begging in the wake of the crisis.[62] In Indonesia, Oxfam reported increased rates of child prostitution among street children.[63]

The Asian financial crisis also had an impact on government spending on health and education in certain countries (see Table 6.2). Several countries afflicted by the crisis witnessed a shift from expensive private health providers to the public health system. Indonesia saw a shift toward private health providers because of insufficient medical supplies and increased user fees in its public health system. Not surprisingly, poorer households dealt with rising health care costs by delaying or avoiding medical care facilities.[64]

The most drastic cuts in education also occurred in Indonesia, where education spending in the post-crisis period was only 72 percent of what was spent in 1996. The cutbacks occurred in spite of a $390 million national education campaign to keep children in school funded by the Indonesian government, World Bank, ADB, and UNICEF. The qualitative impact of these fiscal cuts was not studied. Other countries in the region maintained relatively stable spending on education in the wake of the crisis. Some states mitigated the effects of the crisis through public spending. For example, Thailand created scholarships for 328,000 students by 1999 and provided loans to help parents pay for secondary and tertiary school fees. In 1998/99 there was a fourfold increase over two years in the number of loan recipients with 675,000 students borrowing money from the fund. The government also permitted deferments and waivers of tuition fees to keep students in the education system.[65]

In terms of school enrollment, the ADB estimated that 6 million students in Indonesia dropped out of school after the crisis;[66] however the drop out rates in other crisis countries was milder. Although primary school enrollments were not seriously affected, the crisis did have a significant negative impact on secondary school enrollments particularly among the poor in many of the crisis countries.[67] In Thailand, nearly a third of upper-secondary school children dropped out of school in 1998/99. South Korea actually noted an increase in tertiary education enrollments, possibly reflecting the fact that the 15 to 29 age group witnessed the most dramatic unemployment.[68]

Private expenditures on education (e.g., tutoring) declined significantly, particularly among the poor. In South Korea, household spending on private tutors declined by an average 24 percent, and 39 percent among the lowest income groups compared to 13 percent among the high income groups.[69] In Indonesia, while the body mass index (BMI) fell for all adults regardless of income, there was no decline in children's average height and weight, indicating that parents reduced their own consumption to shield their children from the drop in affordable food.[70]

The crisis also had impacts on practices of social governance and modes of governmentality (the governance of oneself). For example, Korea witnessed a significant discursive shift in its modest welfare provisions away from the traditional homeless population (i.e., the *purangin*) and toward unemployed male workers rendered homeless by the financial crisis (i.e., the "IMF homeless"). The regime of Kim Dae Jung justified its shift on the grounds that these men could be rehabilitated and they were therefore "deserving" of state assistance.[71] Housewives were also targeted through public campaigns and media messages encouraging them to refrain from buying expensive imported goods and to show limitless support for their recently unemployed husbands. Notably these superfluous public campaigns targeting allegedly spendthrift and heartless housewives occurred at a time when real per capita household income had declined by 20 percent.

Two of South Korea's largest corporations, Samsung and Daewoo, initiated public gold collection campaigns to save the nation from the economic crisis. President Kim Dae Jung personally joined in the campaign by donating "a miniature golden tortoise and four golden 'good luck' keys, weighing 393 grams." The President confessed that after accounting for the gold donated by his wife the other day, "This is what was left."[72] Similarly in Malaysia, the government sought to use the crisis to promote individual sacrifice on behalf of the nation. Malaysia's Prime Minister, Mahathir Mohamed urged his countrymen to economize in their daily lives. He went so far as to argue that "Small things like reducing the consumption of sugar from four spoonfuls to three or two will help."[73] Although these campaigns had only a marginal impact on the national economy,[74] they served to socialize the crisis and to divert concerns about regulatory failures and crony capitalism that may have fueled the crisis.

For most of the countries on the front lines, recovery from the financial crisis has been slow whether one compares trend growth rates or trend output levels per capita. On aggregate the economies of the five countries most affected by the crisis (Thailand, Indonesia, Malaysia, South Korea, and the Philippines) grew more slowly from 2000 to 2006 than they did

Table 6.1 Poverty incidence in three East Asian countries before and after the financial crisis (1996, 1998)*

	1996	*1998*	*% Change*
South Korea	9.6	19.2	100
Thailand	11.4	12.9	13.2
Indonesia	11.3	16.7	47.8

Source: Adapted from World Bank (2000b) "Coping with Crises: Social Policy and the Poor in East Asia," by Tamar Manuelyan Atinc (7 April 2000), p. 124.

Note:
* Poverty incidence numbers were derived using national poverty lines and are based on income for Thailand, and on consumption expenditure for South Korea and Indonesia. Poverty incidence numbers for Korea are for urban areas only.

Table 6.2 Government spending on education and health in five East Asian countries since the crisis (ratio of 1998 to 1997)*

	Education	*Health*
South Korea	94.2	96.8
Thailand	98.7	89.3
Indonesia	72.3	87.8
Malaysia	86.3	90.3
Philippines	103.8	92.2

Source: Adapted from World Bank (2000b) "Coping with Crises: Social Policy and the Poor in East Asia," by Tamar Manuelyan Atinc (7 April 2000), p. 124.

Note:
1 *Deflated using GDP deflator from IFS for Korea, Thailand, and the Philippines. GDP deflator for Malaysia from Malaysian Department of Statistics.
2 Education spending for Indonesia is the ratio of 1998 to 1996 and for health is from the World Bank (1999).

from 1990 to 1996 – with annual growth rates an average of 2.5 percent below the previous period.[75] While the annual growth rate in per capita GDP surpassed the pre-crisis peak in the five worst hit countries by 2005, only South Korea appears to have caught back up with the spectacular GDP per capita projected before the crisis. For the other countries, "growth has settled on a lower trajectory."[76]

The crisis has had a lasting impact on investor's confidence in the region. A decade after the crisis, the investment share of GDP is still 10–15 percent below levels seen in the mid-1990s for countries throughout the region, excluding China and Vietnam.[77] In terms of real equity prices, measured in US dollars relative to values in 1990, only South Korea's equities have appreciated nearly a decade after the crisis; Malaysia's equities have also appreciated if values are measured in local currency. In fact, the ADB reports that equity prices are 40 percent lower than their 1990 level in Indonesia and Thailand, and 15 percent lower in Malaysia and the Philippines.

Of course, recovery rates were unevenly distributed across class, region, and country in the initial years after the crisis. While South Korea's economy rebounded relatively quickly only to slow down after 2001, Indonesia's economy remained in recession until the turn of the millennium. In fact, consumer prices in Indonesia skyrocketed after the financial crisis, the government's debt jumped from 27 percent of GDP in 1997 to 103 percent of GDP in 2000, and the recorded unemployment rate was in the double digits.

In general, throughout the Asian region unemployment rates (see Table 6.3), particularly in urban areas, took years to return to pre-crisis levels. Note that even these statistics are slightly misleading as they do not include dropouts from the labor force, i.e., "discouraged workers." Unemployment and underemployment combined with consumer price increases on food items had a disproportionate effect on the living conditions of the poorest segment of the population, because food accounts for a larger share of the consumption basket of the poor. In other words, low-income groups bore a disproportionate brunt of the crisis and they did not immediately share in the economic recovery.[78]

In summary, it becomes apparent that there have been, and will continue to be, social, political, and economic costs related to the development of the technology of risk. The burden of these costs is particularly difficult upon the backs of the poor in the emerging economies who have only recently climbed out of absolute poverty. Nonetheless, the technology of risk promises to transcend political and social instability in the emerging markets generated by events like the Asian financial crisis in order to promote continued economic development. In other words, techniques are being developed to mitigate the costs associated with those political and social phenomena that disrupt business and financial activity. Not surprisingly, however, this technology known as political risk insurance (PRI) or more accurately political risk investment insurance, actually benefits creditors disproportionately relative to the other segments of society that are affected by political and social turmoil. However, in so doing it exposes the raw politics just behind the curtain of technology and rhetoric of mutual gains.

Political risk insurance

PRI reimburses policyholders for financial losses incurred by "politically motivated" actions such as wars, terrorist attacks, civil disorder, sabotage, expropriations, contract repudiation or frustration, etc. in the countries in which the policyholder's firm operates. The insurance does not cover difficulties arising from exchange rate volatility, currency devaluation, or business failure due to general market conditions. Government owned corporations, intergovernmental organizations, and private insurers often sell political risk as part of a broader insurance package and/or export incentives for international enterprises.[79] Although the boundaries between

Table 6.3 Broad economic indicators of the Asian economies since the financial crisis (1997–2000)

		1997	*1998*	*1999*	*2000*
Hong Kong	GDP per capita (US$)	26,049	24,265	23,618	24,066
	GDP (% real change per annum)	4.97	−5.31	3.04	10.48
	Government consumption	8.59	9.35	9.86	9.58
	Budget balance (% of GDP)	5.58	−0.37	−3.98	−0.3
	Consumer prices (% change per annum, average)	5.67	2.84	−3.96	−3.67
	Public debt (% of GDP)	0	0.1	1.3	1.7
	Recorded unemployment (%)	2.43	4.38	6.1	5.08
	Current-account balance/GDP	−3.6	2.39	6.64	5.4
	Foreign-exchange reserves (m$)	92,804	89,601	96,236	107,542
Indonesia	GDP per capita (US$)	1,079	483	681	742
	GDP (% real change per annum)	4.54	−13.2	0.13	4.77
	Government consumption	6.84	5.5	6.49	6.83
	Budget balance (% of GDP)	0.88	−3.06	−3.89	−3.2
	Consumer prices (% change per annum, average)*	6.23	58.44	20.46	3.75
	Public debt (% of GDP)	27.27	76.95	108.91	102.6
	Recorded unemployment (%)	9.7	15.5	17.5	13
	Current-account balance/GDP	−2.27	4.15	4.06	5.6
	Foreign-exchange reserves (m$)	16,587	22,713	26,445	29,120
Malaysia	GDP per capita (US$)	4,626	3,268	3,467	3,780
	GDP (% real change per annum)	7.32	−7.37	5.8	8.5
	Government consumption	10.88	10	11.19	10.4
	Budget balance (% of GDP)	2.35	−1.29	−3.19	−5.9
	Consumer prices (% change per annum, average)*	2.68	5.27	2.74	1.55
	Public debt (% of GDP)	31.9	36.25	37.47	37.7
	Recorded unemployment (%)	2.4	3.2	3.4	3.1
	Current-account balance/GDP	−5.92	13.15	16.01	10.3
	Foreign-exchange reserves (m$)	20,788	25,559	30,588	29,523
Philippines	GDP per capita (US$)	1,117	870	998	959
	GDP (% real change per annum)	5.19	−0.59	3.32	3.95
	Government consumption	13.21	13.28	12.93	12.71
	Budget balance (% of GDP)	0.07	−1.87	−3.73	−4.1
	Consumer prices (% change per annum, average)	5.66	9.66	6.67	4.29
	Public debt (% of GDP)	–	–	–	–
	Recorded unemployment (%)	8.7	10.1	9.7	11.1
	Current-account balance/GDP	−5.3	2.36	10.32	10.9
	Foreign-exchange reserves (m$)	7,266	9,266	12,230	13,054
Singapore	GDP per capita (US$)**	26,205	22,131	21,950	23,500
	GDP (% real change per annum)	8.23	0.31	5.86	9.89
	Government consumption	9.38	10.72	9.7	9.8
	Budget balance (% of GDP)	3.38	2.47	2.55	3.39
	Consumer prices (% change per annum, average)	1.99	−0.25	0.04	1.36
	Public debt (% of GDP)	72.88	83.15	87.36	82.66

Table 6.3 (continued)

		1997	*1998*	*1999*	*2000*
	Recorded unemployment (%)	1.83	3.25	3.5	3.05
	Current-account balance/GDP	17.88	25.4	25.02	23.1
	Foreign-exchange reserves (m$)***	71,288	74,928	76,843	80,127
S. Korea	GDP per capita (US$)	10,360	6,829	8,665	9,670
	GDP (% real change per annum)	5.01	−6.69	10.89	8.81
	Government consumption	10.07	10.98	10.38	10.21
	Budget balance (% of GDP)	−0.02	−2.97	−3.21	−1.1
	Consumer prices (% change per annum, average)	4.44	7.51	0.81	2.26
	Public debt (% of GDP)	9.2	10.7	13.43	13.9
	Recorded unemployment (%)	2.57	6.82	6.25	4
	Current-account balance/GDP	−1.71	12.73	6.03	2.42
	Foreign-exchange reserves (m$)	20,367	51,974	73,987	96,130
Thailand	GDP per capita (US$)	2,487	1,831	2,012	2,910
	GDP (% real change per annum)	−1.45	−10.78	4.23	4.3
	Government consumption	10.13	11.06	11.1	11.8
	Budget balance (% of GDP)	−0.32	−2.69	−2.5	−2.2
	Consumer prices (% change per annum, average)	5.67	8.05	0.25	1.57
	Public debt (% of GDP)	–	–	–	–
	Recorded unemployment (%)	1.5	4.36	4.2	3.61
	Current-account balance/GDP	−2.01	12.72	9.99	8.4
	Foreign-exchange reserves (m$)	26,180	28,825	34,063	32,016

Source: Adapted from Economist Intelligence Unit Country Briefings (1995–2001) available online: www.economist.com/countries.

Notes:
* Consumer Prices are not seasonally adjusted.
** GDP per capita (including foreign workers resident for over one year) based on government figures published before GDP growth rates were revised in mid-1999.
*** Includes gold holdings.

public, multilateral, and private insurers are increasingly porous, government corporations and intergovernmental institutions are usually able to underwrite larger policies and offer longer-term (e.g., 15 to 20 years) insurance packages relative to private insurers.[80] Private insurers are technically free to provide insurance in any country, although many limit the provision of insurance in those areas perceived to be the most risky as a matter to institutional risk management. Only a small fraction on transnational capital flows to emerging markets and developing countries was covered by public, multilateral, or private PRI during the 1990s, but interest and demand is growing.[81] The formal basis for calculating PRI premiums varies widely. While many insurers frankly admit that there is a lack of "off the shelf" statistical data on which to base actuarial estimates,[82] several underwriters claim to use advanced mathematical techniques (e.g., computer driven Monte Carlo simulations) to forecast expected losses and the probability of deviation from expected political phenomena as well as derivatives contracts to minimize disruptions to cash flow. However, PRI is not an actuarial science; it is mired in the political.

OPIC's politics

One of the leading providers of PRI is the American government's Overseas Private Investment Corporation (OPIC). OPIC's clients include large profitable US corporations (e.g., AT&T, Bechtel, Entergy, Freeport-McMoran Copper & Gold Inc., General Electric, McDonalds, Coca-Cola, Citicorp, etc.) as well as some small and medium enterprises that operate in foreign countries. Although the origins of OPIC trace back to the Marshall Plan, the contemporary agency was established by Congress in 1971 in response to a growing balance of payments deficit. OPIC was originally designed to encourage US foreign direct investment in developing countries, but its mission has gradually expanded to include portfolio investments. By the late 1980s, OPIC created venture capital funds to invest in emerging markets and post-Communist transition economies.[83] The funds are structured to protect institutional equity investors from political risks associated with investments located in emerging markets. In the wake of the Asian financial crisis, OPIC announced it would offer PRI for bonds issued in US capital markets to stimulate "project investment" in emerging markets and developing countries.[84] In recent years, OPIC has expanded to offer PRI and insurance against credit risk to support issuers of mortgage backed securities for low-income housing projects in the Caribbean, Africa, and the Middle East.[85]

The US Congress provides partial funding to OPIC, for which it is reimbursed at the end of each year. Congress also sets the cap on the total amount of financing or underwriting that the agency can perform ($29 billion in 2006). The agency charges premiums[86] for its insurance underwriting (roughly equivalent to 1.5 to 2.0 percent of the insured investment's value) but taxpayers are accountable to pay any claims against the agency which cannot be paid out from accumulated reserves. OPIC officials note that less than 1 percent of the PRI sold has resulted in claims and the agency has recovered 98 percent of all claims paid out or settled. In part, OPIC's success rate owes to the fact that foreign governments which expropriate US investments must usually reimburse OPIC before diplomatic relations can be normalized.[87]

As OPIC may only grant PRI in countries approved by Congress, it is an instrument of US foreign policy. For example, after the Tiananmen massacre in 1989, the US congress prohibited the provision of risk insurance for US businesses operating in China. Consequently, the Chinese government lobbied for the removal of this restriction as part of its general bargaining to join the World Trade Organization.[88] Projects supported by OPIC must also comply with set human rights, organized labor, and environmental protection criteria.

Nevertheless, as early as 1973 the US Senate Committee on Foreign Relations concluded that OPIC was only a marginal contributor to economic development and that it increased the likelihood of US involvement in the internal politics of host countries. The committee noted that there was an inherent conflict between the achievement of public policy objectives and sound insurance principles. Although Congress reauthorized funding for OPIC, it instructed the agency to transfer its operations to the private sector by the end of 1980. OPIC was ultimately unable to transfer its operations because of a lack of interest in the private sector. By 1978, Congress withdrew the mandate to shutdown OPIC.[89]

OPIC continues to function as a politicized agency that serves the interests of US industrialists, investors, and politicians. There is a strong correlation between campaign contributions and OPIC support. Bob Hohler, a journalist for the Boston Globe, has stated that,

> Businesses that gave Democratic Party committees more than $2.3 million and won coveted seats on US trade missions during President Clinton's first term secured nearly $5.5 billion to support their foreign business operations from a federal investment agency. In all, 27 corporations that sent executives on trade trips with the late Commerce Secretary Ronald H. Brown obtained part of a multibillion-dollar commitment in federally guaranteed assistance from the Overseas Private Investment Corp., according to a Globe analysis of fundraising records, trip manifests, and OPIC documents. All but three of the 27 OPIC recipients donated to Democratic Party committees, and most of them gave between $50,000 and $358,000 during Clinton's first term.[90]

The average contribution to the Democratic Party from OPIC recipients was $95,000; the average support from OPIC was $200 million per company. The most notorious case was the $544 million in direct loans and $204 million in PRI provided by OPIC to the scandal-ridden Enron Corporation in 1992 and 1993.[91] Enron, which contributed heavily to both major political parties, gave nearly $1 million to the Democratic Party and its politicians during the Clinton presidency.[92] The head of OPIC at that time, Ruth R. Harkin, was the wife of the Democratic Senator from Iowa, Tom Harkin.

The overt cronyism associated with OPIC has made it highly controversial and there are periodic attempts in Congress to choke off funding to OPIC. Proponents of publicly funded PRI, such as Republican Senator Chuck Hagel, argue that OPIC encourages foreign investment in unstable regions and export related job growth in the US. Critics, such as Republican Congressmen John Kasich or Democratic Congressman Jesse Jackson Jr., argue that publicly funded PRI is an unnecessary bureaucratic agency and a mechanism to transfer insurance liability from private firms to public taxpayers.[93]

At a theoretical level, OPIC can be understood as a politicized entity that "*depoliticizes*" as it disguises the political character and underpinnings of financial activity by constructing a discourse in which "politics" is a "risk" which is external, threatening, and alien to financial and business activity. PRI is predicated on making clear conceptual distinctions between political and economic spheres, even though these realms are often overlapping in actual practice. For example, the possibility that "politically motivated" unrest (e.g., sabotage or riots) may be the product of endogenous business practices and labor relations is not seriously contemplated. Moreover, there is an implicit assumption that subjective judgment is not a factor in determining when a political trigger event has happened (e.g., creeping appropriation), if a financial loss can be attributable to a political event, or in interpreting when a political action fits into an insured category (e.g., whether forced conversion of dollar accounts to local currency constitutes currency inconvertibility). Naturally, the element of subjective interpretation introduces the "risk" that insurance claims will not be paid, particularly for private insurers, thereby undermining the rationale for purchasing PRI in the first place. Some of these ambiguities resulted in disputes between private insurers and clients during the Argentinean financial crisis (1999–2002).[94]

Nevertheless, at the same time as it seeks to rhetorically depoliticize and segregate business practices and political actions, OPIC actually entwines the state and market enterprises to achieve its objectives. The discourse on political risk serves to justify further blurring and reconfiguring the boundary between public and private. Companies that could manage without public risk insurance often apply for government funded risk insurance to explicitly interweave their commercial enterprise with the foreign policy objectives of the state. Thus, PRI generates a "halo effect," which signals the general political influence of the company as a deterrent to host governments that may contemplate nationalization or inconvertibility policies and as a sign of low risk/creditworthiness to potential investors.[95] As one company executive told a reporter about an investment in the Middle East:

> We could do it ourselves. We wanted the support and assistance of the U.S. government. It's a very volatile region.[96]

OPIC is able to bring the resources of the US government to negotiate with foreign governments and to secure restitution for its clients. As the US government has the ability to provide or prevent substantial financial assistance and market access to countries in financial distress, not to mention a preponderance of military might, the US has several major bargaining chips with host governments in the emerging markets and developing countries. To this extent, OPIC formalizes and makes explicit the historically semi-formal and implicit relationship between American corporations and the state. Gary Bird, the Director of Risk Management at Phelps Dodge, notes:

> OPIC's greatest value in the political risk arena is that they are a part of the US government," says Bird. "In working with foreign governments that carries a lot of weight.[97]

In fact, OPIC is able to provide insurance against certain political risks, for example currency inconvertibility or prohibitions on repatriation of profits, specifically because it is a part of the US government. If a currency is declared inconvertible to US dollars by a foreign central bank or if a foreign government passes legislation against transferring wealth out of the country, OPIC will purchase its client's local currency in dollars and sell it to the US embassy in that country which can use the currency for local expenses. Of course, by exchanging local currency for dollars, as a former attorney for the agency explained, OPIC performs "the role of the [emerging nation's] central bank, when the central bank wouldn't or couldn't do it."[98]

Private risk insurance corporations compete with OPIC and other public or multilateral risk insurers by similarly blurring the public/private boundary. For example, AIG has recruited a staff of former diplomats and government officials, including: Henry Kissinger, Richard Holbrooke, and Moeen Qureshi (the former World Bank Vice President and the former caretaker Prime Minister of Pakistan) for their political risk subsidiary.[99] The need for a diplomatic contingent is explained by the fact that negotiation with host states remains a major strategy for preventing claims. For example, during the Argentinean crisis (1999–2002), Zurich International negotiated directly with the central bank of Argentina to gain an exception from exchange controls (i.e., full convertibility and transfer of funds) for its clients.[100] Private insurers also form syndicates and work together, at times with public insurers (e.g., through the Berne Union and Prague Club), to negotiate with host states and prevent claims for clients which are co-insured.

Finally, private insurers rely upon derivative instruments (e.g., securitizing future flow receivables in hard currency; utilizing convertibility swaps, etc.) and special purpose vehicles established in offshore markets. The special purpose vehicles manage receivables from customers and ensure that creditors are paid principal and interest first. This technique prevents disruptions due to currency convertibility or restrictions on the transfer capital, particularly during a financial crisis.[101]

PRI in the periphery

For companies and subsidiaries of multinational corporations in the emerging economies, the purchase of PRI and the use of derivatives instruments/offshore structures has been touted as a means of attracting greater private capital investment. Bond issuing companies which have investment grade ratings in local currency and earn hard currency through exports can use these instruments and techniques to achieve credit ratings in excess of their sovereign's ceiling rate, thereby effectively lowering their borrowing costs, lengthening maturities, and accessing institutional investors.[102] For example, the Mexican brewer, Femsa Cerveza, purchased bond insurance from Zurich Insurance which helped the company to secure a rating of "A–" from credit rating agencies, well above the Mexican government's own sovereign rating of "BB+."[103] It should also be noted, however, that this technique cannot help companies which are considered below investment grade in the local currency.

Dan Riordan, the Managing Director of Zurich US and the former Vice President of OPIC, explained that the advantage of purchasing PRI, particularly for subsidiaries of multinational corporations, is that "... you get as much financing off the balance sheet as possible."[104] In essence, PRI and currency convertibility techniques act as a hedge for the main branch of the multinational corporation while also permitting the subsidiary to raise financing directly from the capital markets at investment grade ratings. The subsidiary comes to be treated by bondholders as if it is situated in a politically neutral space.

Of course, the provision of PRI does not neutralize the political; it merely shifts the financial costs of political events onto to public/multilateral/private insurers who are willing to use political influence, pressure, and negotiations to recoup their costs. And although the ingenious arrangements to prevent payment disruptions have survived several financial crises, these arrangements currently represent only a small portion of total debt arrangements in emerging economies and thus have not been severely tested. The techniques for piercing the sovereign's credit ceiling may come to be challenged by states in emerging markets and developing countries if issuing separate credit ratings for investment grade firms is viewed to have adverse effects on the overall sovereign rating.

PRI strategies may also lose favor among businesses in emerging markets. Notably, where the creation of offshore special purpose vehicles is not relevant to the business model, PRI policies generally require that local businesses continue to pay loans into a local currency account if currency inconvertibility is imposed. The rationale is that the domestic company must demonstrate the ability to pay its lenders is being frustrated solely by the currency policies of the host government. The insurance policy may be terminated in cases of nonpayment due to borrower default. However, as one review of the PRI industry notes,

> ... political turmoil is often associated with economic turmoil, which may result in borrower default or devaluation of local currency payments ... PRI offers no protection from such events. Hence, much of the risk of loss in a high-risk market may fall outside the domain of political risk coverage, even though the loss is tied in some way to "political" risk.[105]

It is also important to note that what is being insured by PRI is only the stream of payments to the foreign creditor. The insurer will compensate the lender in hard currency so long as the borrower continues to place deposits in the local currency account. The general impact of political and economic turmoil on borrower's receivables, particularly for nonexport oriented firms, is not considered relevant. Even if there is politically motivated violence to the production facilities, the insurance pays only the lending institution the balance of principal and interest. In cases of total loss, the insurer also has the right to take ownership of damaged property to subrogate and salvage claims in the local judicial system. Finally, there is usually a mandatory waiting period of six months before the insurance policy is activated, which may cause additional hardship and difficulties.[106] Businesses which value PRI for its potential to compensate losses may find less utility than those which seek to acquire PRI for its halo effect.

Nevertheless, sovereign states in the developing world are increasingly providing PRI themselves as a means of attracting foreign investment. For example, the World Bank, Lloyds of London, and seven African countries (i.e., Burundi, Kenya, Malawi, Rwanda, Tanzania, Uganda and Zambia) established the African Trade Insurance agency (ATI) in 2001 to insure investors against embargoes, expropriations and civil disturbances.[107] As the first layer of any losses fall on the $105 million loaned to participating governments by the World Bank,[108] there are strong incentives for these countries to prevent and/or mitigate the causes of claims (e.g., the failure of imports to clear customs because of bribery demands). In essence, states are insuring against political risks over which they have some measure of direct control. Therefore, states are making a public commitment to protect the interests of foreign investors in exchange for a loan from the World Bank. The involvement of the World Bank provides the program with the semblance of a multilateral assistance agreement; however the actual insurance is underwritten by private insurers who also happen to occupy half the seats of the ATI board of directors.[109] Heads of state and political elites in the developing world see little choice but to work with private risk insurers to attract investments. Hakainde Hichilema, Chairman of the ATI, told reporters:

> "In Africa we realise that if we are to achieve the growth rates of 7 per cent per annum over the next 10 to 15 years that will be required to achieve significant and sustainable poverty reduction, we need a vibrant private sector that is willing to invest in Africa's future."[110]

The World Bank estimated that $5 billion worth of trade may be insured by this arrangement over ten years; thus generating additional business for private political risk insurers.

Similarly in South America, five Andean Community countries have undertaken a joint venture with the private American insurer, AIG Global Trade & Political Risk Insurance Company. The joint venture is known as the Latin American Investment Guarantee Company Ltd. (LAIGC). The President of AIG stated, "LAIGC unites the responsiveness, creativity and flexibility of the private sector with the resources of the public sector . . ."[111] Even Cuba has agreed to provide foreign investors with PRI through the Banco Nacional de Cuba.[112]

As the provision of PRI shifts to states in the developing world, a dangerous space opens whereby countries facing serious political instability will be further crippled with the burden of paying foreign investors or their governments (e.g., US State Department and the Office of the US Trade Representative) and multilateral institutions (e.g., MIGA) that will often take over and subrogate the claims of foreign investors if property is damaged or assets are frozen/expropriated. By allowing insurance corporations and governments to pursue lawsuits and intergovernmental arbitration on behalf of the aggrieved investor, host countries may also forfeit a portion of their sovereign right to territorial jurisdiction in disputes between states and foreign investors.[113] Moreover, the cost of paying for claims settled against the host government will undoubtedly be extracted through taxation or reduction of social services.[114]

Conclusion

As noted earlier, the discourse on risk is a transfer point for relations of power across a dense network of state and market actors; the discourse on risk is useful for linking states and markets in new combinations, or ordering states and societies in particular hierarchical relationships. In this vein, the technology of PRI articulates a role for developing countries and emerging economies as not only the legal and coercive guarantors of law and order but also as the *insurers* of law and order.[115] The provision of PRI by developing countries formalizes a different type of accountability. Developing countries become accountable to foreign investors from developed countries and intergovernmental organizations (e.g., the World Bank) in ways that would have been politically unthinkable in the early post-colonial era. Although states have been legally accountable to domestic and foreign subjects for some time, the technology of risk represents a supplement and even an alternative to the juridical sphere.

It should not be surprising that the consequence of the new accountability is to reinforce the *capitalist norm* (see Chapter III) that requires the claims of borrowers be safeguarded by states before the interests of debtors in society. However, to the extent that the insurer role subordinates a "sovereign" state to foreign investors, the technology of risk also becomes instrumental in formalizing the hierarchy of the international political economy. In so far as the insurer role binds states in the developing world from nationalizing the assets of foreign investors, the insurer role is also a step toward the *monetarist norm* of restricting state intervention in the market.

Ultimately, PRI does not represent a solution for the economic, political and social instability generated by the international monetary order. To the contrary, the technology only alleviates anxieties of the owners of capital by reinforcing political and economic hierarchy while socializing risk. The burden of instability will continue to be borne by the people of the emerging markets and developing countries.

The next and final chapter, "Conclusion," locates a root cause of the failure of risk technology to produce relatively stable markets that promote social peace and economic prosperity, especially for the marginalized and economically vulnerable segments of the monetary order. I argue that the technology of risk has failed because it has ignored the moral and ethical basis of economic activity. The technology of risk promotes the transgression of the regulatory framework rather than resolving the disparity between compliance and belief in the operation of financial markets.

7 Conclusion

> Transgression is an action which involves the limit, that narrow zone of a line where it displays the flash of its passage, but perhaps also its entire trajectory, even its origin; it is likely that transgression has its entire space in the line it crosses. The play of limit and transgression seems to be regulated by a simple obstinacy: transgression incessantly crosses and recrosses a line which closes up behind it in a wave of extremely short duration, and thus is made to return once more to the horizon of the uncrossable.[1]
>
> Michel Foucault, 1963

Transgression and limit

The regulation and technology of risk involves the play of limit and transgression. A limit is a restriction, a barrier, or boundary; a limit generally implies an external space beyond itself. Transgression is an excess that challenges and overcomes a limit. It is possible that the limit is known only after transgression occurs. The infinite spiral of limit and transgression generates externalities that have serious economic, political, and social consequences for the subjects of the monetary order. Hence, there is a need to not only understand the dynamics of the discourse on risk, there is a need to explain the reasons why this technology has failed to stabilize markets.

The discourse on risk marks the limit within the firm and designates the firm as a limit. Risk sets the boundaries of prudential behavior within the firm. In fact, risk has become the basis for distinguishing prudent and imprudent behavior, as well as the segregation between the certain and the uncertain in empirical phenomena. Risk designates the limits of regulation and the reach of the state and the monetary order within the firm. Regulations and norms that fail to account for techniques of risk management are resisted and subverted by firms. In essence, the firm's experience of itself is constituted through and circumscribed by risk.

Risk entices the transgression of the limits it establishes only to spawn new limits. Thus, the regulation of risk technology involves not so much a relationship between the prohibited and the lawful, but an inexhaustible spiral of limit and transgression. The transgression of the limit is never a final gesture. The unpunished transgression of a limit often resets the limit further along the trajectory.

As we have seen this process is not unidirectional. If the firm transgresses the rules of the state, the firm's boundary is also transgressed by the state. If firms consistently circumvent regulations, states consistently place more and more activities of the firm under their regulatory gaze. Moreover, this process is not unidimensional; transgression operates across space and time. The monetary order unfolds itself across a space with multiple functional categories of social interaction. This process of mutual transgression played out on the global stage, has worked to reinforce hierarchies within the international monetary order. For instance, under the rubric of minimizing financial risk, developed states have not only increased demands for the self-regulation of market participants, they have also worked with international financial institutions to increase surveillance of developing countries and emerging economies.

The play of limit and transgression generates and incorporates externalities. As risk inevitably enters new frontiers, markets generate instability in the economy and society. In emerging market economies, these "externalities" of the financial system can either have devastating, long-term, and asymmetric impacts or generate the immense profits needed by the relatively powerless. The technology of risk sublates some of the externalities it produces, but only in accordance with dominant capitalist and monetarist norms. In other words, the technology of risk operates normatively in the service of creditors.

The play of limit and transgression has not resulted in deeper wisdom about risk in financial markets. The intensive study of risk, the perpetual invention of speculative and insurance instruments, and the regulation of speculative financial activity has failed to capture or comprehend risk. Risk has been divided, categorized, labeled, and quantified, but risk is not understood. Risk continues to baffle experts, particularly the ability of risk categories to fuse together and form an interconnected continuity in periods of volatility. Thus, each crisis seems to reveal new and unanticipated combinations or sources of risk. Moreover, the standardization of strategies to exploit risk and the harmonization of rules related to the regulation of that technology has proliferated risk across the international system as market participants increasingly follow similar strategies during volatile periods thereby enhancing a herd mentality. Thus, rather than containing volatility by transferring the risk elements of financial contracts to parties with a higher-volatility tolerance, the technology of risk has proliferated the sites and categories of risk to the far corners of the globe, with occasionally devastating results.

Behavior and belief

In so far as the regulation of risk technology has failed to address the moral and ethical basis of economic activity, it has failed to limit the production of risk. The regulation and technology of risk should aim to produce and test the signs of trustworthiness. Financial capitalism cannot operate without the production and occasional verification of the signs of trust. Trust permits the calculation and projection of rates of return on investment, an essential factor in encouraging the reinvestment of capital. The verification of trust enhances confidence in the process of calculation and projection. However, the precise quantification of empirical and social facts cannot substitute for the modification of social behavior. To the extent that the regulation of risk technology fails to address the ethical basis of economic activity, it draws upon the legacy of an earlier age of capitalism.

In the eighteenth century, public intellectuals encouraged market participants to perform the signs of trustworthiness. For instance, Max Weber's shrewd analysis of Benjamin Franklin's popular writings highlighted the ways in which borrowers were encouraged to perform the signs of trust. Franklin wrote:

> The most trifling actions that affect a man's credit are to be regarded. The sound of your hammer at five in the morning, or eight at night, heard by the creditor, makes him easy six months longer; but if he sees you at a billiard-table, or hears your voice at a tavern, when you should be at work, he sends for his money the next day; demands it, before he can receive it, in a lump.
>
> It shows, besides, that you are mindful of what you owe; it makes you appear a careful as well as an honest man, and that still increases your credit.[2]

Weber argues that Franklin was not so concerned about actual virtue, so much as the utility of the appearance of virtue in securing credit. Weber states, "... all Franklin's moral attitudes are coloured with utilitarianism. Honesty is useful, because it assures credit; so are punctuality, industry, frugality, and that is the reason they are virtues."[3] Similarly, Mary Poovey reads Daniel Defoe's *Complete English Tradesman* as arguing that the tradesman's plain style of writing had a performative relationship to the production of honesty. Poovey writes,

> To a large extent, Defoe seems to have thought that a tradesman's plain style of writing had a performative, rather than a mimetic, relation to his subjective feelings. In other words, he believed that a tradesman's plain style encouraged him to be honest, because plain writing inspired *in others* the confidence that underwrote both business and credit; to merit this confidence, the tradesman had to imitate the honesty his writing expressed.[4]

The mode of governmentality or self-government articulated by Franklin and Defoe sought to shape behavior rather than actual belief in the value of a particular set of ethics. If beliefs were transformed through the performance of these signs, so much the better, but changing beliefs was not the primary objective.[5] Thus, the aim was to produce the public signs of trust through rule-governed behavior. The production of public signs was integrated into a social matrix of visual and aural surveillance.

The contemporary regulation of risk technology draws upon this heritage to the extent that it inculcates a similar mode of self-government for market participants. The rules on capital adequacy requirements, for instance, seek to shape a firm's behavior rather than attitudes toward prudential activity. In fact, the technology of risk actually subverts prudential activity by exciting and rewarding speculation. Overall, compliance is more important than belief in the eyes of both state officials and market participants.

Of course, there is a greater emphasis on the written signs of trust over the performance of those signs in person in the contemporary monetary order. As "global" markets imply increasingly anonymous transactions, the publication of the signs of trustworthiness achieves prominence relative to the performance of the signs of trustworthiness for pragmatic reasons. Nevertheless, the role of balance sheets in producing the signs of trustworthiness is a common trait in both ages of capitalism. However, it is illusory to believe that the publication of the signs of trust guarantees virtue any more than the performance of those signs in a public space.

The mounting layers of surveillance within and outside of the firm expose the difficulty of negotiating the range of activity that lies between nominal compliance and actual belief in the moral value of prudential activity. Even the practice of "independent" audits has been called into question with recent scandals in the United States (e.g., the Enron/Arthur Andersen and WorldCom/Arthur Andersen scandals). Ultimately, as the Basel Committee has recognized, the verification of the accuracy (as opposed to the precision) of a document depends upon the judgment and ethics of the accountant or examiner.[6]

The persistence of this flawed strategy of (self-) governance that fails to bridge the chasm between compliance and belief may be a necessary product of a liberal economic order. A liberal order must maintain the illusion of eliciting voluntary compliance from its subjects (whether firms or individuals). Although this illusion is consistently breached through practices of surveillance that map out the interiority of the subject, as well as disciplinary laws and practices that normalize activity and circumscribe the external boundaries of subjects, the liberal state may not demand belief from its subjects.

Thus, the technology of risk can be read as a knowledge project that operates and prospers within the confines of a liberal system. The technology substitutes precision for accuracy and compliance for belief. Moreover, the technology decentralizes the sites of information gathering and analysis. The state serves in a limited capacity scrutinizing and legitimating practices of market participants that are usually already in place.

If changes in belief could be the overt object of knowledge of a liberal state, one could imagine a monetary order that fostered a different array of knowledge projects along side the technology of risk under the guise of self-improvement, confessional conversation, or moral emulation. One might also expect to see a more centralized site for the production and dissemination of knowledge related to prudential market activity. Hence, it must not be assumed that the current technology of risk assessment and management is the manifestation of scientific progress, divorced from the political conditions that make it possible.

Nevertheless, given the confines of a liberal order, why is the gulf between compliance and belief so great? In other words, why does the performance of compliance not result in the transformation of belief? Why do we not see more market participants adopt prudential standards as moral values rather than subverting those standards in the pursuit of profit? Why does an inexhaustible and degenerative spiral of limit and transgression characterize the development of risk technology and regulation?

The answer from the economist is that the behavior of the market participant is merely the manifestation of its (human) nature. In other words, it is natural for the market participant to pursue its short-term self-interest. This naturalized moral philosophy explanation is not convincing. First, it is an abstracted account of motivation that posits a fictional universal subject, which is based on little or no actual observation. Second, it is unable to explain variation in behavior without introducing an even higher level of abstraction. Third, when pressed regarding the absence of evidence and inconsistencies in behavioral patterns, the argument will predictably shift from a descriptive to a prescriptive account of human motivation.

The chasm between belief and compliance cannot be bridged, at least in part, because of the devalued status of non-systematic forms of knowledge in economic discourse. Yet, non-systematic forms of knowledge are almost certainly required as a component in the transformation of beliefs, as the transformation of belief is usually achieved through persuasion. Beliefs are unlikely to be transformed solely through the logic of arguments based on experimentation and the scientific method. The evident signs of belief cannot be produced and verified through the publication of precise quantitative measurements. Hence, the contemporary forms of knowledge that pervade economic discourse are ill suited to transform beliefs.

However, it is also important to state that belief no longer authorizes knowledge. In the contemporary age, belief lacks a consensus about a foundational pillar on which to support the value of values. Thus, there is little reason for a critical subject to believe in the value of prudential behavior. What is needed is not so much a new foundational principle, but the development of an ethical system based on the lack or deferment of foundational principles. The individual cannot develop an ethical system outside of relations of power/knowledge; however, this does not mean that there is no basis on which to reconfigure one's relation to one's self. What is needed is to combine different existing bodies of knowledge in new ways to produce relations with ourselves and others (i.e., ethics) that were not previously possible.

In the absence of serious reforms that emphasize the importance of belief over compliance, the technology of risk will continuously threaten the economic, political, and social fabric of countries around the world. Recurrent financial crises will eventually either significantly impair the operation of the global market system as confidence erodes and/or lead to the resurgence of regional trade and monetary arrangements and the neglect of global institutions. In the near term, the technology of risk and related speculative practices will, on the whole, continue to generate asymmetric economic and social impacts amongst the poorer segments of the global economy.

Notes

Introduction

1 Volatility is the change in the price of a particular asset or set of assets over time. The perception and experience of volatility is constructed in relation to prior experiences and expectations. Economists have developed "formalized measures" of volatility that compare the deviation in the price of the asset relative to the asset itself across time; relative to a group of similar assets; or relative to "rational" expectations and economic "fundamentals." Thus, volatility may be generated through a series of relative comparisons. Many economists believe that exchange rates and stock prices are "too volatile" relative to economic fundamentals, however empirical support for this perception remains tied to model- and data-specific evidence. For a review of the literature and recent developments in the empirical measurement of volatility, see Leonardo Bartolini and Lorenzo Giorgianni, "Excess Volatility of Exchange Rates with Unobservable Fundamentals," Staff Reports No. 103, New York, NY: Federal Reserve Bank of New York, April 2000, pp. 1–26.

2 Jonathan Mitchie and John Grieve, eds., *Global Instability: The Political Economy of World Economic Governance*, London, UK: Routledge, 1999; Eric Helleiner, "From Bretton Woods to Global Finance: A World Turned Upside Down," in *Political Economy and the Changing Global Order*, eds. Richard Stubbs and Geoffrey R. D. Underhill, New York, NY: St. Martin's Press 1994, p. 168; Morris Goldstein and Philip Turner, "Banking Crises in Emerging Economies: Origins and Policy Options," *BIS Economic Papers* 46, October 1996, p. 10; Gordon Thiessen, "Mr. Thiessen Looks at Flexible Exchange Rates in a World of Low Inflation," Remarks by the Governor of the Bank of Canada, Mr. Gordon Thiessen, to the FOREX '97 Conference held in Toronto," Reprinted in *BIS Review* 57, 30 May 1997, pp. 1–5.

3 Barry Eichengreen, Andrew Rose, Charles Wyplosz, Bernard Dumas, and Axel Weber, "Exchange Market Mayhem: The Antecedents and Aftermath of Speculative Attacks," *Economic Policy* 10, no. 21, October 1995, pp. 249–312.

4 See Susan Strange, "An Eclectic Approach," in *The New International Political Economy*, ed. Craig N. Murphy and Roger Tooze, Boulder, CO: Lynne Rienner Publishers, 1991, p. 35.

5 Max Weber, *Economy and Society: An Outline of Interpretive Sociology*, vol. I, eds. Guenther Roth and Claus Wittich, Berkeley, CA: University of California Press, 1978, p. 312.

6 Speculative financial activity may augment (or diminish) the value of a commodity or financial instrument without directly stimulating (or depressing) the production of material goods and services. In other words, speculative financial

activity does not increase value through the efficient exploitation of labor and the production of surplus.

7 Saskia Sassen, *The Global City: New York, London, Tokyo*, Princeton, NJ: Princeton University Press, 1991, pp. 30, 64–78.

8 Susan Strange, *Casino Capitalism*, Manchester, UK: Manchester University Press, 1997, p. 111.

9 Comptroller of the Currency, "OCC's Report on Bank Derivatives Activities, Fourth Quarter 2006," Washington, D.C.: Office of the Comptroller of the Currency, 2007, pp. 1–2, 7.

10 "Struggle is on for the Control of the Lucrative OTC Market," *The Banker*, 1 July 2007.

11 Comptroller of the Currency, "OCC's Report on Bank Derivatives Activities, Fourth Quarter 2006," p. 18, graph 6B.

12 Joseph Radigan, "Playing Catch-up on Risk," *United States Banker* 106, no. 7, July 1996, pp. 32–43.

13 Edgar Meister, "A Timely Discussion of Capital Requirements," *Journal of Lending & Credit Risk Management* 80, no. 6, 1996, pp. 12–22.

14 Keith Redhead and Stewart Hughes, *Financial Risk Management*, Hants, UK: Gower Publishing Company, 1988, p. 11.

15 Peter L. Bernstein, *Against the Gods: The Remarkable Story of Risk*, New York, NY: John Wiley & Sons, Inc., 1996, pp. 335–36.

16 Edward Furash, "Risk Challenges and Opportunities," *Bank Management* 71, no. 3, May-June 1995, pp. 34–39; Steve Cocheo, "Is Your Bank Ready for a Shift in Gears?" *ABA Banking Journal*, November 1998, p. 7.

17 Richard Phillips, "Derivatives Professionals Welcome G30 Attempt to Demystify Market," *Euroweek* 312, 23 July 1993, p. 3.

18 Saul Hansell and Kevin Muehring, "Why Derivatives Rattle Regulators," *Institutional Investor* 26, no. 10, September 1992, pp. 49–62.

19 Susan M. Phillips, "Statement to the Congress," *Federal Reserve Bulletin* 79, no. 12, December 1993, pp. 1137–42.

20 Hansell and Muehring, "Why Derivatives Rattle Regulators."

21 US House of Representatives Committee on Banking and Financial Services, 106th Congress, "Prepared Statement by Karen Shaw Petrou, President ISD/SHAW Inc.," Hearing on "Architecture of International Finance," *Federal Document Clearing House Congressional Testimony*, 20 May 1999.

22 The conceptual meaning of "external" and "internal" regulation varies by author. In some cases "external" regulation may refer to the use of a consulting firm or privately contracted auditing agency, while other authors seem to use the term "external" to refer only to regulation by public officials.

23 Charles A. E. Goodhart, Philip Hartmann, David Llewellyn, Liliana Rojas-Suarez, and Steven Weisbrod, *Financial Regulation: Why, How and Where Now?* London, UK: Routledge Press, 1998, pp. 3–4.

24 "Finance and Economics: Basel Bust," *Economist*, 15 April 2000, pp. 83–84.

25 Goodhart *et. al.*, *Financial Regulation*, p. 39.

26 Hansell and Muehring "Why Derivatives Rattle Regulators."

27 John G. Medlin Jr., "A Timely Discussion of Capital Requirements," in *Journal of Lending & Credit Risk Management* 80, no. 6, February 1998, pp. 54–57.

28 Richard Phillips, "Derivatives Professionals," p. 3.

29 Claudio Borio, Craig Furfine and Philip Lowe, "Procyclicality of the financial system and financial stability: issues and policy options," *BIS Papers* 1, March 2001, p. 4.

30 See Michel Foucault, *The Order of Things: An Archaeology of the Human Sciences*, New York, NY: Vintage Books 1970, p. 312.

31 UK Financial Services Authority, *Risk Based Approach to Supervision of Banks*, London: FSA Publications Department, June 1998, p. 4.
32 US Federal Reserve System, Board of Governors, *85th Annual Report, 1998*, Washington, D.C.: Board of Governors of the Federal Reserve System, Publication Services, 1998, p. 248.
33 Michel Foucault, *The History of Sexuality, vol. I: An Introduction*, trans. Robert Hurley, New York, NY: Vintage Books, 1990, p. 45; Philip Barker, *Michel Foucault: An Introduction*, Edinburgh, UK: Edinburgh University Press, 1998, pp. 29–31.
34 Medlin, "A Timely Discussion," pp. 54–57.
35 "Finance and Economics: Basel Bust," *Economist*, 15 April 2000.
36 Medlin, "A Timely Discussion," pp. 54–57.
37 Andres Green, "The European Capital Adequacy Directive: The Spirit and the Letter," *Credit World* 80, no. 3, January/February 1998, pp. 20–23.
38 Anthony Giddens makes a larger argument that the idea of risk now permeates almost every aspect of our lives. Anthony Giddens, *Runaway World*, London, UK: Profile Books, 1999.
39 Edgar Meister, "Supervising the Quantitative and Qualitative Aspects of Derivatives," *Journal of Lending & Credit Risk Management* 78, no. 8, April 1996, pp. 12–22.
40 See Ian Hacking, *The Emergence of Probability: A Philosophical Study of Early Ideas about Probability, Induction and Statistical Inference*, Cambridge, UK: Cambridge University Press, 1975.
41 Each society in each epoch has its regime of truth. That is to say, each society accepts certain discourses and uses those discourses to distinguish between true and false statements. In our society, the discourse of science plays a foundational role in what we recognize as truth, and at the same time, it disqualifies or delegitimates other knowledge discourses from the regime of truth. In the post-Bretton Woods era, power has reanimated the concept of risk. The contemporary discourse of risk operates within the discourse of science thereby enabling subjects to distinguish between true and false statements about the quality and quantity of risk in a given phenomenon.
42 In other words, these sites of unofficial financial activity are the product of the discourse on risk. The discourse on risk and technologies of risk management that it generates facilitates and encourages the management of risk through transfers of capital between central and parallel markets.
43 Barker, *Michel Foucault*, p. 95.

2 Surfaces of inscription

1 Allen J. Matusow, *Nixon's Economy: Booms, Busts, Dollars, and Votes*, Lawrence, KS: University of Kansas Press, 1998, pp. 148–54; Joanne Gowa, *Closing the Gold Window: Domestic Politics and the End of Bretton Woods*, Ithaca, NY: Cornell University Press, 1983, pp. 150–70.
2 Paul De Grauwe, *International Money: Post-War Trends and Theories*, Oxford, UK: Oxford University Press, 1989, p. 31; Eric Helleiner, *States and the Reemergence of Global Finance: From Bretton Woods to the 1990s*, Ithaca, NY: Cornell University Press, 1994, p. 112.
3 Thiessen, "Mr. Thiessen looks at Flexible Exchange Rates." See also Gowa, *Closing the Gold Window*, p. 37; De Grauwe, *International Money*, pp. 39–41.
4 In 1982, the IMF classified only ten countries as having independently floating exchange rates (prior to 1982 the IMF did not distinguish between independently floating and various other schemes). Of the 146 members of the IMF in the early 1980s, 38 chose to peg their currencies to the US dollar, while an

additional 56 pegged to other currencies or basket of currencies. A few countries do not have a national currency, for example, two states created by the US – Liberia and Panama – used the US dollar as their principal currency in the 1980s. James M. Boughton, *Silent Revolution: The International Monetary Fund, 1979–1989*, Washington, D.C.: International Monetary Fund, 2001, pp. 74, 79.

5 Andrew Leyshon and Nigel Thrift, *Money Space: Geographies of Monetary Transformation*, New York, NY: Routledge, 1997, p. 282.

6 See Kevin A. Froot, "Bank Capital and Risk Management," mimeo, Geneva, CH: IFCI, June 2001. This is a revised version of the paper presented at the IFCI – International Financial Risk Institute's "7th Annual Risk Round Table," 5–6 April 2001, Geneva, Switzerland.

7 Leyshon and Thrift, *Money Space*, p. 13.

8 Mary Poovey, *A History of the Modern Fact: Problems of Knowledge in the Sciences of Wealth and Society*, Chicago, IL: University of Chicago Press, 1998, pp. 29–91.

9 Joël Bessis, *Risk Management in Banking*, Chichester, UK: John Wiley & Sons Ltd., 1998, p. 18.

10 Charles A. E. Goodhart, Philip Hartmann, David Llewellyn, Liliana Rojas-Suarez, and Steven Weisbrod, *Financial Regulation: Why, How and Where Now?* London, UK: Routledge Press, 1998, pp. 38–39.

11 Arupratan Daripa and Simone Varotto, "Value at Risk and Precommitment: Approaches to Market Risk Regulation," *Economic Policy Review* 4, no. 3, October 1998, pp. 137–43.

12 Andres Green, "The European Capital Adequacy Directive: The Spirit and the Letter," *Credit World* 80, no. 3, January/February 1998, pp. 20–23.

13 See "World's Largest Banks: The Top 500 Banks in the World," *Banker*, July 1993, pp. 145–75; "World's Largest Banks: The Top 500 Banks in the World," *Banker*, July 2000, pp. 213–44. Three Chinese banks (Industrial & Commercial Bank of China; Agricultural Bank of China; Bank of China) and one Argentinean bank (Banco Bilbao Bizcaya Argentina) are part of the top 25 banks as measured in terms of "tier one" capital, total assets, and percent return on assets. "Tier One" capital includes common stock, disclosed reserves and retained earnings, but excludes cumulative preference shares, revaluation reserves, hidden reserves, subordinated and other long-term debt. The available asset figures are not risk adjusted; this means that the table underestimates the banks' true capital adequacy. See "World's Largest Banks," *Banker*, July 2000, p. 178.

14 See Bankim Chadha, *et. al.*, *Emerging Market Financing: Quarterly Report on Developments and Prospects, Second Quarter 2000*, Washington, D.C.: International Monetary Fund, 2000; Bankim Chadha, *et. al.*, *Emerging Market Financing: Quarterly Report on Developments and Prospects, Third Quarter 2000*, Washington, D.C.: International Monetary Fund, 2000a; Bankim Chadha, *et. al.*, *Emerging Market Financing: Quarterly Report on Developments and Prospects, February 13, 2001*, Washington, D.C.: International Monetary Fund, 2001; Bankim Chadha, *et. al.*, *Emerging Market Financing: Quarterly Report on Developments and Prospects, May 10, 2001*, Washington, D.C.: International Monetary Fund, 2001a; Bankim Chadha, *et. al.*, *Emerging Market Financing: Quarterly Report on Developments and Prospects, August 8, 2001*, Washington, D.C.: International Monetary Fund, 2001b.

15 Helleiner, *States and the Reemergence of Global Finance*, 1994; Andrew C. Sobel, *Domestic Choices, International Markets: Dismantling National Barriers and Liberalizing Securities Markets*, Ann Arbor, MI: University of Michigan Press, 1994.

16 Saskia Sassen, "Embedding the Global in the National: Implications for the Role of the State," *States and Sovereignty in the Global Economy*, eds. David A. Smith, Dorothy J. Solinger, and Steven C. Topik, London, UK: Routledge Press, 1999, p. 158.
17 Sassen, "Embedding the Global in the National," p. 162.
18 Bank for International Settlements, "Triennial Central Bank Survey – Foreign Exchange and Derivatives Market Activity in 2004," Basel, CH: Bank for International Settlements, 2005, p. 12 – Table B.6. See also Bank for International Settlements, "Triennial Central Bank Survey of Foreign Exchange and Derivatives Market Activity in 2001," Basel, CH: Bank for International Settlements, 2002, p. 10 – Table B.7.
19 Ben Edwards, "Financial Centers: Border Control: Capital Moves Freely Between Financial Centres, But Businesses Do Not," *Economist*, 9 May 1998.
20 The dollar is part of 89 percent of all foreign exchange trades, the euro is part of 37 percent, and the yen is part of 20 percent. In 2004, the most commonly traded currency pair was the dollar/euro (28 percent), followed by dollar/yen (17 percent) and dollar/sterling (14 percent). Trading in the local currencies of emerging market economies accounted for 5.2 percent of foreign exchange activity. See Bank for International Settlements, "Triennial Central Bank Survey," 2005, p. 2.
21 Traditional foreign exchange markets include spot trading and complex forward and swap transactions. A foreign exchange spot contract is an agreement to settle the purchase or sale of a currency not more than two days after the transaction. A foreign exchange forward contract is an agreement to settle the purchase or sale of a currency in the future after at least two business days. A foreign exchange swap is a contractual agreement for the simultaneous exchange of two currencies on a specified date and at a specified rate agreed at the time of the contract, and a reverse exchange of the same two currencies at a date further in the future at a rate agreed at the time of the contract. See Federal Reserve Bank of New York, "The Foreign Exchange and Interest Rate Derivatives Market Survey: Turnover in the United States," New York, NY: Federal Reserve Bank of New York, 2001, p. 10.
22 Peter G. Zhang, *Barings Bankruptcy and Financial Derivatives*, Singapore: World Scientific 1995, pp. 29–30.
23 Barbara B. Diamond and Mark P. Kollar, *24-hour trading: the global network of futures and options markets*, New York, NY: Wiley, 1989, pp. 10–12.
24 Zhang, *Barings Bankruptcy*, pp. 30–33.
25 Zhang, *Barings Bankruptcy*, p. 33.
26 Ibid.
27 SIMEX merged with the Stock Exchange of Singapore in December 1999.
28 John Gapper and Nicholas Denton, *All That Glitters: The Fall of Barings*, New York, NY: Penguin Books, 1997, p. 205.
29 Ibid.
30 Sheelagh McCracken, "Introduction," and "Confronting the Legal Dimension," in *Derivatives: The Risks that Remain*, eds. Elizabeth Sheedy and Sheelagh McCracken, New South Wales, AU: Allen Unwin/ Macquarie Series in Applied Finance, 1997, p. xvii.
31 International Monetary Fund, "Offshore Banking: An Analysis of Micro- and Macro-Prudential Issues," Working Paper, Washington, D.C.: International Monetary Fund, 1999, pp. 4, 10, 13. The share of some offshore financial centers such as Bahrain and Panama has remained static or even declined in the ten-year period from 1987 to 1997.
32 International Monetary Fund, "Measures to Limit the Offshore Use of Currencies: Pros and Cons," Working Paper, Washington, D.C.: International

Monetary Fund, April 2001, p. 7. The prefix "Euro-" (applied to currency, deposits, notes, and commercial paper) simply designates book-entry debt contracts booked outside the country in whose currency they are denominated. For example, "Eurodollar deposits" are dollars deposited in banks outside the United States. The bank accepting the deposit could be a branch of an American bank or a foreign institution that accepts dollar deposits. Borrowers could include governments, enterprises, or individuals that require access to dollars in order to pay their bills. The major borrowers in the marketplace however are generally other banks that require foreign exchange. See Ethan Kapstein, *Governing the Global Economy: International Finance and the State*, Cambridge, MA: Harvard University Press, 1994, p. 32.

33 Gapper and Denton, *All That Glitters*, p. 75.
34 International Monetary Fund, "Offshore Banking," p. 17.
35 International Monetary Fund, "Offshore Banking," p. 16.
36 Kapstein, *Governing the Global Economy*, pp. 32–33.
37 Zhang, *Barings Bankruptcy*, pp. 25–26.
38 Helleiner, "From Bretton Woods to Global Finance," p. 169.
39 Ibid.
40 Alan C. Hudson, "Off-shores On-shore: New Regulatory Spaces and Real Historical Places in the Landscape of Global Money," in *Money and the Space Economy*, Ron Martin, ed., New York, NY: John Wiley & Sons, 1999, pp. 139–54.
41 International Monetary Fund, "Financial Sector Regulation and Supervision: The Case of Small Pacific Island Countries," Policy Discussion Paper, Washington, D.C.: International Monetary Fund, 2001a, p. 7.
42 International Monetary Fund, "Offshore Banking," p. 13.
43 International Monetary Fund, "Financial Sector Regulation and Supervision," p. 3.
44 See International Monetary Fund, "Offshore Banking."
45 Oxfam, "Tax Havens: Releasing the Hidden Billions for Poverty Eradication," *Oxfam Policy Papers*, Oxford, UK: Oxfam, 2000.
46 International Monetary Fund, "Measures to Limit the Offshore Use of Currencies," p. 4.
47 Ibid.
48 Ibid., pp. 6, 8.
49 International Monetary Fund, "Offshore Banking," p. 14.
50 Ibid., p. 15 – footnote 12.
51 Ibid., p. 15.
52 Bank for International Settlements, "Triennial Central Bank Survey," 2005, p. 3; Bank for International Settlements, "Triennial Central Bank Survey," 2002, p. 2.
53 Thomas Krantz, Deputy Secretary General, Fédération Internationale des Bourses de Valeurs, interview by author in London, UK, on 8 November 1999.
54 Susan Strange, *Mad Money*, Manchester, UK: Manchester University Press, 1998, p. 32.
55 Saul Hansell and Kevin Muehring, "Why Derivatives Rattle Regulators," *Institutional Investor* 26, no. 10, 1992, pp. 49–62.
56 Bank for International Settlements, "Triennial Central Bank Survey," 2005, p. 16 – Table C.2.
57 Comptroller of the Currency, "OCC's Report on Bank Derivatives Activities, Fourth Quarter 2006," p. 7.
58 Doug Henwood, *Wall Street: How it Works and for Whom*, New York, NY: Verso Books, 1997, p. 36.
59 Basel Committee on Banking Supervision, "Banks' Interaction with Highly Leveraged Institutions," *Basel Committee Publication No. 45*, Basel, CH: Bank for International Settlements, 1999, p. 2; Financial Stability Forum, "Report of

the Working Group on Highly Leveraged Institutions," Basel, CH: Bank for International Settlements, 2000.

60 Chadha *et al.*, *Emerging Market Financing*, 2000; Chadha *et al.*, *Emerging Market Financing*, 2000a.

61 See Chadha *et al.*, *Emerging Market Financing*, 2000, p. 6; Chadha *et al.*, *Emerging Market Financing*, 2000a, p. 16.

62 See Chadha *et al.*, *Emerging Market Financing*, 2000a, p. 18.

63 Dimitris N. Chorafas, *Risk Management in Financial Services*, London, UK: Butterworths, 1990, p. 52.

3 Theory of risk

1 Walter Bagehot, *Lombard Street: A Description of the Money Market*, Homewood, IL: Richard D. Irwin, Inc., 1962 [1873], p. 61.

2 Joël Bessis, *Risk Management in Banking*, Chichester, UK: John Wiley & Sons Ltd., 1998, p. xii.

3 Bessis, *Risk Management in Banking*, pp. 1–4.

4 For a short list of common financial risks, see Table 3.1.

5 The technology of financial risk is genealogically related to the technology of insurance. The development of insurance as a set of institutions (e.g., marine insurance, health insurance, life insurance, etc.) has been traced back to the development of the actuarial science in the nineteenth century. François Ewald, "Insurance and Risk," in *The Foucault Effect: Studies in Governmentality*, eds. Graham Burchell, Colin Gordon and Peter Miller, London, UK: Harvester Wheatsheaf, 1991.

6 See Michel Foucault, *The History of Sexuality, vol. I: An Introduction*, trans. Robert Hurley, New York, NY: Vintage Books, 1990, pp. 103, 105.

7 Ewald, "Insurance and Risk," p. 198.

8 Ewald, "Insurance and Risk," p. 200.

9 Bessis, *Risk Management in Banking*, p. 47.

10 Institute of International Finance, "Report of the Task Force on Risk Assessment." Washington, D.C.: Institute of International Finance, 1999, p. 4.

11 Andrew Leyshon and Nigel Thrift, *Money Space: Geographies of Monetary Transformation*, New York, NY: Routledge, 1997, pp. 294–95.

12 See Ewald, "Insurance and Risk," p. 197.

13 Bessis, *Risk Management in Banking*, p. xvi.

14 Richard O'Brien, *Global Financial Integration: The End of Geography*, The Royal Institute of International Affairs Chatham House Papers, London, UK: Pinter Publishers, 1992, p. 43.

15 O'Brien, *Global Financial Integration*, p. 43.

16 Bank for International Settlements, "Recent Innovations in International Banking," Basel, CH: Bank for International Settlements, 1986, p. 207.

17 To the extent that the technology of risk management relies on secondary markets to transfer risk as a commodity, the technology of risk appears to conform to the neo-liberal ideological preference for "market" driven solutions. However, the effort at risk management via secondary markets also indicates the aversion of market actors to readily accept market "discipline" when assets are threatened. Short-term fluctuations in exchange rates and interest rates should be reflected in either the price of commodities, the rate of production, or level of capitalization if the logic of free markets is internally consistent.

18 Barbara B. Diamond and Mark P. Kollar, *24-hour trading: the global network of futures and options markets*, New York, NY: Wiley, 1989, pp. 10–12.

19 Charles A. E. Goodhart, *The Central Bank and the Financial System*, London, UK: Macmillan Press, 1995, p. 64.

20 Anthony Giddens, *Modernity and Self-Identity*, Cambridge, UK: Polity Press, 1991, p. 118, as cited in Nigel Thrift, *Spatial Formations*, London, UK: Sage Publications, 1996, p. 219.
21 Bessis, *Risk Management in Banking*, pp. 31–34.
22 Michael Oakeshott, *Rationalism in Politics and Other Essays*, Indianapolis, IN: Liberty Press, 1991, pp. 101, 106–7.
23 Ibid., p. 104.
24 Bessis, *Risk Management in Banking*, p. 13.
25 Ibid., pp. 12–13.
26 Ibid., p. 14.
27 Ibid., p. 26.
28 Ibid., pp. 88–89.
29 Ibid., p. 67.
30 Ibid.
31 Ibid.
32 Katerina Simons, "Model Error: Evaluation of Various Financial Models," *New England Economic Review* 11, no. 21, 1997, pp. 17–28; Darryl Hendricks, "Evaluation of Value-at-Risk Models Using Historical Data Methods for Estimating Market Risk," *Federal Reserve Bank of New York Economic Policy Review* 2, no.1, 1996, pp. 39–69.
33 Simons, "Model Error"; Hendricks, "Evaluation of Value-at-Risk Models."
34 Bessis, *Risk Management in Banking*, pp. 73–74.
35 Ibid., p. 69.
36 Ibid.
37 Ibid., pp. 62, 34.
38 Charles A. E. Goodhart *et. al.*, *Financial Regulation: Why, How and Where Now?* London, UK: Routledge Press, 1998, p. 76.
39 Ibid., pp. 78–79.
40 Ibid., p. 79.
41 Bessis, *Risk Management in Banking*, p. 73.
42 Leyshon and Thrift, *Money Space*, p. 207.
43 Peter L. Bernstein, *Against the Gods: The Remarkable Story of Risk*, New York, NY: John Wiley and Sons, Inc., 1996, p. 335.
44 Bessis, *Risk Management in Banking*, p. 75.
45 Ewald, "Insurance and Risk," p. 200.

4 Theory of regulation

1 Max Weber, *Economy and Society: An Outline of Interpretive Sociology*, vol. II, eds. Guenther Roth and Claus Wittich, Berkeley, CA: University of California Press, 1978, p. 1394.
2 See Ian Hacking, *The Taming of Chance*, Cambridge, UK: Cambridge University Press, 1990, pp. 2–3.
3 Sassen, "Embedding the Global in the National," 158; Immanuel Wallerstein, "States? Sovereignty? The Dilemmas of Capitalists in the Age of Transition," in *States and Sovereignty in the Global Economy*, eds. David A. Smith, Dorothy J. Solinger and Steve C. Topik, London, UK: Routledge Press, 1999.
4 Sassen, "Embedding the Global in the National," p. 159; Saskia Sassen, *Globalization and Its Discontents*, New York, NY: The New Press, 1998, pp. xxvii–xxxiii.
5 For examples, see Frank J. Fabozzi and Franco Modigliani, *Capital Markets: Institutions and Instruments.* 2nd ed., Upper Saddle River, NJ: Prentice Hall, 1996, pp. 20–22.
6 Graham K. Wilson, "Social Regulation and Explanations of Regulatory Failure," *Political Studies* 32, 1984, p. 209.

7 Samantha Barrass, Senior Associate, Markets and Exchanges Division, Financial Services Authority, interview by author in London, UK on 2 November 1999.
8 Michael J. Shapiro, *Reading "Adam Smith": Desire, History and Value*, vol. 4 of *Modernity and Political Thought*, London, UK: Sage Publications, 1993, pp. 2–3.
9 See Strange, *Casino Capitalism*, p. 26.
10 G. F. Knapp, *The State Theory of Money*, [Abridged English edition.] ed. and trans. H.M. Lucas and J. Bonar, London, UK: Royal Economic Society, 1924; Weber, *Economy and Society*, pp. 184–93.
11 Some authors have presented an explicitly Weberian conceptualization of the relationship between the modern state and the economy (see Geoffrey Ingham, "States and Markets in the Production of World Money: Sterling and the Dollar," in *Money, Power and Space*, eds. Stuart Corbridge, Ron Martin, and Nigel Thrift, Oxford, UK: Blackwell Publishers, 1994, pp. 30–31; Stephen Gill and David Law, *The Global Political Economy: Perspectives, Problems and Policies*, Baltimore, MD: Johns Hopkins University Press, 1988, p. 161.
12 Max Weber, *Economy and Society: An Outline of Interpretive Sociology*, vol. I, eds. Guenther Roth and Claus Wittich, Berkeley, CA: University of California Press, 1978, p. 166.
13 Weber, *Economy and Society*, vol. I, p. 178. An alternative view is that money is 'outside money' and thus an asset of private individuals for which the state stands as debtor. However, the historically accurate view is that money is a debt of the issuing authorities. Waltraud Schelkle, *Constitution and Erosion of a Monetary Economy: Problems of India's Development since Independence*, London, UK: Frank Cass; The German Development Institute, 1994, p. 15.
14 Weber, *Economy and Society*, vol. I, p. 172.
15 Ibid., p. 179.
16 Other more subtle instruments are also available to states and their central banks to influence the market value of money by changing the supply of money in circulation. For example, central banks may purchase Treasury bonds, or increase the reserve requirements of banks.
17 Weber, *Economy and Society*, vol. I, p. 178.
18 Grafted onto the international level, one could formulate a model such that a ('hegemonic') state, which comes to provide its currency as the global means of exchange, could use its (market constrained) 'power' to attempt to reflect its ideological or interest group based 'purpose.' See John G. Ruggie, "International Regimes, Transactions and Change: Embedded Liberalism and the Post War Economic Order," *International Organization* 36, 1982, pp. 379–415.
19 Weber, *Economy and Society*, vol. I, p. 79.
20 Ibid., p. 329.
21 Weber, *Economy and Society*, vol. II, p. 668.
22 Weber, *Economy and Society*, vol. I, pp. 161–62.
23 Sassen, "Embedding the Global in the National," pp. 165–66.
24 Ibid., p. 166.
25 Michael Moran "Politics, Banks and Markets: An Anglo-American Comparison," *Political Studies* 32, 1984, pp. 178–79.
26 Michael Moran, *The Politics of the Financial Services Revolution: The USA, UK and Japan*, London, UK: Macmillan Press Ltd., 1991, pp. 24–25.
27 Sobel, *Domestic Choices, International Markets*, pp. 16–17.
28 Even in Europe where international convergent pressures have been coupled with regional harmonization efforts, divergences nevertheless persist between the major states. States differ both in their degree of vulnerability to external economic pressures as well as in their capacity to implement universal standards and deregulatory policies. See Vivien A. Schmidt, "Convergent Pressures, Divergent

Responses: France, Great Britain and Germany between Globalization and Europeanization," in *States and Sovereignty in the Global Economy*, eds. David A. Smith, Dorothy J. Solinger, and Steven C. Topik, London, UK: Routledge Press, 1999, pp. 173–75. In fact, regional harmonization efforts may frustrate the acceptance and implementation of universal standards.

29 Schelkle, *Constitution and Erosion*, pp. 101–2.

30 Barrass interview on 2 November 1999.

31 Schelkle, *Constitution and Erosion*, pp. 3, 101–2.

32 See Foucault *History of Sexuality*, vol. I, pp. 99–100.

33 Philip Barker, *Michel Foucault: An Introduction*, Edinburgh, UK: Edinburgh University Press, 1998, p. 58.

34 Jonathan H. Tattersall, Chairman, Financial Services Regulatory Consulting Group, PriceWaterhouseCoopers, interview by author in London, UK on 8 November 1999.

35 Michael Moran "Theories of Regulation and Changes in Regulation: The Case of Financial Markets." *Political Studies* 34, 1986, p. 185.

36 Meister, "Supervising the Quantitative and Qualitative Aspects of Derivatives," pp. 12–22.

37 See Sobel, *Domestic Choices, International Markets*, pp. 24–45.

38 See Charles E. Lindblom, *Politics and Markets: The World's Political-Economic Systems*, New York, NY: Basic Books, Inc. Publishers, 1977, pp. 181, 185–88.

39 Moran, "Theories of Regulation and Changes in Regulation," p. 186.

40 Moran, "Politics, Banks and Markets," p. 183.

41 Moran, "Theories of Regulation and Changes in Regulation," p. 187; see also Moran, "Politics, Banks and Markets," pp. 182–85; Sobel, *Domestic Choices, International Markets*, pp. 12–13; Bank for International Settlements, "Recent Innovations in International Banking," Basel, CH: Bank for International Settlements, 1986, p. 3.

42 Moran "Theories of Regulation and Changes in Regulation;" Sobel, *Domestic Choices, International Markets*, pp. 21–22.

43 Moran, "Politics, Banks and Markets," p. 187.

44 Colin Gordon, "Governmental Rationality: An Introduction," in *The Foucault Effect: Studies in Governmentality*, eds. Graham Burchell, Colin Gordon, and Peter Miller, London, UK: Harvester Wheatsheaf, 1991, p. 20.

45 Moran, "Theories of Regulation and Changes in Regulation," p. 193.

46 Tattersall interview on 8 November 1999.

47 Board of Governors of the Federal Reserve System, *85th Annual Report, 1998*, Washington, D.C.: Board of Governors of the Federal Reserve System Publication Services, 1998, p. 250; Board of Governors of the Federal Reserve System, *86th Annual Report, 1999* (Washington, D.C.: Board of Governors of the Federal Reserve System, Publication Services, 1999, pp. 120–26.

48 The eleven other countries were Cameroon, Colombia, Czech Republic, Estonia, India, Iran, Israel, Kazakhstan, Lebanon, Slovak Republic, and South Africa. IMF Area departments suggested two countries from each department for the pilot study. Japan declined to participate in the pilot program. El Salvador and Ireland were added to the pilot program.

49 Office Memorandum from IMF Staff on June 30, 1999, Washington, D.C.: International Monetary Fund.

50 The Financial Stability Forum is composed of three members from each of the G7 countries, plus Australia, Canada, France, Germany, Hong Kong, Italy, Japan, Netherlands, Singapore, United Kingdom, United States. The remaining members are drawn from international financial institutions (IMF, World Bank, BIS, OECD), international regulatory and supervisory groups (BCBS, IOSCO, International Association of Insurance Supervisors), and committees of central

bank (Committee on the Global Financial System, and Committee on Payment and Settlement Systems).

51 The FSF did recommend increased voluntary surveillance of Highly Leveraged Institutions (i.e., hedge funds) and their creditors in April 2000, however progress toward that objective has been slow. See Financial Stability Forum, "Report of the Working Group on Highly Leveraged Institutions," Basel, CH: Bank for International Settlements, 2000. The US introduced legislation to require mandatory disclosure of risk at HLIs after the collapse of LTCM. However, the US later decided to reconsider this legislation as media attention faded and the HLIs made some improvement in disclosure of (qualitative but not quantitative) credit risks to their creditors. No other country has introduced mandatory disclosure legislation. See Financial Stability Forum, "Progress in Implementing the Recommendations of the Working Group on Highly Leveraged Institutions (HLIs): A Note to the FSF by the Chairman of the HLI Working Group," Basel, CH: Bank for International Settlements, 2001; Financial Stability Forum, "The FSF Recommendations and Concerns Raised by Highly Leveraged Institutions (HLIs): An Assessment," Basel, CH: Bank for International Settlements, 2002. Recent public concerns about the role of hedge funds in financing terrorism and engaging in short-selling after the September 11th attacks on the US, may focus regulatory attention on these institutions once again.

5 Regulating risk

1 Howard Davies, Chairman of Britain's Financial Services Authority, explained to the House of Commons the role of institutions such as the Basel Committee or IOSCO, 'I think it is important to note what the Basel Committee and IOSCO and IAIS, the insurance one, of which we are now a member of all three, can do and essentially they are trade unions of regulators, if you like, and what they can do is determine best practice internationally and the Basel Committee has been pretty successful in that generally in the past with a code of practice on principles of good banking supervision and capital agreement about how much capital banks should hold as a minimum, et cetera. IOSCO has set out a group of principles of securities regulation which speaks to issues of market transparency and price formation and all of these good things, but they are clubs of regulators. We pay a subscription and we go along as part of the club and the club can set up some rules and say, "This is what we should all do", but the Basel Committee and IOSCO do not have an army of inspectors or enforcers to go around and insist that people actually do it. That is not what they are; they are voluntary clubs of regulators. Therefore, I do not think it is entirely fair to point the finger at the clubs. I think those clubs did what good clubs can do which is to say, "If you really want to be a good banking supervisor, this is what you ought to do", but in individual jurisdictions around the world, it was not necessarily so easy to implement those principles. Perhaps the banking supervisors were not totally independent or perhaps, dare I say it, they were too close to politicians or perhaps they did not have the degree of independence from the institutions they supervised, such that imposing capital standards or rigorous standards of accounting was not terribly easy for them, or perhaps the standards of accounting and disclosure in that country were not such as to allow them to do it in any very easy way. So I think the issue is how do you translate those good practice principles into action on the ground in markets where currently those principles are not properly followed. … ' United Kingdom, House of Commons "Treasury – Minutes of Evidence on October 29, 1998," London, UK: Her Majesty's Stationary Office, Question 281.

2 Spain joined the Basel Committee in February 2001.
3 The United States has four representatives on the Basel Committee because of its dispersed regulatory structure: two officials from the US Federal Reserve Bank, and one from the Office of the Comptroller of the Currency and the FDIC respectively.
4 Michael Moran, *The Politics of Banking: The Strange Case of Credit Control*, New York, NY: St. Martin's Press, 1984, p. 13.
5 Informal networks continue to be a major basis through which central banks regulate the market. In 1995, after the collapse of Johnson Matthey, BCCI, and Barings Bank, Gordon Brown lambasted the Bank of England for continuing to rely upon its old-boy and other informal networks in order to regulate banks, 'The report [on the collapse of Barings] reveals that just about everyone in the know in Singapore, including many newspapers – and, indeed, many in London – was aware of the problems of Barings; but not, it seems, the Bank of England, which should have been the first to know, but apparently was the last to be told. Is it not clear that the report has provided a damning indictment of the Bank of England's whole approach to the supervision of the banking system? On page 244, the Bank admits that it relied on an informal network of understanding, and made informal concessions – as the Chancellor said – to a management that it now concedes were shambolic. It was thought reasonable to rely on local regulators – regulators who have refused to co-operate in the investigation. A statement on page 245 symbolises the whole problem: "There does not appear to have been any guideline or system in place within the Bank for determining ... the situation". Does that not illustrate everything that is wrong with the Bank's approach – an excessive reliance on the old boys network – and does it not demonstrate the need for tougher regulatory controls? Can the Chancellor really be satisfied with a concluding statement in the report that says only: "the Bank should explore ways of increasing its understanding of the non-banking business"? Why is it only now that the Bank proposes to co-operate with the SFA in a better way, and why does it propose only at this stage "to prepare internal guidelines to assist its staff"? Is it not symptomatic of the whole culture of complacency that the Governor said only last August that there was no need to worry about the derivatives market, because "We now have an expert team monitoring derivatives", getting better all the time? Was it not also over-complacent to dismiss the Americans as "over-excited" by the need for regulation, and to say of derivatives traders such as Barings: "These people know what they are doing, whether it's at director level or the chaps on the desk"? These failures reflect not just incompetence, but a flawed structure of regulation. ... ' United Kingdom Hansard Parliamentary Debates, "Barings: Testimony of the Chancellor of the Exchequer, Mr. Kenneth Clarke," 4th ser., vol. 255, July 18, 1995.
6 The link between the simultaneous collapses of Franklin National Bank and Banca Privata was the Italian financier, Michele Sindona. He owned Banca Privata as well as a controlling share in Franklin National, the nineteenth largest bank in the US. Apparently, Sindona had ransacked the banks he owned in Italy and Switzerland of $225 million in order to acquire a controlling share in Franklin National in 1972. Then Sindona took $15 million from Franklin National to partially repay his banks in Italy. He lost another $30 million in foreign exchange speculation. He altered bank records for sixteen months to conceal his actions. Sindona was sentenced by the US to 25 years in prison for fraud in connection with the collapse of Franklin National. Other top officials at Franklin National were also convicted of falsifying records to hide losses from foreign exchange and bond losses. James L. Rowe and John Kennedy, "Sindona Hit with 99-Count Indictment," *Washington Post*, 20 March 1979.

Bankhaus ID Herstatt, West Germany's third largest bank, lost $453 million in foreign exchange speculation. Prior to liquidation settlements, a host of German, British, and American banks lost large amounts of money due to the collapse of Herstatt bank. For example, Chase Manhattan lost $156 million on deposits from Herstatt in their New York City branch office. Seattle First National bank lost $22.5 million in a foreign exchange transaction that was not completed when Herstatt bank was closed by German authorities. Most counterparties eventually recovered nearly 90 percent of their losses. However, in the month after these major bank collapses, Eurocurrency trading declined by 50 percent as confidence in the financial system declined. Most importantly, these bank collapses revealed the flaws that stemmed from the ambiguous authority structures in the post-Bretton Woods monetary order.

7 Ethan B. Kapstein, "Resolving the Regulator's Dilemma: International Coordination of Banking Regulation," *International Organization* 43, no. 2, 1989, p. 329.
8 Basel Committee on Banking Supervision, "Principles for the Supervision of Banks' Foreign Establishments," in *Compendium of documents produced by the Basel Committee on Banking Supervision*, vol. III, Basel, CH: Bank for International Settlements, 1983.
9 Ibid., p. 2.
10 See Ronald MacDonald, "Consolidated Supervision of Banks," in *Handbooks in Central Banking* 15, London, UK: Centre for Central Banking Studies, Bank of England, 1997, p. 6.
11 Michel Foucault "Governmentality," in *The Foucault Effect: Studies in Governmentality*, eds. Graham Burchell, Colin Gordon, and Peter Miller, Chicago, IL: University of Chicago Press, 1991; See also Stephen D. Krasner, "Globalization and Sovereignty," in *States and Sovereignty in the Global Economy*, eds. David A. Smith, Dorothy J. Solinger, and Steven C. Topik, London, UK: Routledge Press, 1999.
12 Foucault "Governmentality," p. 93.
13 Ibid., p. 95.
14 See Foucault "Governmentality."
15 Kapstein, "Resolving the Regulator's Dilemma," p. 330.
16 Monroe Davis, "Capital Ratios Are Only One Step," *Banker* 137, no. 735, 1987, p. 57; Basel Committee on Banking Supervision, "Consolidated Supervision of Banks' International Activities." in *Compendium of documents produced by the Basel Committee on Banking Supervision*, vol. I, Basel, CH: Bank for International Settlements, 1979; Basel Committee on Banking Supervision, "Principles for the Supervision of Banks' Foreign Establishments," in *Compendium of documents produced by the Basel Committee on Banking Supervision*, vol. III, Basel, CH: Bank for International Settlements, 1983.
17 Steve Lohr, "BCCI's Fall Shows Gaps in Policing Global Fraud," *New York Times*, 14 July 1991.
18 Neil Bennett, "Bankers Tighten Rules in Fight Against Fraud," *Times*, 7 July 1992; Basel Committee on Banking Supervision, "Minimum Standards for the Supervision of International Banking Groups and Their Cross-Border Establishments." in *Compendium of documents produced by the Basel Committee on Banking Supervision*, vol. III, Basel, CH: Bank for International Settlements, 1992.
19 Kapstein, "Resolving the Regulator's Dilemma," p. 330.
20 Ibid.
21 Wolfgang H. Reinicke, *Banking, Politics and Global Finance: American Commercial Banks and Regulatory Change, 1980–1990*, Hants, UK: Edward Elgar Publishing Co., 1995, pp. 134–35.
22 Ibid., p. 135.

23 Basel Committee on Banking Supervision, "Supervision of Banks' Foreign Exchange Positions." in *Compendium of documents produced by the Basel Committee on Banking Supervision*, vol. I, Basel, CH: Bank for International Settlements, 1980, p. 1. During the 1980s, exchange rate movements in excess of 30 percent a year were not unusual. For example, the pound sterling traded at $2.40 in 1981, fell to over $1.00 in 1985, and swung back to $1.50 in 1986. It has been argued that the collapse of one-fifth of the UK manufacturing industry during 1979 to 1982 can be ascribed to the loss of markets caused by the strengthening of the pound sterling and the rise of interest rates. Keith Redhead and Steward Hughes, *Financial Risk Management*, Hants, UK: Gower Publishing Co., 1988, p. 1.

24 I. G. Patel, *Glimpses of Indian Economic Policy: An Insider's View*, Oxford, UK: Oxford University Press, 2002, p. 168. Wriston's theory ignores the distinction between internal and external debt. External debt must usually be paid in foreign currency. Unlike internal debt, which can be paid through an expansion of the money supply, external debt must be paid out of foreign currency reserves. Thus, a country can go bankrupt once it runs out of a sufficient supply of foreign reserves to repay loans.

25 John Train, "Banking and the Bottom Line," *Washington Post*, 13 May 1984.

26 Reinicke, *Banking, Politics and Global Finance*, p. 142.

27 Train, "Banking and the Bottom Line," p. 11.

28 Bank of England, "Banking Act 1979 Annual Report by the Bank of England 1982/83," London, UK: Bank of England; Hertford, UK: Stephen Austin and Sons, Ltd., 1983, p. 4.

29 See Ibid., p. 4.

30 Kapstein, *Governing the Global Economy*, p. 103.

31 Ibid., p. 108.

32 Reinicke, *Banking, Politics and Global Finance*, pp. 137–38.

33 The FDIC's argument, although it did not propose a two-tier system of capital adequacy, would eventually serve as the backbone for the Basel Accord of 1988. Ibid., p. 140.

34 Ibid., pp. 148–49, 158.

35 Public Law 98–101, Sec. 908, (b)(3)(C), 97 Stat. 1281, as quoted in Reinicke, *Banking, Politics and Global Finance*, p. 162.

36 Ibid., p. 163; Kapstein, *Governing the Global Economy*, pp. 107–8.

37 Reinicke, *Banking, Politics and Global Finance*, p. 163.

38 Ibid., p. 165.

39 Specifically, the 1988 Basel Capital Accord stated that the capital base for all banks and bank holding companies (with consolidated assets over $150 million) would be 8 percent of total risk-weighted assets derived from two tiers. The two tiers framework provided a common standard while respecting national differences. See Kapstein, *Governing the Global Economy*, p. 117. In the first tier, 4 percent of the base would come from core capital (i.e., equity plus disclosed reserves). The remainder (i.e., loan-loss reserves, perpetual and limited-life preferred stock, subordinated debt and hybrid capital instruments, such as derivatives) could come from a second tier composed of supplementary capital. There were five risk-weighted categories in the Accord (0, 10, 20, 50, and 100 percent of the 8 percent minimum capital requirement). Short-term obligations, such as balances due from the US Federal Reserve, were in the 0 percent category. Longer-term US obligations were in the 10 percent category. All claims on domestic banks were in the 20 percent category, etc. All corporate loans were assigned the full 100 percent or 8 percent minimum requirement. Off-balance-sheet items were translated into a credit equivalence and then assigned a risk-weighted category. Weights assigned to each category were determined arbitrarily with no reference to any particular insolvency probability. The Accord

was to be implemented by the end of 1992. Basel Committee on Banking Supervision, "International Convergence of Capital Measurement and Capital Standards," *Basel Committee Publication No. 4*, Basel, CH: Bank for International Settlements, 1988; Basel Committee on Banking Supervision, "Risk Management Guidelines for Derivatives, July 1994," in *Compendium of Documents Produced by the Basel Committee on Banking Supervision,* vol. I–III, Basel, CH: Bank for International Settlements, 1994; Robert L. Bevan, "Risk-Based Capital," *United States Banker* 94, no. 4, 1988, p. 60; Alan Greenspan, "Moving with the Times: Need to Reform the Basel Accord of 1988," *Banker* 148, no. 867, 1998, p. 16.

40 The appearance of uniformity masked the compromises embedded in the final agreement. Calomiris and Litan note, "... Germany was influential in gaining a discounted risk weight for mortgage loans (which survives to this day) and also held up the most recent proposal to ensure favorable treatment for its banks' mortgages." See Charles W. Calomiris and Robert E. Litan, "Financial Regulation in a Global Marketplace," *Brookings-Wharton Papers on Financial Services*, 2000, p. 294.

41 Basel Committee on Banking Supervision, "Banks' Interaction with Highly Leveraged Institutions," *Basel Committee Publication No. 45*, Basel, CH: Bank for International Settlements, 1999, p. 1.

42 Reserve Bank of India, "Comments of the Reserve Bank of India on A New Capital Adequacy Framework," Bombay, IN: Reserve Bank of India, 2000, pp. 5, 10.

43 "Capital Punishment," *Economist*, 12 April 1997. Ironically, the Basel Committee issued a report two months after the start of the Asian financial crisis urging emerging market economies to adopt capital adequacy reserve standards that were even more stringent than the Basel Accord. See Charles W. Calomiris and Robert E. Litan, "Financial Regulation in a Global Marketplace," *Brookings-Wharton Papers on Financial Services*, 2000, p. 294.

44 Sunanda Sen, "Basel Norms and Bank Restructuring," *The Hindu*, 8 April 2005.

45 Kapstein, *Governing the Global Economy*, p. 107.

46 Ibid., pp. 110–11.

47 William Hall, "Supervisory Authorities Take a Fresh Look," *Financial Times*, 4 May 1982.

48 See Andrew Leyshon and Nigel Thrift, *Money Space: Geographies of Monetary Transformation*, New York, NY: Routledge Press, 1997, p. 308.

49 Max Weber, *Economy and Society: An Outline of Interpretive Sociology.* vol. 2, eds. Geunther Roth and Claus Wittich, Berkeley, CA: University of California Press, 1978, p. 1206.

50 John Gapper and Nicholas Denton, *All That Glitters: The Fall of Barings*, New York, NY: Penguin Books, 1997, p. 2.

51 A loan-loss provision refers to the capital set aside as an allowance to cover loan default or renegotiation.

52 A netting arrangement is essentially one where bankruptcy arrangements are pre-specified by the contracting parties. Bankers believe that these arrangements constitute a form of insurance as contractual counterparties do not need to wait for liquidation and court settlements to retrieve their investments after a bank collapse.

53 Basel Committee on Banking Supervision, "History of the Basel Committee and its Membership," in *Compendium of Documents Produced by the Basel Committee on Banking Supervision,* vol. I, Basel, CH: Bank for International Settlements, 2001, p. 3.

54 Basel Committee on Banking Supervision & International Federation of Accountants, "The Relationship between Banking Supervisors and Banks' External Auditors," Basel, CH: Bank for International Settlements, 2001.

55 Basel Committee on Banking Supervision, "Internal Audit in Banks and the Supervisor's Relationship with Auditors," *Basel Committee Publication No. 84*, Basel, CH: Bank for International Settlements, 2001a, p. 1.
56 Edith Kurzweil, *The Age of Structuralism: Levi-Strauss to Foucault*, New York, NY: Columbia University Press, 1980, p. 219. For example, after the Asian Financial Crisis, Arthur Andersen revealed its new business risk model, called the "Business Audit," that organized and defined 78 separate business risks, industry by industry, enabling clients to see '. . . a comprehensive map of their businesses across all 78 dimensions.' *Australian Financial Review*, 28 May 1998.
57 Basel Committee on Banking Supervision, "Framework for Internal Control Systems in Banking Organisations." *Basel Committee Publication No. 40*, Basel, CH: Bank for International Settlements, 1998, p. 3; see also John I. Tiner, and Joe M. Conneely, *Accounting for Treasury Products: A Practical Guide to Accounting, Tax and Risk Control*, Cambridge, UK: Woodhead-Faulkner Ltd.; Arthur Andersen and Co., 1987, pp. 136–37.
58 Basel Committee on Banking Supervision & International Organization of Securities Commissions, "Review of Issues Relating to Highly Leveraged Institutions (HLIs)," *Basel Committee Publication No. 79*, Basel, CH: Bank for International Settlements, 2001, p. 5.
59 Basel Committee on Banking Supervision, "Internal Audit in Banks and the Supervisor's Relationship with Auditors," *Basel Committee Publication No. 84*, Basel, CH: Bank for International Settlements, 2001a, p. 1.
60 Basel Committee on Banking Supervision & International Federation of Accountants, "The Relationship between Banking Supervisors and Banks' External Auditors," Basel, CH: Bank for International Settlements, 2001, p. 6.
61 Reserve Bank of India, "Comments of the Reserve Bank of India on A New Capital Adequacy Framework," pp. 7, 11.
62 Basel Committee on Banking Supervision, "Letter from William J. McDonough to International Federation of Accountants, Re: Code of Ethics for Professional Accountants," Basel, CH: Bank for International Settlements, 24 October 2000, Annex.
63 Basel Committee on Banking Supervision, "Letter from William J. McDonough to IAPC Review Task Force – International Federation of Accountants, Re: Report and Recommendations from the IAPC Review Task Force," Basel, CH: Bank for International Settlements, 21 September 2001b, Annex.
64 Basel Committee on Banking Supervision, "Supervision of Banks' Foreign Exchange Positions," in *Compendium of documents produced by the Basel Committee on Banking Supervision*, vol. I. Basel, CH: Bank for International Settlements, 1980, p. 5.
65 Basel Committee on Banking Supervision & International Federation of Accountants, "The Relationship between Banking Supervisors and Banks' External Auditors," p. 10.
66 Ibid., p. 10.
67 Charles A. E. Goodhart, Philip Hartmann, David Llewellyn, Liliana Rojas-Suarez, and Steven Weisbrod, *Financial Regulation: Why, How and Where Now?* London, UK: Routledge Press, 1998, p. 74.
68 Basel Committee on Banking Supervision, "The Supervisory Treatment of Market Risk," Basel, CH: Bank for International Settlements, 1993.
69 "Banking Regulations: A Brush with Basel," *Economist*, 16 September 1995, p. 89.
70 Goodhart *et al.*, *Financial Regulation*, p. 75.
71 Richard Dale, *Risk and Regulation in Global Securities Markets*, Chichester, UK: John Wiley and Sons, 1996, p. 137.
72 Group of Thirty, "Derivatives: Practices and Principles," Washington, D.C.: Group of Thirty, 1993; Group of Thirty, "Derivatives: Practices and Principles,

Appendix I: Working Papers," Washington, D.C.: Group of Thirty, 1993a. The VaR estimates how the value of an individual position or the whole portfolio changes with a change in the prices of the underlying instruments. The VaR is the maximum amount the portfolio can lose with a given probability in a given time period. For example, if the daily VaR were estimated to be $1 million at the 95th percent confidence level, one would expect to lose no more than $1 million in one day 95 percent of the time. Industry practice was to use a 95 percent confidence level and a time period (or 'holding period') of two days. To arrive at a VaR estimate, one generally assumes that returns are independently distributed over time and identically distributed over time (IID), and that they are normally distributed. Critics argue that these assumptions make the model analytically tractable but they are not necessarily close to reality. For example, the normal distribution assumption is used routinely in modeling asset returns, it has been widely recognized for many years that financial markets exhibit significant non-normalities. In particular, asset returns exhibit 'fat tails,' meaning that more of their probability is to be found at the tail ends of the distribution and less at the center. Katerina Simons, "Model Error: Evaluation of Various Financial Models," *New England Economic Review* 11, no. 21, 1997, p. 17–28; Darryl Hendricks, "Evaluation of Value-at-Risk Models Using Historical Data Methods for Estimating Market Risk," *Federal Reserve Bank of New York Economic Policy Review* 2, no.1, 1996, p. 39–69.

73 Group of Thirty, "Derivatives: Practices and Principles," pp. i–ii, 2.

74 Group of Thirty, "Derivatives: Practices and Principles," pp. 8, 22–24.

75 Richard Lapper, "Basel Accord to Include Market Risk," *Financial Times*, 11 April 1995.

76 "Banking Regulations: A Brush with Basel," *Economist*, 16 September 1995, p. 89.

77 Basel Committee on Banking Supervision, "Consultative Paper: A New Capital Adequacy Framework," Basel, CH: Bank for International Settlements, 1999a, p. 2.

78 Basel Committee on Banking Supervision, "The Management of Banks' Off-Balance-Sheet Exposures, March 1986," in *Compendium of documents produced by the Basel Committee on Banking Supervision*, vols. I–III, Basel, CH: Bank for International Settlements, 1986, p. 157.

79 Bank of England, "Banking Act 1979 Annual Report by the Bank of England 1986/87," Hertford, UK: Stephen Austin and Sons, Ltd., 1987, p. 5.

80 Dimitris N. Chorafas, *Risk Management in Financial Services*, London, UK: Butterworths, 1990, p. 75.

81 Ibid., p. 76.

82 Bank for International Settlements, "Recent Innovations in International Banking," Basel, CH: Bank for International Settlements, 1986, p. 3.

83 Bank of England, "Banking Act 1979 Annual Report by the Bank of England 1986/87," p. 7.

84 Basel Committee on Banking Supervision, "History of the Basel Committee and its Membership." In *Compendium of Documents Produced by the Basel Committee on Banking Supervision*, vol. I, Basel, CH: Bank for International Settlements, 2001, p. 2.

85 Basel Committee on Banking Supervision, "Principles for the Supervision of Banks' Foreign Establishments," in *Compendium of documents produced by the Basel Committee on Banking Supervision*, vol. III, Basel, CH: Bank for International Settlements, 1983, p. 3.

86 See U.S. House Committee on Banking and Financial Services, "Financial Institutions And Consumer Credit Unions Hedge Funds," testimony of Marge Roukeman, Representative and Chairwoman of the House Committee on Banking

and Financial Services, 106th Cong., 1st sess., 24 March 1999; William Kay, "Jury's Still Out on the Hedge Fund," *Independent*, 7 July 2001. All of these figures must be treated with special caution. As an IMF report states, 'It is important to emphasize the fragmentary nature of information on this subject. Hedge funds are a rapidly growing part of the financial sector, but they are not subject to reporting and disclosure requirements of the sort that typically apply to banks and mutual funds. . . . Offshore funds typically domicile in jurisdictions where they are subject to even less regulation. This makes it difficult to construct a comprehensive enumeration of hedge funds, much less to assemble information on their activities.' International Monetary Fund, EBS/98/9, 16 January 1998, 4. See also US President's Working Group on Financial Markets, "Hedge Funds, Leverage, and the Lessons of Long-Term Capital Management," Washington, D.C., 1999, pp. 1–2.

87 See Anatole Kaletsky, "How Mr. Soros Made a Billion by Betting Against the Pound." *Times,* 26 October 1992; Richard Thompson and Michael Marray, "White-knuckle Ride on the Soros Express: The Wall Street Wizard is Having Take More and More Risk to Maintain the Huge Returns for Investors," *Independent*, 6 June 1993; Alicia Wyllie, "Hedge Funds Come In Out of the Cold," *Sunday Times*, 24 September 2001.

88 The term "hedge fund" dates to 1949 when an investment partnership established by the sociologist and financial journalist, Alfred Winslow Jones, combined the practices of short selling and leverage. See also US President's Working Group on Financial Markets, "Hedge Funds, Leverage, and the Lessons of Long-Term Capital Management," Washington, D.C., 1999, p. 1; Monetary Authority of Singapore, "Hedge Funds," Singapore: Monetary Authority of Singapore, 1999; IMF Document: EBS/98/9, 16 January 1998, p. 8. Contemporary hedge funds employ a wider array of financial instruments and strategies. Most importantly, contemporary hedge funds are specifically designed to evade regulatory scrutiny.

89 "Soul-Searching by Regulators After LTCM: The Increasingly Mainstream View is that Many Leveraged Funds Have Grown Large Enough to Pose a Systemic Risk," *Financial Times*, 28 September 1998.

90 In the UK, unit trusts may qualify as an "unregulated scheme" if they agree not to advertise or otherwise solicit investments from the general public. However, unregulated schemes are still subject to the self-regulating-organisation rules promulgated by the Investment Management Regulatory Organisation (IMRO). Thus, these schemes are required to produce periodic accounting statements, information about management, and asset valuation. Standards are relaxed for funds whose shareholders are "nonprivate customers," a category roughly equivalent to high net worth individuals in the United States. In these cases, IMRO is required to verify that the fund has adequate control of customer money, managers are "fit and proper," and that there is a absence of fraud. See IMF Document: EBS/98/9, 16 January 1998, pp. 19–20.

91 Individuals who do not have sufficient portfolios are beginning to pool their money in order to invest in hedge funds as a group of investors. See William Kay, "Jury's Still Out on the Hedge Fund," *Independent*, 7 July 2001.

92 U.S. House Committee on Banking and Financial Services, "Prepared Statement by Michael L. Brosnan, Deputy Comptroller for Risk Evaluation: Hearing of the Financial Institutions Consumer Subcommittee," 106th Cong., 1st sess., 24 March 1999, footnote 1.

93 Junichi Miura, "Crisis Clarified Risky Operations of Hedge Funds," *Daily Yomiuri*, 30 October 1998.

94 "Soul-Searching by Regulators after LTCM," *Financial Times*, 28 September 1998. Market participants distinguish between two main types of hedge funds:

macro-hedge funds and relative value funds. Macro funds tend to take large, unhedged positions in national markets based on a top-down analysis of macroeconomic and financial conditions. Relative value funds take positions on the relative prices of closely related securities (e.g., Treasury bills and bonds). As relative value funds are less exposed to macroeconomic fluctuations, they tend to be more highly leveraged. Relative value funds are also more likely to use derivative products. See Monetary Authority of Singapore. "Hedge Funds." Singapore: Monetary Authority of Singapore, 1999. See also IMF Document: EBS/98/9, 16 January 1998, pp. 7, 12.

95 US House, *Prepared Statement by Michael L. Brosnan*, 24 March 1999, footnote 1.

96 Federal Reserve System, Board of Governors, *85th Annual Report, 1998*, Washington, D.C.: Board of Governors of the Federal Reserve System Publication Services, 1998, p. 25.

97 Notably, even though no financial institutions failed as a result of the LTCM debacle, private "market-disciplining" mechanisms completely failed to prevent the build-up and concentration of counterparty risk exposures within the internationally active financial institutions. See International Monetary Fund, "Offshore Financial Centers: The Role of the IMF," Washington, D.C.: International Monetary Fund 2000a, p. 49.

98 Jane Martinson, "International Lenders to Face More Detailed Regulation," *Guardian*, 17 January 2001.

99 IMF Document: EBS/98/9, 16 January 1998, pp. 3, 23–24.

100 Alan Beattie, "Banks Lacking Data on Hedge Funds They Lend To." *Financial Times*, 23 March 2001.

101 See Bank of England, "Bank of England Banking Act [1987] Report 1987/88," London, UK: Bank of England; Stephen Austin and Sons, Ltd., 1988, pp. 9, 12; Bank of England, "Bank of England Banking Act [1987] Report 1989/90," London, UK: Bank of England; Stephen Austin and Sons, Ltd., 1990, p. 10. Provisioning problems were also evident in 1991, but loan problems were associated with the United States and the former communist countries. Latin American debt was reassessed allowing provisions set aside in previous years to be released. Bank of England, "Bank of England Banking Act [1987] Report 1991/92," London, UK: Bank of England; Stephen Austin and Sons, Ltd., 1992, p. 13.

102 Bank of England, "Bank of England Banking Act [1987] Report 1987/88," p. 9.

103 Bank for International Settlements, "Recent Innovations in International Banking," pp. 2, 130–37.

104 Saskia Sassen, *The Global City: New York, London, Tokyo*. Princeton, NJ: Princeton University Press, 1991, p. 30, 64–78.

105 Bank for International Settlements, "Recent Innovations in International Banking," Basel, CH: Bank for International Settlements, 1986, p. 129.

106 Alexander Nicoll, "Morgan Guaranty Warns on 'Paper' Loans," *Financial Times*, 30 July 1985.

107 Maggie Urry, "Set for Further Expansion," *Financial Times*, 7 May 1985.

108 Hamish McRae, "Securitisation: Comments on BIS Annual Report," *Guardian*, 11 June 1985.

109 Bank of England, "Bank of England Banking Act [1987] Report 1987/88," p. 8.

110 Basel Committee on Banking Supervision, "Consultative Paper: A New Capital Adequacy Framework," Basel, CH: Bank for International Settlements, 1999a, p. 3.

111 International Monetary Fund, *International Capital Markets: Developments and Prospects*, eds. Mark Allen, *et al.*, Washington, D.C.: International Monetary Fund, 1990, p. 45.

112 Deutsche Bundesbank, "Report of the Deutsche Bundesbank for the Year 1991," Frankfurt, DE: Deutsche Bundesbank, 1992, p. 75. It was also possible

to use short-term subordinated debt to the extent that it did not exceed 250 percent of equity capital. The German delegation tried hard to get the securities supervisors to a more stringent definition of capital, which did not diverge from the capital concept used for banks. However, the securities supervisors were unwilling to accept this, so the bank supervisors considered applying a wider definition of capital to the banks' securities business as well.

113 International Monetary Fund, *International Capital Markets*, p. 46.

114 "Lex Column: Financial Regulation." *Financial Times*, 21 May 1996.

6 The political arena

1 Steven Radelet and Jeffrey Sachs, "The Onset of the East Asian Financial Crisis," Harvard Institute for International Development Working Paper, 30 March 1998, p. 5.

2 World Bank, "Global Economic Prospects and the Developing Countries – Beyond Financial Crisis," Washington, D.C.: The World Bank Group, 1998/99, p. 59.

3 David Crane, "Time to Review Role, Resources of IMF," *Toronto Star*, 13 January 1998.

4 Although Singapore had effectively established an Asian dollar market in 1968, the rise of competing offshore markets increased business and helped to funnel additional foreign capital to the emerging market countries.

5 Chalongphob Sussangkarn, "Directions of East Asian Regional Financial Cooperation," *Asian Economic Papers*, Cambridge, MA: The Center for Strategic and International Studies and MIT, Fall 2006.

6 Francis C. Nantha, "Labuan Offered as Location for Proposed Trading Center," *New Straits Times* (Malaysia), 10 October 1997; See also Alvin Tay and Leslie Yee, "New Centres Challenge Singapore's Offshore Banking," *Business Times* (Singapore), 3 October 1992.

7 Harish Mehta, "Massive Capital Outflows Mean Bumpy Ride to Recovery for Thailand," *Business Times* (Singapore), 17 September 1999.

8 Eisuke Sakakibara, "Mr. Yen Looking Back: The Makings of a Crisis," *Daily Yomiuri*, 13 November 1999.

9 Chalongphob Sussangkarn, "Directions of East Asian Regional Financial Cooperation," *Asian Economic Papers*, (Fall 2006); see also Jeff Gerth and Richard W. Stevenson, "Inadequate Regulation Seen in Asia's Banking Crises," *New York Times*, 22 December 1997.

10 Ibid.

11 World Bank, "Global Economic Prospects," pp. 60–67.

12 Brett D. Fromson, "Bank Profits to Gauge Asian Impact; Earnings Reports Expected Today from Chase, Citicorp, J.P. Morgan," *Washington Post*, 20 January 1998.

13 Sakakibara, "Mr. Yen;" see also Jonathan Fuerbringer, "How Asian Currencies Tumbled So Quickly," *New York Times*, 10 December 1997.

14 Paul Blustein, *The Chastening: Inside the Crisis that Rocked the Global Financial System and Humbled the IMF*, New York, NY: Public Affairs, 2001, p. 75.

15 Sussangkarn, "Directions."

16 Fromson, "Bank Profits."

17 "J.P. Morgan's Woes Could Hurt Asian Bailout," *Saint Louis Post-Dispatch*, 21 January 1998.

18 Brett D. Fromson, "Asian Crisis Takes Toll on Three US Banks," *Washington Post*, 21 January 1998.

19 Edmund L. Andrews, "German Bank Acts to Shield Itself of Asia," *New York Times*, 29 January 1998; Brett D. Fromson, "Asian Crisis."

20 Nicholas D. Kristoff and Edward Wyatt, "Who Went Under in the World's Sea of Cash," *New York Times*, 15 February 1999; Sakakibara, "Mr. Yen."
21 Gary J. Schinasi, R. Sean Craig, Burkhard Drees, and Charles Kramer, *Modern Banking and OTC Derivatives Markets: The Transformation of Global Finance and Its Implications for Systemic Risk*, Occasional Paper 203 (Washington, DC.: International Monetary Fund, 2000), p. 50.
22 Ibid., pp. 8–9.
23 Samer Iskander, "Put Option Triggered of IFCT Bond," *Financial Times*, 8 January 1998.
24 Ibid., p. 8.
25 Ibid., p. 5.
26 Fromson, "Bank Profits."
27 Meredith Woo-Cummings, ed., *The Developmental State*, Ithaca, NY: Cornell University Press, 1999, p. 13.
28 Blustein, *Chastening*, p. 8.
29 Eric van Wincoop and Kei Mu-Yi (29 February 2000) "Asian Crisis Post-Mortem: Where did the Money Go and Did the United States Benefit?" BIS Conference Papers, Basel, CH: Bank for International Settlements, March 2000, 282.
30 Schinasi, *Modern Banking*, p. 8.
31 US House Committee on Banking and Financial Services, *Financial Institutions and Consumer Credit Unions Hedge Funds*. Testimony of Marge Roukeman, Representative and Chairwoman of the House Committee on Banking and Financial Services. 106th Cong., 1st sess., 24 March 1999; Junichi Miura, "Crisis Clarified Risky Operations of Hedge Funds," *Daily Yomiuri*, 30 October 1998.
32 Donald MacKenzie, "How a Superportfolio Emerges: Long-Term Capital Management and the Sociology of Arbitrage," in *The Sociology of Financial Markets*, Karin Knorr Cetina and Alex Preda, eds., Oxford, UK: Oxford University Press, 2005, pp. 71–72.
33 Phillip J. Longman, Jack Egan, Pamela Sherrid, and Fred Vogelstein, "Close to the Brink," *U.S. News & World Report* 125, no. 13 (5 October 1998), p. 48.
34 MacKenzie, "Superportfolio Emerges," p. 74.
35 MacKenzie, "Superportfolio Emerges," p. 75.
36 "Long-term Sickness?" *The Economist*, 3 October 1998, p. 81.
37 Alison Warner, "Behind the Hedges," *The Banker* 148, no. 873, 1 November 1998, pp. 24–28.
38 Even in industrialized countries, economic shocks may have lasting effects. For example, European employment rates have yet to recover from the oil crisis thirty years ago. Economists generally explain the phenomenon as the result of an attrition in skills from prolonged unemployment. World Bank, "Global Economic Prospects," x.
39 John H. Boyd, Sungkyu Kwak, and Bruce Smith, "The Real Output Losses Associated with Modern Banking Crises," *Journal of Money, Credit, and Banking* 37, no. 6, December 2005, p. 979.
40 World Bank, *Annual Report 1999*, Washington, D.C.: World Bank Group, 2000, p. 3.
41 World Bank, "Global Economic Prospects," p. 9.
42 Asian Development Bank, *Asian Development Outlook 2001*, Manila, Phillippines: Asian Development Bank, 2001, p. 180.
43 Measuring poverty through a constant measure facilitates comparison between countries, however national statistics are usually more reliable measures of poverty. National statistics permit researchers to capture a greater degree of the contextual character of poverty. For example, while \$1 per day (even if adjusted for purchasing power parity) may be adequate to meet the needs of a citizen in country X, citizens of country Y may find even \$5 per day grossly inadequate to

meet the needs for survival. A shift toward measuring poverty through daily caloric intake does not resolve the contextual problem. In fact, even national statistics must be considered suspect where there are large income disparities between urban and rural areas or between geographic regions of a country.

44 Tamar Manuelyan Atinc and Michael Walton, "Responding to the Financial Crisis: Social Consequences of the East Asian Financial Crisis," Washington, D. C.: World Bank, 1998, 4–5. In these statistics, the East Asia region included Malaysia, Thailand, Indonesia, China, Philippines, Papua New Guinea, Lao PDR, Vietnam, and Mongolia.

45 Nevertheless, nearly 50 percent of Thailand's wealth was owned by less than 10 percent of the population. Alternative calculations for the poverty rate argue that 60 percent of the country's 60 million people still lived in poverty. Seth Mydans, "Thailand's Economic Crash Crushes Working Poor," *New York Times*, 15 December 1997.

46 Tamar Manuelyan Atinc, "Coping with Crises: Social Policy and the Poor in East Asia," Washington, D.C.: World Bank, 2000, 123; see also: Andrew Pollack, "Koreans Worry About Increasing Layoffs." *New York Times*, p. 17 December 1997. For a similar story on unemployment in Indonesia, see Seth Mydans, "Once-Buoyant Hopes Sink in Indonesia's Slump," *New York Times*, 13 December 1997; Edmund L. Andrews, "German Bank Acts to Shield Itself on Asia," *New York Times*, 29 January 1998.

47 World Bank, "Thailand Economic Monitor: Executive Summary," *Thailand Economic Monitor*, Washington, D.C.: World Bank, 2001, p. ii.

48 Frank Ching, "Social Impact of the Regional Financial Crisis," *Asia Society* (February 1999). Available on-line at < http://www.asiasociety.org/publications/update_crisis_ching.html > accessed June 20, 2007.

49 World Bank, "Global Economic Prospects," p. 105.

50 Tayyeb Shabbir, "The Social Costs of the Asian Financial Crisis," Working paper, Philadelphia, PA: University of Pennsylvania Department of Economics, 1998, p. 3.

51 Seung-Kyung Kim and John Finch, "Living with Rhetoric, Living Against Rhetoric: Korean Families and the IMF," *Korean Studies* 26, no. 1, 2002, p. 123.

52 Ibid., p. 128.

53 H. P. Moon, H. H. Lee, and G. J. Yoo, "Social Impact of the Financial Crisis in Korea: Economic Framework," Paper presented at the Finalization Conference on Assessing the Social Impact of the Financial Crisis in Selected Asian Developing Economies, Asian Development Bank, Manila, Philippines (17–18 June 1999) cited in James Knowles, Ernesto M. Pernia, and Mary Racelis, "Social Consequences of the Financial Crisis in Asia: The Deeper Crisis," *Economics and Development Resource Center Briefing Notes*, no. 16, Manila, Philippines: Asian Development Bank, July 1999, p. 2.

54 International Labour Organisation, "Crisis-Affected Peoples and Countries," Geneva, CH: International Labour Organisation, Recovery & Reconstruction Departments, 2001, p. 83.

55 Knowles, Pernia, and Racelis, "Social Consequences," p. 5.

56 Stephen Haggard, "The Politics of the Asian Financial Crisis," *Journal of Democracy* 11, no. 2, April 2000, p. 142.

57 For a discussion of existing social protection arrangements in Thailand, Indonesia, and South Korea, see: Sanjeev Gupta, Calvin McDonald, Christian Schiller, Marinus Verhoeven, *et al.*, "Mitigating the Social Costs of the Asian Crisis," *Finance and Development* 35, no. 3, September 1998, pp. 18–21.

58 Edmund L. Andrews, "German Bank Acts to Shield Itself on Asia," *New York Times*, 29 January 1998; Sidney Jones, "Social Cost of Asian Crisis," *Financial Times*, 26 January 1998.

59 Paul Blustein, "Dreams Tumble with the Rupiah; Indonesia's Workers Put Hopes for a Better Life on Hold," *Washington Post*, 23 January 1998; Seth Mydans, "Indonesia Turns Its Chinese into Scapegoats," *New York Times*, 2 February 1998; Paul Blustein, "Worries Grow About Indonesia; US, IMF Officials Fear Unrest Could Spell Financial Trouble for Asian Neighbors," *Washington Post*, 7 March 1998.

60 Mark Atkinson, John Aglionby, and Larry Elliot, "Brown Warns Suharto as Asian Crisis Deepens: Six Die in Indonesian Riots as Markets Continue to Plummet," *Guardian*, 7 May 1998; Greg Torode, "Jakarta Troops Kill Six Students; People Were Screaming, But the Soldiers Wouldn't Stop Firing. I Saw Dozens of People Hit," *South China Morning Post*, 13 May 1998; Mark Landler, "Indonesian Riot Police Open Fire at Protests, Killing Six Students," *New York Times*, 13 May 1998; Cindy Shiner, "Rioting Spreads in Indonesia; Looters Set Shops Ablaze as Protests Move Beyond Campuses," *Washington Post*, 14 May 1998; Mark Landler, "Riots Break Out in Jakarta After Shooting of Students." *New York Times*, 14 May 1998; Keith B. Richburg, "Riots Rage in Indonesian Capital; Suharto Returns; Violence Reveals Deep Rift in Military," *Washington Post*, 15 May 1998; Mark Landler, "Unrest in Indonesia: An Overview." *New York Times*, 15 May 1998; Peter G. Gosselin, "Indonesia Woes Darken Asian Comeback Prospects; After Brief Rebound, Region Faces Another Round of Declines," *Boston Globe*, 16 May 1998.

61 Shabbir, "Social Costs," p. 3.

62 Ching, "Social Impact."

63 Oxfam International, "East Asian 'Recovery' Leaves the Poor Sinking," Press Briefing, October 1998.

64 Knowles, Pernia, and Racelis, "Social Consequences," p. 8.

65 Jonathan Ablett and Ivar-André Slengesol, "Education in Crisis: The Impact and Lessons of the East Asian Financial Shock, 1997–99," Paris, France: UNESCO, 2001, p. 21.

66 Alison Warner, "Asia Remains Unstable," *The Banker* 148, no. 869, July 1998, pp. 94–98; Asian Development Bank, "News Release: Asia's Crisis Plagues the Poor," Manila, Philippines: Asian Development Bank, 1999.

67 See Ablett and Slengesol, "Education in Crisis."

68 Ibid., pp. 19, 22.

69 Knowles, Pernia, and Racelis, "Social Consequences," pp. 6–7.

70 Ablett and Slengesol, "Education in Crisis," p. 13.

71 Jesook Song, "Family Breakdown and Invisible Homeless Women: Neoliberal Governance during the Asian Debt Crisis in South Korea, 1997–2001," *Positions* 14, no. 1, Spring 2006, pp. 37–65.

72 Seung-Kyung and Finch, "Living with Rhetoric," pp. 120–39.

73 Seth Mydans, "Malaysia Is Ready to Inflict its own Economic Medicine," *New York Times*, 16 December 1997.

74 Approximately 23 percent of Korean household participated in the gold collection drives, donating 65 grams per household; however almost all Koreans sold their gold rather than donating to the drive. Seung-Kyung Kim and John Finch argue that the nationalist rhetoric obscured the mixed motivation and desperation of families who sold their gold. Seung-Kyung and Finch, "Living with Rhetoric," p. 127.

75 Keith Bradsher, "Asia's Long Road Back," *The New York Times*, 28 June 2007; Asian Development Bank, *Beyond the Crisis: Emerging Trends and Challenges*, Manila, Philippines: Asian Development Bank, 2007, p. 1.

76 Asian Development Bank, *Beyond the Crisis*, p. 1.

77 David Hale, "It is a big mistake to Kill Bush's Trade Deal with Seoul," *The Financial Times*, 18 July 2007; Asian Development Bank, *Beyond the Crisis*, p. 12.

78 Jayasankar Shivakumar, Gamini Abeysekera, Amara Pongsapich, and Bencha Yoddumnern-Attig, "Social Capital and the Crisis," in *Thailand Social Monitor*, Washington, D.C.: World Bank, 2000, p. 42; Knowles, Pernia, and Racelis, "Social Consequences," p. 2.

79 For examples of political risk insurers see: Multilateral Investment Guarantee Agency (MIGA) www.miga.org; Overseas Private Insurance Corporation (OPIC) www.opic.gov; and Risk Protection International, LLC (RPI) www.riskprotection.com.

80 OPIC offers significantly more risk insurance than the World Bank's MIGA. Moreover, fully one-third of MIGA political risk insurance is given to US firms. "Prospect for Investment Insurance Seen Improving, *Journal of Commerce*, 20 August 1997. However, the distinction between public and private reinsurance has become blurred as governmental corporations sign agreements with private reinsurers to cover risks. Ronald G. Mullins, "World Bank Unit in Deal with Private Reinsurer," *Journal of Commerce*, 25 April 1997; Andrew Jack, "France to Share Risk on China Guarantees," *Financial Times*, 23 March 1998.

81 Meg Green, "As US Companies Increase International Investing, Political Risk Insurers Find New Markets," *Best's Review* 104, no. 11, 2004, p. 54.

82 Kausar Hamdani, Elise Liebers, and George Zanjani, "An Overview of Political Risk Insurance: Executive Summary," Federal Reserve Bank of New York and Committee on the Global Financial System Working Group, May 2005, p. 4. When a President of OPIC was asked how the agency calculated risk for investments in Russia in 1995, she replied: "You don't. To invest in Russia in 1995 for instance, there would have been no way to genuinely calculate the risks. There was no history upon which to make any kind of calculation. So all you can really say is that the risk is high. This isn't very comforting. Obviously, as countries develop a record of doing business, you then have something to evaluate. The threshold question for us always is: is this going to be profitable." A. J. Vogl, "Risky Business," *Across the Board* 34, no. 5, May 1997, p. 37–40.

83 Edward Royce, "OPIC is not the Way to Promote Free Trade; If Merrill Lynch won't Insure DuPont in Russia, Why Should the American Taxpayer?" *Christian Science Monitor*, 30 September 1996.

84 Nancy Dunne and Jeremy Grant, "OPIC Seeks to Boost Emerging Market," *Financial Times*, 6 November 1998.

85 Tamar Hahn, "OPIC to Insure EM Mortgage-Backeds," *Emerging Markets Report*, 17 April 2000.

86 OPIC claim that they charge market rates for their insurance. However, this claim is contradicted by the fact that the agency also claims that it only provides political risk insurance when private markets are insufficiently developed. For a defense of OPIC practices, see Mildred O. Callear, "'Corporate Welfare' that Isn't?" *Washington Post*, 11 May 1997.

87 "OPIC Signs Pact with Vietnam," *Journal of Commerce*, 23 March 1998.

88 James Kynge, "China Calls on US to Lift Trade Sanctions at Summit," *Financial Times*, 23 June 1998.

89 John S. Diaconis, "Political Risk Insurance: OPIC's Use of a "Fiduciary Agent to Facilitate Resolution of Subrogation Claims," *The International Lawyer* 23, no. 271, Spring 1989.

90 Bob Hohler, "Trade-trip Firms Netted $5.5bn in Aid; Donated $2.3m to Democrats." *Boston Globe*, 30 March 1997.

91 The Export-Import Bank of the US also provided Enron with an additional $675 million in loans. Richard W. Stevenson, "Enron Received Many Loans from US for Foreign Projects During the 1990's," *New York Times*, 21 February 2002.

92 Patrice Hill, "Clinton Helped Enron Finance Projects Abroad; Maintained Close Ties to Lay," *Washington Times*, 21 February 2002.

93 "OPIC Comes Under Ideological Fire." *Financial Times*, 6 March 1997; Jonathan Riskind, "Agency Intact Despite Kasich's Best Efforts," *Columbus (Ohio) Dispatch*, 16 November 1997; Riskind, "Public Agency Acting Too Privately," *Columbus (Ohio) Dispatch*, 2 May 1997.
94 Hamdani, Liebers, and Zanjani, "Overview," p. 1.
95 Committee on the Global Financial System, "Foreign Direct Investment in the Financial Sector of Emerging Market Economies," Report submitted by a Working Group established by the Committee on the Global Financial System, Basel, CH: Bank for International Settlements, March 2004, p. 19; Gerald T. West, "Political Risk Investment Insurance: A Renaissance," *Journal of Project Finance*, vol. 5, no. 2, Summer 1999, pp. 29–30.
96 Riskind, "Public Agency."
97 Ellen Leander, "Is OPIC Funding Corporate Welfare?" *Treasury & Risk Management* 7, no. 2, March 1997.
98 Parenthesis original. Nikos Valance, "Defusing Global Bond Risk," *CFO* 16, no. 6, May 2000, pp. 133–37.
99 Joseph B. Treaster, "Insurers find Profit in a new Risk Consciousness," *New York Times*, 24 February 2002.
100 "Locals Seek Protection," *Latin Finance*, July/August 2007, p. 1.
101 For a detailed explanation, see: Suhas Ketkar and Dilip Ratha, "Securitization of Future Flow Receivables: A Useful Tool for Developing Countries," *Finance and Development*, 38, no. 1, March 2001.
102 Richard Barovick, "Covering Bonds in New Markets." *Journal of Commerce*, 23 May 2000, p. 8.
103 Ibid.
104 Valance, "Defusing Global Bond Risk," 134. See also West, "Political Risk Investment Insurance," p. 30.
105 Hamdani, Liebers, and Zanjani, "Overview," p. 8.
106 Ibid., p. 3.
107 Mary Lacey, "World Briefing Africa: Insurance For Risky Region," *New York Times*, 21 August 2001; Andrew Bolger, "African Insurance Initiative Aims to Boost Trade," *Financial Times*, 7 August 2001.
108 Ironically, a portion of the funds used by the World Bank to support projects like this come from the net income generated by World Bank loans to developing countries. See Robert Chote, "More Cash Urged for World Bank Risk Unit," *Financial Times*, 17 September 1997.
109 Steward Fleming, "Taking the Risk out of Trading with Africa," *The Evening Standard* (London), 2 August 2001.
110 Bolger, "African Insurance," p. 14.
111 "AIG in Joint Venture to Offer Risk Cover." *Journal of Commerce*, 31 March 2000, p. 7.
112 Pascal Fletcher, "Havana Signs Insurance Deal," *Financial Times*, 7 November 1998.
113 Diaconis, "Political Risk Insurance."
114 Of course, developing states could also use the threat of nationalization to extract rents from investors, states, and multilateral institutions. For example, Peru extracted funds and technology from the US government and AIG to help it bolster earnings from oil and nonferrous metals production that could then be used to pay a claim against Peru for nationalizing an oil drilling operation. However, very few developing countries are in a position to effectively use the threat of nationalization, particularly when they face possible political and economic sanctions from developed countries and multilateral institutions in retaliation. Peru only avoided the most serious economic sanctions from the US because of its cooperation in the "war on drugs." Clyde H. Farnsworth, "Insurer Offers Peru Proposal on Oil Claim," *New York Times*, 12 June 1989.

115 See also David A. Moss, *When All Else Fails: Governments as the Ultimate Risk Manager*, Cambridge, MA: Harvard University Press, 2002.

7 Conclusion

1 Michel Foucault, *Language, Counter-memory, Practice: Selected Essays and Interviews*, ed. Donald F. Bouchard, trans. Donald F. Bouchard and Sherry Simon, Ithaca, NY: Cornell University Press, 1977, pp. 33–34.

2 Max Weber, *The Protestant Ethic and the Spirit of Capitalism*, New York, NY: Charles Scribner's Sons, 1958, pp. 49–50.

3 Ibid., p. 52.

4 Poovey, *History of the Modern Fact*, p. 167.

5 Ibid., p. 169. In fact, Defoe goes on to argue that a "complete" tradesman may need to be duplicitous to counter the unsociable (i.e., slanderous and libelous) behavior of his customers. In addition, he even argues that customers *like* to be lied to because they experience the consumption of goods and services as an affective and even aesthetic act.

6 Basel Committee on Banking Supervision, "Letter from William J. McDonough to International Federation of Accountants, Re: Code of Ethics for Professional Accountants," (Basel, CH: Bank for International Settlements, 2000), Annex.

Bibliography

Ablett, Jonathan and Ivar-André Slengesol. "Education in Crisis: The Impact and Lessons of the East Asian Financial Shock, 1997–99." Thematic study originally published by UNESCO for the International Consultative Forum on Education for All 2000 and the World Education Forum in Dakar, Senegal, 26–28 April 2000. Paris, France: UNESCO, 2001.

Acker, Bill. "Another Fine Mess: The Barings Crisis Highlights the New Style of Management in Banking." *Banker* 145, no. 830 (1995): 57–59.

Adams, John. "Cars, Cholera, and Cows: The Management of Risk and Uncertainty." *Policy Analysis* 335 (1999): 1–49.

Andrews, Edmund L. "German Bank Acts to Shield Itself on Asia." *New York Times*, 29 January 1998.

Angelini, Anthony, Maximo Eng and Francis A. Lees. *International Lending, Risk and the Euromarkets.* New York, NY: John Wiley and Sons, 1979.

Asian Development Bank. "News Release: Asian Exports Plummet Due to Financial Crisis." Manila, Philippines: Asian Development Bank, 1999.

——. "News Release: Asia's Crisis Plagues the Poor." Manila, Philippines: Asian Development Bank, 1999.

——. *Annual Report of the Bank 2000.* Manila, Philippines: Asian Development Bank, 2001.

——. *Asian Development Outlook 2001.* Manila, Philippines: Asian Development Bank, 2001.

——. *Beyond the Crisis: Emerging Trends and Challenges*, Manila, Philippines: Asian Development Bank, 2007.

Atinc, Tamar Manuelyan. "Coping with Crises: Social Policy and the Poor in East Asia." Washington, D.C.: World Bank, 2000.

Atinc, Tamar Manuelyan and Michael Walton. "Responding to the Financial Crisis: Social Consequences of the East Asian Financial Crisis." Washington, D.C.: World Bank, 1998.

Atkinson, Mark, John Aglionby and Larry Elliot. "Brown Warns Suharto as Asian Crisis Deepens: Six Die in Indonesian Riots as Markets Continue to Plummet." *Guardian*, 7 May 1998.

Bäckström, Urban. *Annual General Meeting: Address by the President of the Bank for International Settlements.* Press release. Basel, CH: Bank for International Settlements, 7 June 1999.

Bagehot, Walter. *Lombard Street: A Description of the Money Market.* Homewood, IL: Richard D. Irwin, Inc., 1962.

Banker. "You'd Better Ask Murphy: Regulators Worry That Derivatives Are Too Risky – Bankers More Phlegmatic," vol. 143, no. 803 (1993): 48–52.

——. "World's Largest Banks: The Top 500 Banks in the World," vol. 143, no. 803 (1993): 145–75.

——. "World's Largest Banks: The Top 500 Banks in the World," vol. 150, no. 887 (2000): 213–44.

Bank of England. *Banking Act 1979 Annual Report by the Bank of England 1979/80*. London, UK: Bank of England, 1980.

——. "Banking Act 1979 Annual Report by the Bank of England 1980/81." London, UK: Bank of England; Hertford, UK: Stephen Austin and Sons, Ltd., 1981.

——. *Banking Act 1979 Annual Report by the Bank of England 1981/82*. London, UK: Bank of England; Harrison and Sons, Ltd., 1982.

——. *Banking Act 1979 Annual Report by the Bank of England 1982/83*. London, UK: Bank of England; Hertford, UK: Stephen Austin and Sons, Ltd., 1983.

——. "Agreed Proposal of the United States Federal Banking Supervisory Authorities and the Bank of England on Primary Capital and Capital Adequacy Assessment." *Bank of England Quarterly Bulletin* 27(1987): 87–93.

——. "Banking Act 1979 Annual Report by the Bank of England 1986/87." London, UK: Bank of England; Hertford, UK: Stephen Austin and Sons, Ltd., 1987.

——. "Convergence of Capital Adequacy in the UK and the US." *Bank of England Quarterly Bulletin* 27 (1987): 85–86.

——. "Bank of England Banking Act [1987] Report 1987/88." London, UK: Bank of England; Stephen Austin and Sons, Ltd., 1988.

——. "Bank of England Banking Act [1987] Report 1988/89." London, UK: Bank of England; Stephen Austin and Sons, Ltd., 1989.

——. "Bank of England Banking Act [1987] Report 1989/90." London, UK: Bank of England; Stephen Austin and Sons, Ltd., 1990.

——. "Bank of England Banking Act [1987] Report 1990/91." London, UK: Bank of England; Stephen Austin and Sons, Ltd., 1991.

——. "Bank of England Banking Act [1987] Report 1991/92." London, UK: Bank of England; Stephen Austin and Sons, Ltd., 1992.

——. "Bank of England Banking Act [1987] Report 1992/93." London, UK: Bank of England; Stephen Austin and Sons, Ltd., 1993.

——. "Bank of England Banking Act [1987] Report 1993/94." London, UK: Bank of England; Stephen Austin and Sons, Ltd., 1994.

——. "Bank of England Banking Act [1987] Report 1994/95." London, UK: Bank of England; Stephen Austin and Sons, Ltd., 1995.

——. "Bank of England Banking Act [1987] Report 1995/96." London, UK: Bank of England; Pillans & Wilson Greenaway, 1996.

——. "Bank of England Banking Act [1987] Report 1996/97." London, UK: Bank of England; Pillans & Wilson Greenaway, 1997.

——. "Bank of England Banking Act [1987] Report 1997/98." London, UK: Bank of England; Pillans & Wilson Greenaway, 1998.

Bank for International Settlements. "Recent Innovations in International Banking." Basel, CH: Bank for International Settlements, 1986.

——. *Press Release on Market Risk*. Press Release. Basel, CH: Bank for International Settlements, 10 December 1996.

——. "OTC Derivatives: Settlement Procedures and Counterparty Risk Management: Report by the Committee on Payment and Settlement Systems and the

Euro-currency Standing Committee of the Central Banks of the Group of Ten Countries." Basel, CH: Bank for International Settlements, 1998.
——. "The Global OTC Derivatives Market at End-June 2001: Second Part of the Triennial Central Bank Survey of Foreign Exchange and Derivative Market Activity." Basel, CH: Bank for International Settlements, 2001.
——. "Multidisciplinary Working Group on Enhanced Disclosure: Final Report to Basel Committee on Banking Supervision, Committee on the Global Financial System of the G-10 Central Banks, International Association of Insurance Supervisors, International Organisation of Securities Commissions." Basel, CH: Bank for International Settlements, 2001.
——. "Triennial Central Bank Survey of Foreign Exchange and Derivatives Market Activity in 2001." Basel, CH: Bank for International Settlements, 2002.
——. "Triennial Central Bank Survey of Foreign Exchange and Derivatives Market Activity in 2004." Basel, CH: Bank for International Settlements, 2005.
Banking World, "Barings' Collapse." vol. 13, no. 4 (1995): 16.
Barbash, Fred. "Huge Losses Sing Bank in London." *Washington Post*, 27 February 1995.
Barker, Philip. *Michel Foucault: An Introduction*. Edinburgh, UK: Edinburgh University Press, 1998.
Barovick, Richard. "Covering Bonds in New Markets." *Journal of Commerce*, 23 May 2000.
Barrass, Samantha. Senior Associate, Markets and Exchanges Division, Financial Services Authority. Interview by author. London, UK, 2 November 1999.
Bartolini, Leonardo and Lorenzo Giorgianni. *Excess Volatility of Exchange Rates with Unobservable Fundamentals*, Staff Reports No. 103. New York, NY: Federal Reserve Bank of New York (April 2000): 1–26.
Basel Committee on Banking Supervision. "Consolidated Supervision of Banks' International Activities." In *Compendium of documents produced by the Basel Committee on Banking Supervision*. Vol. I. Basel, CH: Bank for International Settlements, 1979.
——. "Supervision of Banks' Foreign Exchange Positions." In *Compendium of documents produced by the Basel Committee on Banking Supervision*. Vol. I. Basel, CH: Bank for International Settlements, 1980.
——. "Principles for the Supervision of Banks' Foreign Establishments." In *Compendium of documents produced by the Basel Committee on Banking Supervision*. Vol. III. Basel, CH: Bank for International Settlements, 1983.
——. "The Management of Banks' Off-Balance-Sheet Exposures (March 1986)." In *Compendium of documents produced by the Basel Committee on Banking Supervision*. Vols. I–III. Basel, CH: Bank for International Settlements, 1986.
——. "International Convergence of Capital Measurement and Capital Standards." *Basel Committee Publication No. 4*. Basel, CH: Bank for International Settlements, 1988.
——. "Minimum Standards for the Supervision of International Banking Groups and Their Cross-Border Establishments." In *Compendium of documents produced by the Basel Committee on Banking Supervision*. Vol. III. Basel, CH: Bank for International Settlements, 1992.
——. "The Supervisory Treatment of Market Risk." Basel, CH: Bank for International Settlements, 1993.
——. "Risk Management Guidelines for Derivatives (July 1994)." In *Compendium of Documents Produced by the Basel Committee on Banking Supervision*. Vol. I–III. Basel, CH: Bank for International Settlements, 1994.

Basel Committee on Banking Supervision & Offshore Group of Banking Supervisors. "The Supervision of Cross-Border Banking." Basel, CH: Bank for International Settlements, 1996.

——. "Explanatory Note: Modification of the Basel Capital Accord of July 1988, as amended in January 1996." Press Release. 19 September 1997.

——. "Framework for Internal Control Systems in Banking Organisations." *Basel Committee Publication No. 40*. Basel, CH: Bank for International Settlements, 1998.

——. "Banks' Interaction with Highly Leveraged Institutions." *Basel Committee Publication No. 45*. Basel, CH: Bank for International Settlements, 1999.

——. "Consultative Paper: A New Capital Adequacy Framework." Basel, CH: Bank for International Settlements, 1999a.

——. "Letter from William J. McDonough to International Federation of Accountants, Re: Code of Ethics for Professional Accountants." Basel, CH: Bank for International Settlements, 2000.

——. "History of the Basel Committee and its Membership." In *Compendium of Documents Produced by the Basel Committee on Banking Supervision*. Vol. I. Basel, CH: Bank for International Settlements, 2001.

——. "Internal Audit in Banks and the Supervisor's Relationship with Auditors." *Basel Committee Publication No. 84*. Basel, CH: Bank for International Settlements, 2001a.

——. "Letter from William J. McDonough to IAPC Review Task Force – International Federation of Accountants, Re: Report and Recommendations from the IAPC Review Task Force." Basel, CH: Bank for International Settlements, 2001b.

Basel Committee on Banking Supervision & International Federation of Accountants. "The Relationship between Banking Supervisors and Banks' External Auditors." Basel, CH: Bank for International Settlements, 2001.

Basel Committee on Banking Supervision & International Organization of Securities Commissions. "Review of Issues Relating to Highly Leveraged Institutions (HLIs)." *Basel Committee Publication No. 79*. Basel, CH: Bank for International Settlements, 2001.

Basel Committee on Banking Supervision & Offshore Group of Banking Supervisors. "The Supervision of Cross-Border Banking." Basel, CH: Bank for International Settlements, 1996.

Bataille, Georges. *Theory of Religion*. Translated by Robert Hurley. New York, NY: Zone Books, 1992.

Beattie, Alan. "Banks Lacking Data on Hedge Funds They Lend To." *Financial Times*, 23 March 2001.

Behrmann, Neil. "Bank of England to Lose Its Supervisory Role." *Business Times* (Singapore), 22 May 1997.

Bennett, Neil. "Bankers Tighten Rules in Fight Against Fraud." *Times*, 7 July 1992.

——. "G30 Calls for Tighter Control of Trading in Derivatives." *Times*, 22 July 1993.

——. "The Week the Barings Reaped Its Own Seeds of Disaster." *Times*, 4 March 1995.

——. "Authorities Told Barings It Was At Risk of Collapse." *Times*, 6 March 1995.

Bernstein, Edward M. "The Making and Remaking of the Bretton Woods Institutions." In *The Bretton Woods-GATT System: Retrospect and Prospect after Fifty Years*, edited by Orin Kirshner. Armonk, NY: M.E. Sharpe, 1996.

Bernstein, Peter L. *Against the Gods: The Remarkable Story of Risk*. New York, NY: John Wiley and Sons, Inc., 1996.

Bessis, Joël. *Risk Management in Banking*. Chichester, UK: John Wiley and Sons, Ltd., 1998.

Bevan, Robert L. "Risk-Based Capital." *United States Banker* 94, no. 4 (1988): 60.

Bide, Paul. "Flight to Quality at the Core of Widening Spreads." *Australian Financial Review*, 27 December 1997.

Blanden, Michael. "Can the Risks Be Seen?" *Banker* 147, no. 855 (1997): 32–37.

Blustein, Paul. *The Chastening: Inside the Crisis that Rocked the Global Financial System and Humbled the IMF.* New York, NY: Public Affairs, 2001.

——. "Dreams Tumble with the Rupiah; Indonesia's Workers Put Hopes for a Better Life on Hold." *Washington Post*, 23 January 1998.

——. "Worries Grow About Indonesia; US, IMF Officials Fear Unrest Could Spell Financial Trouble for Asian Neighbors." *Washington Post*, 7 March 1998.

Bolger, Andrew. "African Insurance Initiative Aims to Boost Trade." *Financial Times*, 7 August 2001.

Borch, Karl. *Economics of Insurance*. Edited and completed by Knut K. Aase and Agnar Sandmo. Amsterdam, Netherlands: Elsevier Science Publishers, B.V., 1990.

Borio, Claudio E.V. and Renato Filosa. "The Changing Borders of Banking: Trends and Implications." *BIS Economic Papers* 43. Basel, CH: Bank for International Settlements, Monetary and Economic Department, 1994.

Borio, Claudio, Craig Furfine and Philip Lowe. "Procyclicality of the Financial System and Financial Stability: Issues and Policy Options." *BIS Papers* 1. Basel, CH: Bank for International Settlements, 2001.

Boughton, James M. *Silent Revolution: The International Monetary Fund, 1979–1989*. Washington, D.C.: International Monetary Fund, 2001.

Boyd, John H., Sungkyu Kwak, and Bruce Smith. "The Real Output Losses Associated with Modern Banking Crises." *Journal of Money, Credit, and Banking* 37, no. 6 (December 2005): 977–99.

Boyer, Robert. *The Regulation School: A Critical Introduction*. Translated by Crain Charney. New York, NY: Columbia University Press, 1990.

Bradsher, Keith. "Asia's Long Road Back." *The New York Times*, 28 June 2007.

Brady, Simon. "Basel Turns the Screw." *Euromoney*, September 1990.

Brealey, Richard A. and Stewart A. Myers. *Principles of Corporate Finance*. 4th edn., international edn. New York, NY: McGraw Hill, Inc., 1991.

Breen, Stephen and Bob Newton. "Far East Hunt for Rogue Barings Dealer Goes On." *Scotsman*, 1 March 1995.

Bunker, Ted. "Power Grab Threatens OTC Derivatives Market." *Boston Herald*, 22 June 1998.

Burnside, Craig, Marin Eichenbaum and Sergio Rebelo. "What Caused the Recent Asian Currency Crises." In *The Asian Financial Crisis: Origins, Implications and Solutions*, edited by William C. Hunter, George G. Kaufman and Thomas H. Kreuger. Boston, MA: Kluwer Academic Publishers, 1999.

Business World, "Commentary: The Leaders They Deserve." 13 November 2000.

Callear, Mildred O. "'Corporate Welfare' that Isn't?" *Washington Post*, 11 May 1997.

Callelo, David and Susan Strange. "Money and World Politics." In *Paths to International Political Economy*, edited by Susan Strange. London, UK: George Allen and Unwin, 1984.

Callon, Michel. "Some Elements of a Sociology of Translation: Domestication of the Scallops and the Fishermen of St. Brieuc Bay." In *Power, Action and Belief: A*

New Sociology of Action? Edited by John Law. London, UK: Routledge and Kegan Paul, 1986.

——. "Actor Network Theory – the Market Test." In *Actor Network Theory and After*, edited by John Law and John Hassard. Oxford, UK: Blackwell Publishers, 1999.

Calomiris, Charles W. and Robert E. Litan. "Financial Regulation in a Global Marketplace." *Brookings-Wharton Papers on Financial Services*, 2000.

Camdessus, Michel. "Stable and Efficient Financial Systems for the 21st Century: A Quest for Transparency and Standards." Working paper, International Organization of Securities Commissions, Lisbon, Portugal, 25 May 1999.

Cameron, Rondo E. *A Concise Economic History of the World: From Paleolithic Times to the Present*. New York, NY: Oxford University Press, 1989.

Cerney, Philip. "The Dynamics of Financial Globalization." *Policy Sciences* 27 (1994): 319–42.

——. "Globalization and the Changing Logic of Collective Action." *International Organization* 49 (1995): 595–625.

Chadha, Bankim, *et al. Emerging Market Financing: Quarterly Report on Developments and Prospects*, Second Quarter 2000. Washington, D.C.: International Monetary Fund, 2000.

——. *Emerging Market Financing: Quarterly Report on Developments and Prospects*, Third Quarter 2000. Washington, D.C.: International Monetary Fund, 2000a.

——. *Emerging Market Financing: Quarterly Report on Developments and Prospects*, February 13, 2001. Washington, D.C.: International Monetary Fund, 2001.

——. *Emerging Market Financing: Quarterly Report on Developments and Prospects*, May 10, 2001. Washington, D.C.: International Monetary Fund, 2001a.

——. *Emerging Market Financing: Quarterly Report on Developments and Prospects*, August 8, 2001. Washington, D.C.: International Monetary Fund, 2001b.

——. *Emerging Market Financing: Quarterly Report on Developments and Prospects*, November 14, 2001. Washington, D.C.: International Monetary Fund, 2001c.

Chapman, Alger B. "International Securities Regulation in a Global Electronic Environment." In *Innovation and Technology in the Markets: A Reordering of the World's Capital Market Systems*, edited by Daniel R. Siegel. London, UK: McGraw-Hill Book Co., 1990.

Chen, Zhou. "Speculative Market Structure and the Collapse of an Exchange Rate Mechanism." In *LSE Financial Markets Group Discussion Paper Series* 202. London, UK: London School of Economics, 1995.

Chicago Sun-Times. "Fed, CFTC Chiefs Air Differences on Regulating Derivatives Trade." 24 July 1998.

Ching, Frank "Social Impact of the Regional Financial Crisis," Asia Society (February 1999) http://www.asiasociety.org/publications/update_crisis_ching.html (accessed June 20, 2007).

Chorafas, Dimitris N. *Risk Management in Financial Services*. London, UK: Butterworths, 1990.

Chote, Robert. "More Cash Urged for World Bank Risk Unit." *Financial Times*, 17 September 1997.

Cocheo, Steve "Is Your Bank Ready for a Shift in Gears?" *ABA Banking Journal*, November 1998.

Cohen, Benjamin J. "Phoenix Risen: The Resurrection of Global Finance." *World Politics* 48 (1996): 268–96.

Committee on the Global Financial System. "Foreign Direct Investment in the Financial Sector of Emerging Market Economies." Report submitted by a Working Group established by the Committee on the Global Financial System. Basel, CH: Bank for International Settlements, March 2004.

Confidential Interview. Interview with author. London, UK, 3 November 1999.

Corrigan, Tracy. "Committee Publishes Supervision Principles." *Financial Times*, 29 October 1992.

——. "SEC and Regulators Deadlocked Over Capital Requirements." *Financial Times*, 30 October 1992.

——. "Banks Offer Lesson in Regulation – Derivatives." *Financial Times*, 7 July 1994.

Cox, Robert W. "Global Restructuring: Making Sense of the Changing International Political Economy." In *Political Economy and the Changing Global Order*, edited by Richard Stubbs and Geoffrey R.D. Underhill. New York, NY: St. Martin's Press, 1994.

Cozens, Diane. "Basel Guidelines on Innovative Tier 1 Capital Instruments." *Compliance Monitor*, March 1999.

Crane, David. "Time to Review Role, Resources of IMF." *Toronto Star*, 13 January 1998.

Dale, Richard. *International Banking Deregulation: The Great Banking Experiment*. Oxford, UK: Blackwell Publishers, 1992.

——. *Risk and Regulation in Global Securities Markets*. Chichester, UK: John Wiley and Sons, 1996.

Dalglish, Brenda. "A High Stakes Game." *Maclean's* 107, no. 22 (1994): 20.

Daripa, Arupratan and Simone Varotto. "Value at Risk and Precommitment: Approaches to Market Risk Regulation." *Economic Policy Review* 4, no. 3 (1998): 137–43.

Davis, E.P. "Portfolio Behaviour of the Non-Financial Private Sectors in the Major Economies." In *BIS Economic Papers* 17. Basel, CH: Bank for International Settlements, Monetary and Economic Department, 1986.

Davis, Monroe. "Capital Ratios Are Only One Step." *Banker* 137, no. 735 (1987): 55–59.

Day, Kathleen. "Top Regulator Was Aware of Fund's Debt." *Washington Post*, 18 November 1998.

De Grauwe, Paul. *International Money: Post-War Trends and Theories*. Oxford, UK: Oxford University Press, 1989.

Denny, Charlotte. "Warning of 'Lost Decade' for the Poor." *Guardian*, 27 April 1999.

Derivatives Week. "Official Calls for Basel to Address Credit Swaps." 24 March 1997.

Deutsche Bundesbank. "Report of the Deutsche Bundesbank for the Year 1991." Frankfurt, DE: Deutsche Bundesbank, 1992.

De Vries, Margaret Garritsen. "The Bretton Woods Conference and the Birth of the International Monetary Fund." In *The Bretton Woods – GATT System: Retrospect and Prospect after Fifty Years*, edited by Orin Kirshner. Armonk, NY: M.E. Sharpe, Inc., 1996.

Diaconis, John S. "Political Risk Insurance: OPIC's Use of a "Fiduciary Agent to Facilitate Resolution of Subrogation Claims." *The International Lawyer*, 23, no. 271 (Spring 1989).

Diamond, Barbara B. and Mark P. Kollar. *24-hour Trading: The Global Network of Futures and Options Markets.* New York, NY: Wiley and Sons, 1989.

Dimson, Elroy and Paul Marsh. "The Debate on International Capital Requirements: Evidence on Equity Positions Risk for UK Securities Firms." City Research Project. London, UK: London Business School, 1994.

——. "Capital Requirements for Securities Firms." *Journal of Finance* 50, no. 3 (1995): 821–51.

Donovan, Patrick and Kevin Rafferty. "Initial Barings Panic is Over: Three Quarters of Rogue Contracts Find Buyers." *Guardian*,1 March 1995.

Dreyfus, Hubert L. and Paul Rabinow. *Michel Foucault: Beyond Structuralism and Hermeneutics.* Brighton, UK: Harvester Press Ltd., 1982.

Dunne, Nancy and Jeremy Grant. "OPIC Seeks to Boost Emerging Market." *Financial Times*, 6 November 1998.

Duran, Nicole. "Corporate Debt Led to Derivatives Profit Rise." *American Banker* 166, no. 117 (2001): 1.

Dyrberg, Torben Bech. *The Circular Structure of Power: Politics, Identity, Community.* London, UK: Verso Books, 1997.

Economist. "Tighter Belts: Securities Regulation." 5 October 1991.

——. "The Capital Handicap." 26 February 1994.

——. "Banking Regulations: A Brush with Basel." 16 September 1995.

——. "Capital Punishment." 12 April 1997.

——. "Long-term Sickness?" 3 October 1998.

——. "A New Approach to Financial Risk." 17 October 1998.

——. "Finance and Economics: Basel Bust." 15 April 2000.

Edwards, Ben. "Financial Centers, Border Control: Capital Moves Freely Between Financial Centres, but Businesses Do Not." *Economist*, 9 May 1998.

Eichengreen, Barry. *Globalizing Capital: A History of the International Monetary System.* Princeton, NJ: Princeton University Press, 1996.

Eichengreen, Barry, *et al.* "Hedge Funds and Financial Market Dynamics." Occasional Paper 166. Washington D.C.: International Monetary Fund, 1998.

Eichengreen, Barry, Andrew Rose, Charles Wyplosz, Bernard Dumas, and Axel Weber. "Exchange Market Mayhem: The Antecedents and Aftermath of Speculative Attacks." *Economic Policy*, no. 21 (October 1995): 249–312.

Evans, Michael. "The Classical Economists, Laissez-Faire and the State." In *The Market and the State: Studies in Interdependence*, edited by Michael Moran and Maurice Wright. New York, NY: St. Martin's Press, 1991.

Ewald, François. "Insurance and Risk." In *The Foucault Effect: Studies in Governmentality*, edited by Graham Burchell, Colin Gordon and Peter Miller. London, UK: Harvester Wheatsheaf, 1991.

Fabozzi, Frank J. and Franco Modigliani. *Capital Markets: Institutions and Instruments.* 2nd edn. Upper Saddle River, NJ: Prentice Hall, 1996.

Farnsworth, Clyde H. "Insurer Offers Peru Proposal on Oil Claim." *New York Times*, 12 June 1989.

Federal Reserve Bank of New York. "The Foreign Exchange and Interest Rate Derivatives Market Survey: Turnover in the United States." New York, NY: Federal Reserve Bank of New York, 2001.

Federal Reserve System, Board of Governors. *85th Annual Report, 1998*. Washington, D.C.: Board of Governors of the Federal Reserve System Publication Services, 1998.

——. *86th Annual Report, 1999*. Washington, D.C.: Board of Governors of the Federal Reserve System, Publication Services, 1999.

Financial Services Authority. *Risk Based Approach to Supervision of Banks*. London, UK: Financial Services Authority Publications Department, 1998.

Financial Stability Forum. "Report of the Working Group on Highly Leveraged Institutions." Basel, CH: Bank for International Settlements, 2000.

——. "Progress in Implementing the Recommendations of the Working Group on Highly Leveraged Institutions (HLIs): A Note to the FSF by the Chairman of the HLI Working Group." Basel, CH: Bank for International Settlements, 2001.

——. "The FSF Recommendations and Concerns Raised by Highly Leveraged Institutions (HLIs): An Assessment." Basel, CH: Bank for International Settlements, 2002.

Financial Times. "Trouble at the Regulators' Ball." 30 October 1992.

——. "The Barings Crisis: Clarke Promises 'Rigorous' Regulatory Review – Chancellor of the Exchequer's Statement to the House of Commons." 28 February 1995.

——. "The Barings Crisis – Why it Happened." 4 March 1995.

——. "Lex Column: Financial Regulation." 21 May 1996.

——. "OPIC Comes Under Ideological Fire," 6 March 1997.

——. "More Equity." 8 April 1998.

——. "Soul-Searching by Regulators after LTCM: The Increasingly Mainstream View is that Many Leveraged Funds Have Grown Large Enough to Pose a Systemic Risk." 28 September 1998.

Fleming, Steward. "Taking the Risk out of Trading with Africa." *The Evening Standard* (London), 2 August 2001.

Fletcher, Pascal. "Havana Signs Insurance Deal." *Financial Times*, 7 November 1998.

Foley, Bernard J. *Capital Markets*. New York, NY: St. Martin's Press, 1991.

Foucault, Michel. *The Order of Things: An Archaeology of the Human Sciences*. New York, NY: Vintage Books, 1970.

——. *The Archaeology of Knowledge & The Discourse on Language*. Translated by A. M. Sheridan Smith. New York, NY: Pantheon Books, 1972.

——. *Language, Counter-memory, Practice: Selected Essays and Interviews*. Edited by Donald F. Bouchard. Translated by Donald F. Bouchard and Sherry Simon. Ithaca, NY: Cornell University Press, 1977.

——. *Discipline and Punish: The Birth of the Prison*. Translated by Alan Sheridan. New York, NY: Vintage Books, 1979.

——. *The History of Sexuality, vol. I: An Introduction*. Translated by Robert Hurley. New York, NY: Vintage Books, 1990.

——. "Governmentality." In *The Foucault Effect: Studies in Governmentality*. Edited by Graham Burchell, Colin Gordon and Peter Miller. Chicago, IL: University of Chicago Press, 1991.

——. *Ethics: Subjectivity and Truth*, vol. 1 of *The Essential Works of Michel Foucault, 1954–1984*. Edited by Paul Rabinow. Translated by Robert Hurley, *et al.* London, UK: Allen Lane, 1997.

Frankel, S. Herbert. *Two Philosophies of Money*. New York, NY: St. Matin's Press, 1977.

Freeland, Charles. Deputy Secretary General, Basel Committee on Banking Supervision, Bank for International Settlements. Interview by author. Basel, CH, 14 January 2000.

Fromson, Brett D. "Bank Profits to Gauge Asian Impact; Earnings Reports Expected Today from Chase, Citicorp, J.P. Morgan." *Washington Post*, 20 January 1998.

——. "Asian Crisis Takes Toll on Three US Banks." *Washington Post*, 21 January 1998.

Froot, Kevin A. "Bank Capital and Risk Management." In proceedings, 7th Annual Risk Round Table. Geneva, Switzerland: International Financial Risk Institute, 2001.

Fuerbringer, Jonathan. "How Asian Currencies Tumbled So Quickly." *New York Times*, 10 December 1997.

Furash, Edward. "Risk Challenges and Opportunities" *Bank Management* 71, no. 3 (1995): 34–39.

Gapper, John. "The Barings Crisis: Why Did Directors Not Recognise the Risks?" *Financial Times*, 2 March 1995.

——. "George Warns on Bank Chain Reaction Collapses." *Financial Times*, 27 October 1995.

Gapper, John and Nicholas Denton. *All That Glitters: The Fall of Barings*. New York, NY: Penguin Books, 1997.

Gerth, Jeff and Richard W. Stevenson. "Inadequate Regulation Seen in Asia's Banking Crises." *New York Times*, 22 December 1997.

Giddens, Anthony. *Modernity and Self-Identity*. Cambridge, UK: Polity Press, 1991.

——. *Runaway World*. London, UK: Profile Books, 1999.

Gill, Stephen and David Law. *The Global Political Economy: Perspectives, Problems and Policies*. Baltimore, MD: Johns Hopkins University Press, 1988.

Glassman, James K. "Big Money: The Barings Bank Debacle; Nick Leeson's Legacy: Little People Can Still Make Big Waves." *Washington Post*, 1 March 1995.

Gledhill, Dan. "Creditors to Sue Bank of England; Barings Backlash over Weak Regulation." *Independent*, 27 February 2000.

Gold, Joseph. "Strengthening the Soft International Law of Exchange Arrangements." *American Journal of International Law* 77, no. 3 (1983): 443–89.

Goldstein, Morris. *The Asian Financial Crisis: Causes, Cures and Systemic Implications*. Washington, D.C.: Institute for International Economics, 1998.

Goldstein, Morris and Philip Turner. "Banking Crises in Emerging Economies: Origins and Policy Options." *BIS Economic Papers* 46. Basel, CH: Bank for International Settlements, Monetary and Economic Department (October 1996): 1–67.

Goodman, John B. *Monetary Sovereignty: The Politics of Central Banking in Western Europe*. Ithaca, NY: Cornell University Press, 1992.

Goodhart, Charles A.E. *Money, Information and Uncertainty*. 2nd edn. London, UK: Macmillan Press, 1989.

——. *The Central Bank and the Financial System*. London, UK: Macmillan Press, 1995.

Goodhart, Charles A.E., Philip Hartmann, David Llewellyn, Liliana Rojas-Suarez, and Steven Weisbrod. *Financial Regulation: Why, How and Where Now?* London, UK: Routledge Press, 1998.

Gordon, Colin. "Governmental Rationality: An Introduction." In *The Foucault Effect: Studies in Governmentality*. Edited by Graham Burchell, Colin Gordon and Peter Miller. London, UK: Harvester Wheatsheaf, 1991.

Gosselin, Peter G. "Indonesia Woes Darken Asian Comeback Prospects; After Brief Rebound, Region Faces Another Round of Declines." *Boston Globe*, 16 May 1998.

Gowa, Joanne. *Closing the Gold Window: Domestic Politics and the End of Bretton Woods.* Ithaca, NY: Cornell University Press, 1983.

Graham, George. "Regulators Stand Firm on Bank Rules." *Financial Terms*, 11 December 1996.

——. "Harassed Regulators Try to Draw the Line: Basel Accord Capital Adequacy Rules at Centre of Dispute." *Financial Times*, 6 April 1998.

——. "Fresh Drive to Reform Bank Capital Rules." *Financial Times*, 14 May 1999.

Green, Andres. "The European Capital Adequacy Directive: The Spirit and the Letter." *Credit World* 80, no. 3 (1998): 20–23.

Green, Meg. "As US Companies Increase Intenational Investing, Political Risk Insurers Find New Markets," *Best's Review* 104, no. 11 (2004): 54–57.

Gray, John. *Hayek on Liberty.* Oxford, UK: Basil Blackwell, 1984.

Gray, Simon and Joanna Place. "Financial Derivatives." In *Handbooks in Central Banking* 17. London, UK: Centre for Central Banking Studies, Bank of England, 1999.

Greenspan, Alan. "Moving with the Times: Need to Reform the Basel Accord of 1988." *Banker* 148, no. 867 (1998): 16–18.

Group of Thirty. "The Outlook for International Bank Lending: A Survey of Opinion Among Leading International Bankers." Edited by M. S. Mendelsohn. New York, NY: Group of Thirty, 1981.

——. "How Bankers See the World Financial Market." New York, NY: Group of Thirty, 1982.

——. "Risks in International Bank Lending." New York, NY: Group of Thirty, 1982a.

——. "Derivatives: Practices and Principles." Washington, D.C.: Group of Thirty, 1993.

——. "Derivatives: Practices and Principles, Appendix I: Working Papers." Washington, D.C.: Group of Thirty, 1993a.

Gupta, Sanjeev, Calvin McDonald, Christian Schiller, Marinus Verhoeven, *et al.* "Mitigating the Social Costs of the Asian Crisis." *Finance and Development*, vol. 35, no. 3 (September 1998): 18–21.

Hacking, Ian. *The Emergence of Probability: A Philosophical Study of Early Ideas about Probability*, Induction and Statistical Inference. Cambridge, UK: Cambridge University Press, 1975.

——. "The Archaeology of Foucault." In *Foucault: A Critical Reader*, edited by David Couzens Hay. Oxford, UK: Basil Blackwell, 1986.

——. *The Taming of Chance.* Cambridge, UK: Cambridge University Press, 1990.

Haggard, Stephen. "The Politics of the Asian Financial Crisis." *Journal of Democracy* 11, no. 2 (April 2000): 130–44.

Hahn, Tamar. "OPIC to Insure EM Mortgage-Backeds." *Emerging Markets Report*, 17 April 2000.

Hale, David. "It is a big mistake to Kill Bush's Trade Deal with Seoul." *The Financial Times*, 18 July 2007.

Hall, John A. and G. John Ikenberry. *The State.* Milton Keynes, UK: Open University Press, 1989.

Hall, William. "Supervisory Authorities Take a Fresh Look." *Financial Times*, 4 May 1982.

Hamdani, Kausar, Elise Liebers, and George Zanjani. "An Overview of Political Risk Insurance: Executive Summary." Report for the Federal Reserve Bank of

New York and Committee on the Global Financial System Working Group, May 2005.

Hamilton-Hart, Natasha. "Indonesia: Reforming the Institutions of Financial Governance." In *The Asian Financial Crisis and the Architecture of Global Finance*, edited by Gregory Noble and John Ravenhill. Cambridge, UK: Cambridge University Press, 2000.

Hansell, Saul and Kevin Muehring. "Why Derivatives Rattle Regulators." *Institutional Investor* 26, no. 10 (1992): 49–62.

Harris, William F. *The Interpretable Constitution*. Baltimore, MD: Johns Hopkins University Press, 1993.

Hayek, F.A. *Individualism and Economic Order*. Chicago, IL: Chicago University Press, 1948.

——. "Economic Freedom and Representative Government" 4th Wincott Memorial Lecture, Royal Society of Arts. Kent, UK: Institute of Economic Affairs, 1973.

——. *Denationalisation of Money: An Analysis of the Theory and Practice of Concurrent Currencies*. Lancing, UK: Institute of Economic Affairs, 1976.

——. *Economic Freedom*. Cambridge, MA: Basil Blackwell, 1991.

Helleiner, Eric. *States and the Reemergence of Global Finance: From Bretton Woods to the 1990s*. Ithaca, NY: Cornell University Press, 1994.

——. "From Bretton Woods to Global Finance: A World Turned Upside Down." In *Political Economy and the Changing Global Order*, edited by Richard Stubbs and Geoffrey R.D. Underhill. New York, NY: St. Martin's Press, 1994a.

——. "Sovereignty, Territoriality and the Globalization of Finance." In *States and Sovereignty in the Global Economy*, edited by David A. Smith, Dorothy J. Solinger and Steven C. Topik. London, UK: Routledge Press, 1999.

Hendricks, Darryl. "Evaluation of Value-at-Risk Models Using Historical Data Methods for Estimating Market Risk." *Federal Reserve Bank of New York Economic Policy Review* 2, no.1 (1996): 39–69.

Henwood, Doug. *Wall Street: How it Works and for Whom*. New York, NY: Verso Books, 1997.

Herde, Robert B. Market Policy Division, Deutsche Börse AG. Interview by author. Frankfurt, GER, 12 January 2000.

Hill, Patrice. "Clinton Helped Enron Finance Projects Abroad; Maintained Close Ties to Lay." *Washington Times*, 21 February 2002.

Hindess, Barry. "Politics and Liberation." In *The Later Foucault: Politics and Philosophy*, edited by Jeremy Moss. London, UK: Sage Publications, 1998.

Hirschman, Albert O. *The Strategy of Economic Development*. New Haven, CT: Yale University Press, 1958.

Hohler, Bob. "Trade-trip Firms Netted $5.5bn in Aid; Donated $2.3m to Democrats." *Boston Globe*, 30 March 1997.

Horsefield, J. Keith. *The International Monetary Fund 1945–1965: Twenty Years of International Monetary Cooperation*, vol. 1. Washington, DC: International Monetary Fund, 1969.

Hu, Henry T.C. "Misunderstood Derivatives: The Causes of Informational Failure and the Promise of Regulatory Incrementalism." *Yale Law Journal* 102, no. 6 (1993): 1457–1513.

Hudson, Alan C. "Off-shores On-shore: New Regulatory Spaces and Real Historical Places in the Landscape of Global Money." In *Money and the Space Economy*. Edited by Ron Martin. New York, NY: John Wiley & Sons, 1999.

Hughes, Duncan, Michael Lipin and Fung Wai-Kong. "Government Vows Vigilance After Acting on Currency Speculation Scare; Dollar Defense Cost US $1bn." *South China Morning Post*, 13 August 1997.

Ikenberry, G. John. "Conclusion: An Institutional Approach to American Foreign Economic Policy." *International Organization* 42, no. 1 (1988): 219–43.

——. "Rethinking the Origins of American Hegemony." *Political Science Quarterly* 104, no. 3 (1989): 375–400.

——. "A World Economy Restored: Expert Consensus and the Anglo-American Postwar Settlement." *International Organization* 46, no. 1 (1992): 289–321.

Ingham, Geoffrey. "States and Markets in the Production of World Money: Sterling and the Dollar." In *Money, Power and Space*, edited by Stuart Corbridge, Ron Martin and Nigel Thrift. Oxford, UK: Blackwell Publishers, 1994.

Institute of International Finance. "Report of the Task Force on Risk Assessment." Washington, D.C.: Institute of International Finance, 1999.

International Labour Organisation. "Crisis-Affected Peoples and Countries." Geneva, CH: International Labour Organisation, Recovery & Reconstruction Departments, 2001.

International Monetary Fund. "Managing Financial Risks in Indebted Developing Countries." *IMF Occasional Paper* 65. Edited by Donald J. Mathieson, David Folkerts-Landau, Timothy Lane, and Iqbal Zaidi. Washington, D.C.: International Monetary Fund, 1989.

——. *International Capital Markets: Developments and Prospects.* Edited by Mark Allen, *et al.* Washington, D.C.: International Monetary Fund, 1990.

——. *International Capital Markets: Part II. Systemic Issues in International Finance.* World Economic and Financial Surveys Series. Edited by Morris Goldstein and David Folkerts-Landau. Washington, D.C.: International Monetary Fund, 1993.

——. *International Capital Markets: Developments, Prospects, and Policy Issues.* World Economic and Financial Surveys Series. Edited by Morris Goldstein and David Folkerts-Landau. Washington, D.C.: International Monetary Fund, 1994.

——. "Offshore Banking: An Analysis of Micro- and Macro-Prudential Issues." Working Paper. Washington, D.C.: International Monetary Fund, 1999.

——. *World Economic Outlook*. Washington, D.C.: International Monetary Fund, 1999a.

——. *International Capital Markets: Developments, Prospects, and Policy Issues.* World Economic and Financial Surveys Series. Edited by Donald J. Mathieson and Garry J. Schinasi. Washington, D.C.: International Monetary Fund, 2000.

——. "Measures to Limit the Offshore Use of Currencies: Pros and Cons." Working Paper. Washington, D.C.: International Monetary Fund, 2001.

——. "Financial Sector Regulation and Supervision: The Case of Small Pacific Island Countries." Policy Discussion Paper. Washington, D.C.: International Monetary Fund, 2001a.

International Monetary Fund, Monetary and Exchange Affairs Department. "Offshore Financial Centers: IMF Background Paper." Washington, D.C.: International Monetary Fund, 2000.

——. "Offshore Financial Centers: The Role of the IMF." Washington, D.C.: International Monetary Fund 2000a.

Iskander, Samer. "Put Option Triggered of IFCT Bond." *Financial Times*, 8 January 1998.

Jack, Andrew. "France to Share Risk on China Guarantees." *Financial Times*, 23 March 1998.

Jackson, Patricia, *et al.* "Capital Requirements and Bank Behavior: The Impact of the Basel Accord." *Working Papers No. 1*. Basel, CH: Bank for International Settlements, 1999.

Jakarta Post, "Rupiah Attacked," 23 July 1997.

James, Harold. *International Monetary Cooperation Since Bretton Woods*. Washington, D.C.: International Monetary Fund and Oxford University Press, 1996.

Jerusalem Post. "Bonfire of the Vanities." 1 March 1995.

Jones, Sidney. "Social Cost of Asian Crisis." *Financial Times*, 26 January 1998.

Journal of Commerce, "AIG in Joint Venture to Offer Risk Cover," 31 March 2000.

Journal of Commerce. "OPIC Signs Pact with Vietnam," 23 March 1998.

—— "Prospect for Investment Insurance Seen Improving." 20 August 1997.

Kahler, Miles. "Capital Flows and Financial Crises." In *Capital Flows and Financial Crises*, edited by Miles Kahler. Manchester, UK: Manchester University Press, 1998.

——. "The New International Financial Architecture and Its Limits." In *The Asian Financial Crisis and the Architecture of Global Finance*, edited by Gregory Noble and John Ravenhill. Cambridge, UK: Cambridge University Press, 2000.

Kaletsky, Anatole. "How Mr. Soros Made a Billion by Betting Against the Pound." *Times*, 26 October 1992.

Kapstein, Ethan B. "Resolving the Regulator's Dilemma: International Coordination of Banking Regulation." *International Organization* 43, no. 2 (1989): 323–47.

——. *Governing the Global Economy: International Finance and the State*. Cambridge, MA: Harvard University Press, 1994.

——. "Supervising International Banks: Origins and Implications of the Basel Accord." In *Global Risk Based Capital Regulations*. Vol. 1. Edited by Charles A. Stone and Anne Zissu. Burr Ridge, IL: Irwin Professional Publishing, 1994a.

——. "Shockproof: The End of Financial Crisis." *Foreign Affairs*, 75, no. 1 (January/February 1996): 2–8.

Kay, William. "Jury's Still Out on the Hedge Fund." *Independent*, 7 July 2001.

Keely, James F. "Toward a Foucauldian Analysis of International Regimes." *International Organization* 44 (1990): 83–105.

Kennedy, Dominic. "Nick Leeson in German Court Today." *Times*, 3 March 1995.

Ketkar, Suhas and Dilip Ratha. "Securitization of Future Flow Receivables: A Useful Tool for Developing Countries." *Finance and Development*, 38, no. 1 (March 2001).

Keynes, John Maynard. *The General Theory of Employment Interest and Money*. Vol. VII of *The Collected Writings of John Maynard Keynes*. London, UK: Macmillan; London: Cambridge University Press for the Royal Economic Society, 1973.

——. *A Treatise on Probability*. Vol. VIII of *The Collected Writings of John Maynard Keynes*. London, UK: Macmillan Press for the Royal Economic Society, 1973a.

Khan, Saleheen, Faridul Islam, and Syed Ahmed. "The Asian Crisis: An Economic Analysis of the Causes." *Journal of Developing Areas* 39, no. 1, (Fall 2005): 169–90.

Kim, Seung-Kyung and John Finch, "Living with Rhetoric, Living Against Rhetoric: Korean Families and the IMF." *Korean Studies* 26, no. 1 (2002): 120–39.

Kindleberger, Charles P. *International Capital Movements: Based on the Marshall Lectures given at the University of Cambridge 1985*. Cambridge, UK: Cambridge University Press, 1987.

Knapp, G.F. *The State Theory of Money*. Abridged English edition. Edited and translated by H.M. Lucas and J. Bonar. London, UK: Royal Economic Society, 1924.

Knight, Frank H. *Risk, Uncertainty and Profit*. Reprint of Scarce Texts in Economic and Political Science 16. London, UK: London School of Economic and Political Science, 1948.

Knight, Jerry. "Agencies Try to Block Study on Derivatives." *Washington Post*, 6 June 1998.

Knowles, James, Ernesto M. Pernia, and Mary Racelis. "Social Consequences of the Financial Crisis in Asia: The Deeper Crisis." *Economics and Development Resource Center Briefing Notes*, no. 16, Manila, Philippines: Asian Development Bank (July 1999): 1–17.

Krantz, Thomas. Deputy Secretary General, Fédération Internationale des Bourses de Valeurs. Interview by author. London, UK, 8 November 1999.

Krasner, Stephen D. "Globalization and Sovereignty." In *States and Sovereignty in the Global Economy*, edited by David A. Smith, Dorothy J. Solinger and Steven C. Topik. London, UK: Routledge Press, 1999.

Kristoff, Nicholas D. and Edward Wyatt. "Who Went Under in the World's Sea of Cash." *New York Times*, 15 February 1999.

Krugman, Paul. "The Fall and Rise of Developmental Economics." In *Rethinking the Development Experience*, edited by Lloyd Rodwin and Donald Schön. Washington, D.C.: Brookings Institution, 1994.

——. "Rupiah Rasputin: A Currency Board Won't Solve Indonesia's Woes." *Fortune*, 13 April 1998.

Kumar, Krishan. *Utopia and Anti-Utopia in Modern Times*. Cambridge, MA: Basil Blackwell, 1987.

Kurzweil, Edith. *The Age of Structuralism: Levi-Strauss to Foucault*. New York, NY: Columbia University Press, 1980.

Kynge, James. "China Calls on US to Lift Trade Sanctions at Summit." *Financial Times*, 23 June 1998.

Labaton, Stephen and Timothy O'Brien. "Financiers Plan to Put Controls on Derivatives." *New York Times*, 7 January 1999.

Lacey, Mary. "World Briefing Africa: Insurance For Risky Region." *New York Times*, 21 August 2001

Lamfalussy, Alexander. "Letters to the Editor – Asian Debt: The Signs Were There for All to See." *Financial Times*, 13 February 1998.

Landler, Mark. "Indonesian Riot Police Open Fire at Protests, Killing Six Students." *New York Times*, 13 May 1998.

——. "Riots Break Out in Jakarta After Shooting of Students." *New York Times*, 14 May 1998.

——. "Unrest in Indonesia: An Overview." *New York Times*, 15 May 1998.

Lapper, Richard. "Basel Accord to Include Market Risk." *Financial Times*, 11 April 1995.

——. "Regulators Aim to Gird the Globe: Enthusiasm is Growing for an International Framework for Supervising Financial Markets." *Financial Markets*, 10 July 1995.

——. "Survey of Derivatives: Evolution in the Face of Disaster – After a Series of Financial Losses Dealers in Derivatives Have Become More Cautious." *Financial Times*, 16 November 1995.

Latin Finance. "Locals Seek Protection." July/August 2007.

Latour, Bruno. "The Powers of Association." In *Power, Action and Belief: A New Sociology of Action*, edited by John Law. London, UK: Routledge and Kegan Paul, 1986.

Latter, Tony. "The Causes and Management of Banking Crises." In *Handbooks in Central Banking* 12. London, UK: Centre for Central Banking Studies, Bank of England, 1997.

Law, John. "After ANT: Complexity, Naming and Topology." In *Actor Network Theory and After*, edited by John Law and John Hassard. Oxford, UK: Blackwell Publishers, 1999.

Law, John and John Hassard, eds. *Actor Network Theory and After*. Oxford, UK: Blackwell Publishers, 1999.

Leander, Ellen. "Is OPIC Funding Corporate Welfare?" *Treasury & Risk Management*, 7, no. 2 (March 1997).

Levinsohn, James, Steven Barry and Jed Friedman. "Impacts of the Indonesian Economic Crisis: Price Changes and the Poor." Working Paper 7194. Cambridge, MA: National Bureau of Economic Research, 1999.

Lewis, Alfred and Gioia Pescetto. *EU and US Banking in the 1990s*. San Diego, CA: Academic Press, Inc., 1996.

Leyshon, Andrew and Nigel Thrift. *Money Space: Geographies of Monetary Transformation*. New York, NY: Routledge Press, 1997.

Lindblom, Charles E. *Politics and Markets: The World's Political-Economic Systems*. New York, NY: Basic Books, Inc. Publishers, 1977.

Lissakers, Karin. "The IMF and the Asian Crisis: A View from the Executive Board." In *The Asian Financial Crisis: Origins, Implications and Solutions*, edited by William C. Hunter, George G. Kaufman and Thomas H. Kreuger. Boston, MA: Kluwer Academic Publishers, 1999.

Lohr, Steve. "BCCI's Fall Shows Gaps in Policing Global Fraud." *New York Times*, 14 July 1991.

Longman, Phillip J., Jack Egan, Pamela Sherrid, and Fred Vogelstein. "Close to the Brink." *U.S. News & World Report* 125, no. 13 (5 October 1998).

Lomax, David F. *London Markets after the Financial Services Act*. London, UK: Butterworth and Co., 1987.

MacDonald, Ronald. "Consolidated Supervision of Banks." In *Handbooks in Central Banking* 15. London, UK: Centre for Central Banking Studies, Bank of England, 1997.

MacKenzie, Donald. "How a Superportfolio Emerges: Long Term Capital Management and the Sociology of Arbitrage." In *The Sociology of Financial Markets*. Edited by Karin Knorr Cetina and Alex Preda. Oxford, UK: Oxford University Press, 2005.

Marsh, David. *The Bundesbank: The Bank the Rules Europe*. Great Britain: Mandarin Paperback, 1992.

Martinson, Jane. "International Lenders to Face More Detailed Regulation." *Guardian*, 17 January 2001.

Matusow, Allen J. *Nixon's Economic Policy: Booms, Busts, Dollars and Votes*. Lawrence, KS: University of Kansas Press, 1998.

McCarthy, Ed. "Derivatives Revisited." *Journal of Accountancy* 189, no. 5 (2000): 35.

McCloskey, Donald N. *Knowledge and Persuasion in Economics*. Cambridge, UK: Cambridge University Press, 1994.

McCracken, Sheelagh. "Introduction" and "Confronting the Legal Dimension." In *Derivatives: The Risks the Remain*, edited by Elizabeth Sheedy and Sheelagh McCracken. New South Wales, AU: Allen Unwin/Macquarie Series in Applied Finance, 1997.

McKinnon, Ronald I. *Money and Capital in Economic Development*. Washington, D. C.: Brookings Institution, 1973.

McNay, Lois. *Foucault: A Critical Introduction*. Cambridge, UK: Polity Press, 1994.

McRae, Hamish. "Securitisation: Comments on BIS Annual Report." *Guardian*, 11 June 1985.

Medlin, John G. Jr. "A Timely Discussion of Capital Requirements." *Journal of Lending and Credit Risk Management* 80, no. 6 (1998): 54–57.

Mehta, Harish. "Massive Capital Outflows Mean Bumpy Ride to Recovery for Thailand." *Business Times* (Singapore), 17 September 1999.

Mehta, Kamalakshi. "Interview – J.P. Morgan Touts New Credit Risk Tool." *Reuters Financial News Service*, 9 April 1997.

Meister, Edgar. "Supervising the Quantitative and Qualitative Aspects of Derivatives." *Journal of Lending and Credit Risk Management* 78, no. 8 (1996): 12–22.

Merquior, J. G. *Foucault*. 2nd edn. London, UK: Fontana Press, 1991.

Miller, Merton H. *Financial Innovations and Market Volatility*. Oxford, UK: Basil Blackwell Ltd., 1991.

Mishkin, Frederic S. *The Next Great Globalization: How Disadvantaged Nations Can Harness Their Financial Systems to Get Rich*. Princeton, NJ: Princeton University Press, 2006.

Mitchell, Timothy. "The Limits of the State: Beyond Statist Approaches and Their Critics." *American Political Science Review* 85 (1991): 77–96.

Mitchie, Jonathan and John Grieve Smith, eds. *Global Instability: The Political Economy of World Economic Governance*. London, UK: Routledge Press, 1999.

Miura, Junichi. "Crisis Clarified Risky Operations of Hedge Funds." *Daily Yomiuri*, 30 October 1998.

Monetary Authority of Singapore. "Hedge Funds." Singapore: Monetary Authority of Singapore, 1999.

Mongelluzzo, Bill. "Signs of Recovery: After Two Years of Decline, Volume is Rising in Trade Between the United States and the West Coast of South America." *Journal of Commerce*, 9 April 2001.

Moon, H.P., H.H. Lee, and G.J. Yoo. "Social Impact of the Financial Crisis in Korea: Economic Framework." Paper presented at the Finalization Conference on Assessing the Social Impact of the Financial Crisis in Selected Asian Developing Economies, Asian Development Bank, Manila, Philippines (17–18 June 1999).

Moran, Michael. *The Politics of the Financial Services Revolution: The USA, UK and Japan*. London, UK: Macmillan Press Ltd., 1991.

——. *The Politics of Banking: The Strange Case of Credit Control*. New York, NY: St. Martin's Press, 1984.

——. "Politics, Banks and Markets: An Anglo-American Comparison." *Political Studies* 32 (1984): 173–89.

——. *The Politics of Banking: The Strange Case of Credit Control*. 2nd edn. London, UK: Macmillan Press Ltd., 1986.

——. "Theories of Regulation and Changes in Regulation: The Case of Financial Markets." *Political Studies* 34 (1986): 185–201.

——. *The Politics of the Financial Services Revolution: The USA, UK and Japan*. London, UK: Macmillan Press Ltd., 1991.

Moss, David A. *When All Else Fails: Governments as the Ultimate Risk Manager*. Cambridge, MA: Harvard University Press, 2002.

Mullins, Ronald G. "World Bank Unit in Deal with Private Reinsurer." *Journal of Commerce*, 25 April 1997.

Mydans, Seth. "Malaysia Is Ready to Inflict its own Economic Medicine." *New York Times*, 16 December 1997.

——. "Once-Buoyant Hopes Sink in Indonesia's Slump." *New York Times*, 13 December 1997.

——. "Thailand's Economic Crash Crushes Working Poor." *New York Times*, 15 December 1997.

——. "Newly Jobless – and Newly Angry – Threaten Indonesia's Stability." *New York Times*, 29 January 1998.

——. "Indonesia Turns Its Chinese into Scapegoats." *New York Times*, 2 February 1998.

Nantha, Francis C. "Labuan Offered as Location for Proposed Trading Center," *New Straits Times* (Malaysia), 10 October 1997.

New York Stock Exchange. *The Fact Book*. New York, NY: New York Stock Exchange, 2000.

New York Times. "Currency Markets: Speculators Press Attack on South Asian Countries." 22 July 1997.

Nicholls, David. *The Pluralist State: The Political Ideas of J.N. Figgis and His Contemporaries*. 2nd edn. London, UK: Macmillan Press; Oxford, UK: St. Antony's College, 1994.

Nicoll, Alexander. "Morgan Guaranty Warns on 'Paper' Loans." *Financial Times*, 30 July 1985.

Noble, Gregory and John Ravenhill, eds. *The Asian Financial Crisis and the Architecture of Global Finance*. Cambridge, UK: Cambridge University Press, 2000.

O'Brien, Richard. *Global Financial Integration: The End of Geography*. The Royal Institute of International Affairs Chatham House Papers. London, UK: Pinter Publishers, 1992.

O'Brien, Timothy. "A Federal Turf War Over Derivatives Control." *New York Times*, 8 May 1999.

Oakeshott, Michael. *Rationalism in Politics and Other Essays*. Indianapolis, IN: Liberty Press, 1991.

Oatley, Thomas and Robert Nabors. "Redistributive Cooperation." *International Organization* 52 (1998): 35–54.

Oil and Gas Journal. "Weather Derivatives." 3 September 2001.

Ordeshook, Peter C. *Game Theory and Political Theory: An Introduction*. New York, NY: Cambridge University Press, 1986.

Organisation for Economic Co-operation and Development. "Systemic Risks in Securities Markets." Paris, FR: Organisation for Economic Co-operation and Development, 1991.

Owen, Richard. "Volatility Rears Its Ugly Head." *Courier Mail*, 9 October 2001.

Oxfam International. "East Asian 'Recovery' Leaves the Poor Sinking." Press Briefing, October 1998.

——. "Tax Havens: Releasing the Hidden Billions for Poverty Eradication." In *Oxfam Policy Papers*. Oxford, UK: Oxfam, 2000.

Patel, I.G. *Glimpses of Indian Economic Policy: An Insider's View*. Oxford, UK: Oxford University Press, 2002.

Pauly, Louis W. "Promoting a Global Economy: The Normative Role of the International Monetary Fund." In *Political Economy and the Changing Global Order*, edited by Richard Stubbs and Geoffrey R.D. Underhill. New York, NY: St. Martin's Press, 1994.

Peltzman, Sam. "Toward a More General Theory of Regulation" in *Chicago Studies in Political Economy*, edited by George Stigler. Chicago, IL: University of Chicago Press, 1988.

Phillips, Richard. "Derivatives Professionals Welcome G30 Attempt to Demystify Market." *Euroweek*, 23 July, 1993.

Phillips, Susan M. "Statement to the Congress." *Federal Reserve Bulletin* 79, no. 12 (1993): 1137–42.

Pollack, Andrew. "Koreans Worry About Increasing Layoffs." *New York Times*, 17 December 1997.

Poovey, Mary. *A History of the Modern Fact: Problems of Knowledge in the Sciences of Wealth and Society*. Chicago, IL: University of Chicago Press, 1998.

Porter, Tony. *States, Markets and Regimes in Global Finance*. London, UK: Macmillan Press, 1993.

Radelet, Steven and Jeffrey Sachs. "The Onset of the East Asian Financial Crisis," Harvard Institute for International Development Working Paper, 30 March 1998.

Radigan, Joseph. "Playing Catch-up on Risk." *United States Banker* 106, no. 7 (1996): 32–43.

Redhead, Keith and Steward Hughes. *Financial Risk Management*. Hants, UK: Gower Publishing Co., 1988.

Rees-Mogg, William. "How a Great Bank was Brought Low." *Times*, 27 February 1995.

Reinicke, Wolfgang H. *Banking, Politics and Global Finance: American Commercial Banks and Regulatory Change, 1980–1990*. Hants, UK: Edward Elgar Publishing Co., 1995.

Reserve Bank of India. "Comments of the Reserve Bank of India on A New Capital Adequacy Framework." Bombay, IN: Reserve Bank of India, 2000.

Reynolds, Kathleen. "CFTC Chair Brooksley Born Shakes Up Agency with Derivatives Policies." *Bond Buyer*, 1 June 1998.

Richburg, Keith B. "Riots Rage in Indonesian Capital; Suharto Returns; Violence Reveals Deep Rift in Military." *Washington Post*, 15 May 1998.

Ringshaw, Grant. "Focus the Leeson Effect: Victims of the Rogue Trader." *Telegraph*, 4 July 1999.

Riskind, Jonathan. "Public Agency Acting Too Privately." *Columbus* (Ohio) *Dispatch*, 2 May 1997.

——. "Agency Intact Despite Kasich's Best Efforts." *Columbus* (Ohio) *Dispatch*, 16 November 1997.

Rodgers, Peter. "If the Bank's Policing is Flawed – What About the Rest of the City?/ Questions Raised by the Rescue of Johnson Matthey Bank." *Guardian*, 24 October 1984.

Roeder, David. "CFTC Boss Accepts CBOT's Olive Branch." *Chicago Sun-Times*, 20 January 1998.

Rothstein, Robert. "Consensual Knowledge and International Collaboration: Some Lessons from the Commodity Negotiations." *International Organization* 38, no. 4 (1984): 733–62.

Rowe, James L. and John Kennedy. "Sindona Hit with 99-Count Indictment." *Washington Post*, 20 March 1979.

Royce, Edward. "OPIC is not the Way to Promote Free Trade; If Merrill Lynch won't Insure Du Pont in Russia, Why Should the American Taxpayer?" *Christian Science Monitor*, 30 September 1996.

Ruggie, John G. "International Regimes, Transactions and Change: Embedded Liberalism and the Post War Economic Order." *International Organization* 36 (1982): 379–415.

Saint Louis Post-Dispatch, "J.P. Morgan's Woes Could Hurt Asian Bailout," 21 January 1998.

Sakakibara, Eisuke. "Mr. Yen Looking Back: The Makings of a Crisis," *Daily Yomiuri*, 13 November 1999.

Sanström, Sven. "The East Asia Crisis and the Role of the World Bank: Statement to the Bretton Woods Committee." Washington, D.C.: World Bank Group, 1998.

Sassen, Saskia. *The Global City: New York, London, Tokyo.* Princeton, NJ: Princeton University Press, 1991.

——. *Globalization and Its Discontents.* New York, NY: The New Press, 1998.

——. "Embedding the Global in the National: Implications for the Role of the State." In *States and Sovereignty in the Global Economy*, edited by David A. Smith, Dorothy J. Solinger and Steven C. Topik. London, UK: Routledge Press, 1999.

Sawicki, Jana. "Feminism, Foucault and 'Subjects' of Power and Freedom." In *The Later Foucault: Politics and Philosophy*, edited by Jeremy Moss. London, UK: Sage Publications, 1998.

Schattney, Georg. Market Policy Division, Deutsch Börse AG. Interview by author. Frankfurt, GER, 12 January 2000.

Schekle, Waltraud. *Constitution and Erosion of a Monetary Economy: Problems of India's Development since Independence.* London, UK: Frank Cass; The German Development Institute, 1994.

Schinasi, Gary J., R. Sean Craig, Burkhard Drees and Charles Kramer. *Modern Banking and OTC Derivatives Markets: The Transformation of Global Finance and Its Implications for Systemic Risk.* Occasional Paper 203. Washington, D.C.: International Monetary Fund, 2000.

Schmidt, Vivien A. "Convergent Pressures, Divergent Responses: France, Great Britain and Germany between Globalization and Europeanization." In *States and Sovereignty in the Global Economy*, edited by David A. Smith, Dorothy J. Solinger and Steven C. Topik. London, UK: Routledge Press, 1999.

Scott, James C. *Seeing Like a State: How Certain Schemes to Improve the Human Condition Have Failed.* New Haven, CT: Yale University Press, 1998.

Sen, Sunanda. "Basel Norms and Bank Restructuring," *The Hindu*, 8 April 2005.

Shabbir, Tayyeb. "The Social Costs of the Asian Financial Crisis." Working paper. Philadelphia, PA: University of Pennsylvania Department of Economics, 1998.

Shapiro, Michael J. Reading "Adam Smith": Desire, History and Value. Vol. 4 of Modernity and Political Thought. London, UK: Sage Publications, 1993.

Shaw, Edward S. *Financial Deepening in Economic Development.* New York, NY: Oxford University Press, 1973.

Sheedy, Elizabeth and Sheelagh McCracken, eds. *Derivatives: The Risks that Remain.* New South Wales, AU: Allen Unwin/Macquarie Series in Applied Finance, 1997.

Shiner, Cindy. "Rioting Spreads in Indonesia; Looters Set Shops Ablaze as Protests Move Beyond Campuses." *Washington Post*, 14 May 1998.

Shivakumar, Jayasankar, Gamini Abeysekera, Amara Pongsapich and Bencha Yoddumnern-Attig. "Social Capital and the Crisis." In *Thailand Social Monitor.* Washington, D.C.: World Bank, 2000.

Simons, Katerina. "Model Error: Evaluation of Various Financial Models." *New England Economic Review* 11, no. 21 (1997): 17–28.

Sivell, George and Patricia Tehan. "Barings Borrowed Pounds 400m to Support Leeson Deals." *Times*, 2 March 1995.

Skocpol, Theda. *States and Social Revolutions: A Comparative Analysis of France, Russia and China.* Cambridge, UK: Cambridge University Press, 1979.

Sleeper, Robert. Head of Banking, Banking for International Settlements. Interview by author. Basel, CH, 17 January 2000.

Smith, Adam. *An Inquiry into the Nature and Causes of the Wealth of Nations.* Edited by R.H. Campbell and A.S. Skinner. Indianapolis, IN: Liberty Fund, 1981.

Sobel, Andrew C. *Domestic Choices, International Markets: Dismantling National Barriers and Liberalizing Securities Markets.* Ann Arbor, MI: University of Michigan Press, 1994.

Song, Jesook. "Family Breakdown and Invisible Homeless Women: Neoliberal Governance during the Asian Debt Crisis in South Korea, 1997–2001." *Positions* 14:1 (Spring 2006): 37–65.

Steil, Benn. "International Securities Markets Regulation." In *International Financial Market Regulation*, edited by Benn Steil. New York, NY: J. Wiley and Sons, 1994.

Stigler, George J. *The Citizen and the State: Essays on Regulation.* Chicago, IL: University of Chicago Press, 1975.

——. "The Theory of Economic Regulation." In *Chicago Studies in Political Economy*, edited by George Stigler. Chicago, IL: University of Chicago Press, 1988.

Stiglitz, Joseph *et al. The Economic Role of the State.* Edited by Arnold Heertje. Southampton, UK: Camelot Press; Bank Isinger de Beaufort NV, 1989.

Stiglitz, Joseph E. *The Roaring Nineties: A New History of the World's Most Prosperous Decade.* New York, NY: W. W. Norton & Company, 2003.

——. "Road to Recovery: Restoring Growth in the Region Could be a Long and Difficult Process." *Asia Week*, 17 July 1998.

——. "What We Have Learned from Recent Crises: Implications for Banking Regulations" Working Paper, Global Financial Crises: Implications for Banking and Regulation Conference, Federal Reserve Bank of Chicago, Chicago, IL, 1999.

Strange, Susan. "An Eclectic Approach." In *The New International Political Economy*, edited by Craig N. Murphy and Roger Tooze. Boulder, CO: Lynne Rienner Publishers, 1991.

——. *Casino Capitalism.* Manchester, UK: Manchester University Press, 1997.

——. *Mad Money.* Manchester, UK: Manchester University Press, 1998.

Stevenson, Richard W. "Enron Received Many Loans from U.S. for Foreign Projects During the 1990s." *New York Times*, 21 February 2002.

Summers, Lawrence H. and Victoria P. Summers. "When Financial Markets Work Too Well: A Case for a Securities Transaction Tax." In *Innovation and Technology in the Markets: A Reordering of the World's Capital Market Systems*, edited by Daniel R. Siegel. London, UK: McGraw-Hill Book Co., 1990.

Sussangkarn, Chalongphob. "Directions of East Asian Regional Financial Cooperation." *Asian Economic Papers.* Cambridge, MA: The Center for Strategic and International Studies and MIT, Fall 2006.

Tait, Nikki. "Concession Buys Time in Turf Battle to Regulate Over-the-Counter Derivatives Trading in the U.S." *Financial Times*, 27 July 1998.

——. "Bail-Out Prompts CFTC Rule Probe." *Financial Times*, 1 October 1998.

——. "CFTC Seeks More OTC Transparency." *Financial Times*, 16 October 1998.

——. "Commodity Futures Regulator to Step Down." *Financial Times*, 20 January 1999.

Tamber, Gurinder. Global Commodities Trader, Global Markets Division, Deutsche Bank AG. Multiple interviews and consultations by author. London, UK, 2000–2001.

Tan, Angela. "Political Risk Insurance Seen Rising After ISD Arrests." *Business Times* (Singapore), 15 January 2002.

Tattersall, Jonathan H. Chairman, Financial Services Regulatory Consulting Group, PricewaterhouseCoopers. Interview by author. London, UK, 8 November 1999.

Tay, Alvin and Leslie Yee. "New Centres Challenge Singapore's Offshore Banking." *Business Times* (Singapore), 3 October 1992.

Thiessen, Gordon. "Mr. Thiessen Looks at Flexible Exchange Rates in a World of Low Inflation." Remarks by the Governor of the Bank of Canada, Mr. Gordon Thiessen, to the FOREX '97 Conference held in Toronto." Reprinted in *BIS Review* 57 (30 May 1997): 1–5.

Thompson, Richard and Michael Marray. "White-knuckle Ride on the Soros Express: The Wall Street Wizard is Having the Take More and More Risk to Maintain the Huge Returns for Investors." *Independent*, 6 June 1993.

Thrift, Nigel. *Spatial Formations*. London, UK: Sage Publications, 1996.

Tiner, John I. and Joe M. Conneely. *Accounting for Treasury Products: A Practical Guide to Accounting, Tax and Risk Control*. Cambridge, UK: Woodhead-Faulkner Ltd.; Arthur Andersen and Co., 1987.

Torode, Greg. "Jakarta Troops Kill Six Students; People Were Screaming, But the Soldiers Wouldn't Stop Firing. I Saw Dozens of People Hit." *South China Morning Post*, 13 May 1998.

Train, John. "Banking and the Bottom Line." *Washington Post*, 13 May 1984.

Treaster, Joseph B. "Insurers find Profit in a new Risk Consciousness." *New York Times*, 24 February 2002.

Triffin, Robert. *Gold and the Dollar Crisis: The Future of Convertibility*. New Haven, CT: Yale University Press, 1960.

Turner, Philip. "Capital Flows in the 1980s: A Survey in Major Trends." In *BIS Economic Papers* 30. Basel, CH: Bank for International Settlements, Monetary and Economic Department, 1991.

Underhill, Geoffrey R.D. "Private Markets and Public Responsibility in a Global System: Conflict and Cooperation in Transnational Banking and Securities Regulation." In *The New World Order in International Finance*, edited by Geoffrey R. D. Underhill. New York, NY: St. Martin's Press, 1997.

——. Professor, Afdeling Politicologie. Interview by author. Oxford, UK, 3 December 1999.

United Kingdom Hansard Parliamentary Debates. "Barings." 4th ser., vol. 255. (1995).

Urry, Maggie. "Set for Further Expansion." *Financial Times*, 7 May 1985.

US House Committee on Agriculture. Application of the Commodity Exchange Act to Transactions in Over-the-Counter Derivatives: Submitted by the Board of Governors of the Federal Reserve System to the Subcommittee on Risk Management and Specialty Crops. 105th Cong., 2nd session, 10 June 1998.

——. Testimony of Commodity Futures Trading Commission Chairperson Brooksley Born: Hearing before the Subcommitte on Risk Management and Specialty Crops. 105th Cong., 2nd sess., 10 June 1998.
US House Committee on Banking and Financial Services. The Regulation of OTC Derivatives: Testimony of Chairman of the Board of Governors of the Federal Reserve System Alan Greenspan before the Committee on Banking and Financial Services. 105th Cong., 2nd sess., 24 July 1998.
——. *Financial Institutions and Consumer Credit Unions Hedge Funds.* Testimony of Marge Roukeman, Representative and Chairwoman of the House Committee on Banking and Financial Services. 106th Cong., 1st sess., 24 March 1999.
——. Prepared Statement by Michael L. Brosnan, Deputy Comptroller for Risk Evaluation: Hearing of the Financial Institutions Consumer Subcommittee. 106th Cong., 1st sess., 24 March 1999.
——. Prepared statement by Shaw Petrou, President ISD/SHAW, Inc. "International Financial Architecture: Hearing before the Committee on Banking and Financial Services. 106th Cong., 1st sess., 20 May 1999.
US President's Working Group on Financial Markets. "Hedge Funds, Leverage, and the Lessons of Long-Term Capital Management." Washington, D.C., 1999.
US Senate Committee on Banking, Housing and Urban Affairs. Deposit Insurance Revision and Financial Services Industry Restructuring: Hearing before the Committee on Banking, Housing and Urban Affairs. 101st Cong., 2nd sess., 12 July 1990.
Valance, Nikos. "Defusing Global Bond Risk." *CFO* 16, no. 6 (May 2000): 133–37.
Velloor, Ravi. "Tighter Controls after Barings Debacle." *Strait Times* (Singapore), 4 July 1999.
Vogel, David. "The Power of Business in American: A Re-appraisal." *British Journal of Political Science* 13 (1983): 19–43.
Vogl, A. J. "Risky Business." *Across the Board*, 34, no. 5 (May 1997): 37–40.
Volcker, Paul A. "Remarks by Paul A. Volcker at the Annual Dinner of the Institute of International Finance." Washington, D.C.: Institute of International Finance, 1998.
Wagster, John D. "Impact of the 1988 Basel Accord on International Banks." *Journal of Finance* 51 (1996): 1321–46.
Wallerstein, Immanuel. "States? Sovereignty? The Dilemmas of Capitalists in the Age of Transition." In *States and Sovereignty in the Global Economy*, edited by David A. Smith, Dorothy J. Solinger and Steve C. Topik. London, UK: Routledge Press, 1999.
Warner, Alison. "Asia Remains Unstable." *The Banker* 148, no. 869 (July 1998): 94–98.
——. "Behind the Hedges." *The Banker* 148, no. 873 (1 November 1998): 24–28.
Warner, Jeremy, John Eisenhammer and Donald MacIntyre. "Barings Dealer's Pound 1m Boast; Bonus Claim Just Weeks Before Bank's Collapse." *Independent*, 28 February 1995.
Walter, Ingo. *Global Competition in Financial Services: Market Structure, Protection and Trade Liberalization.* Cambridge, MA: Ballinger Publishing; American Enterprise Institute, 1988.
Waters, Richard. "IOSCO Drops Common Capital Plan." *Financial Times*, 11 February 1993.
Weber, Max. *From Max Weber: Essays in Sociology.* Translated by H.H.Gerth and C. Wright Mills. New York, NY: Oxford University Press, 1946.
——. *The Protestant Ethic and the Spirit of Capitalism.* New York, NY: Charles Scribner's Sons, 1958.

——. *Economy and Society: An Outline of Interpretive Sociology.* 2 vols. Edited by Geunther Roth and Claus Wittich. Berkeley, CA: University of California Press, 1978.

Weever, Patrick and Robert Tyerman. "The Futures that Finished Barings." *Telegraph*, 5 March 1995.

Weisweiller, Rudy. *How the Foreign Exchange Market Works.* New York, NY: New York Institute of Finance, 1990.

West, Gerald T. "Political Risk Investment Insurance: A Renaissance." *Journal of Project Finance* 5, no. 2 (Summer 1999): 27–36.

White, William R. "International Agreements in the Area of Banking and Finance: Accomplishments and Outstanding Issues." In *BIS Working Papers* 38. Basel, CH: Bank for International Settlements, Monetary and Economic Department, 1996.

Williamson, John. *The Failure of World Monetary Reform, 1971–74.* Southampton, UK: Thomas Nelson and Sons Ltd., 1977.

Wilson, Graham K. "Social Regulation and Explanations of Regulatory Failure." *Political Studies* 32 (1984): 203–25.

Wincoop, Eric van and Kei Mu-Yi. "Asian Crisis Post-Mortem: Where did the Money Go and Did the United States Benefit?" BIS Conference Papers. Basel, CH: Bank for International Settlements, 2000.

Woo-Cummings, Meredith ed. *The Developmental State.* Ithaca, NY: Cornell University Press, 1999.

World Bank. *Annual Report 1999*. Washington, D.C.: World Bank Group, 2000.

——. "Global Economic Prospects and the Developing Countries – Beyond Financial Crisis." Washington, D.C.: The World Bank Group, 1998/99.

——. "Thailand Economic Monitor: Executive Summary." In *Thailand Economic Monitor.* Washington, D.C.: World Bank, 2001.

Wyllie, Alicia. "Hedge Funds Come In Out of the Cold." *Sunday Times*, 24 September 2001.

Zhang, Peter G. *Barings Bankruptcy and Financial Derivatives.* Singapore: World Scientific, 1995.

Index